BRITISH GEOLOGICAL SURVEY

J H POWELL
A H COOPER
A C BENFIELD

Geology of the country around Thirsk

Memoir for 1:50 000 geological sheet 52
(England and Wales)

CONTRIBUTORS

Palaeontology
B M Cox
H C Ivimey-Cook
G Warrington
I P Wilkinson

Geophysics
J M Allsop
B C Chacksfield

Hydrocarbons
D W Holliday

Hydrogeology
R A Monkhouse

LONDON: HMSO   1992

© *NERC copyright 1992*

First published 1992

ISBN 0 11 884481 4

Bibliographical reference

Powell, J H, Cooper, A H, and Benfield, A C. 1992. Geology of the country around Thirsk. *Memoir of the British Geological Survey*, Sheet 52 (England and Wales).

Authors

J H Powell, BSc, PhD
British Geological Survey
Keyworth

A H Cooper, BSc, PhD, CGeol
British Geological Survey
Newcastle upon Tyne

A C Benfield, BSc, CGeol
formerly British Geological Survey

Contributors

J M Allsop, BSc
B C Chacksfield, BSc
B M Cox, BSc, PhD
D W Holliday, MA, PhD, CGeol
H C Ivimey-Cook, BSc, PhD
G Warrington, BSc, PhD, CGeol
I P Wilkinson, BSc, PhD
British Geological Survey
Keyworth

R A Monkhouse, BSc, CGeol
British Geological Survey
Wallingford

Other publications of the Survey dealing with this and adjoining districts

BOOKS

British Regional Geology
Eastern England from the Tees to The Wash 2nd edition, 1980

Memoirs
Geology of the country around Harrogate (Sheet 62), *in press*

Mineral Assessment Reports: resources of 1:25 000 sheets; Sand and Gravel
No. 119   Bedale, North Yorkshire, 1982
No. 135   West Tanfield, North Yorkshire, 1983
No. 143   Ripon, North Yorkshire, 1984

MAPS

1:625 000

Solid geology (South sheet), 1979
Quaternary geology (South sheet), 1977
Aeromagnetic map (South sheet), 1965

1:250 000
Solid geology, Tyne Tees, 1981
Aeromagnetic anomaly, Tyne Tees, 1981
Bouguer gravity anomaly, Tyne Tees, 1978

1:50 000 or 1:63 360

Sheet 41   Richmond (Solid) 1970, (Drift) 1970
Sheet 42   Northallerton (Solid and Drift) pre-1900
Sheet 43   Egton (Solid and Drift) pre-1900
Sheet 51   Masham (Solid) 1985, (Drift) 1985
Sheet 52   Thirsk (Solid and Drift) 1992
Sheet 53   Pickering (Solid and Drift) 1973
Sheet 62   Harrogate (Solid) 1987, (Drift) 1987
Sheet 63   York (Solid and Drift) 1983

Printed in the UK for HMSO
Dd 0291140 12/92 C10 531/3 12521

Geology of the country around Thirsk

The district described in this memoir incorporates the central part of the largely drift-covered Vale of York, which is predominantly underlain by Triassic and Lower Jurassic rocks. This vale is fringed by higher ground to the south-west, where Carboniferous and Permian rocks crop out, and to the east by the prominent Hambleton and Howardian Hills formed by Middle and Upper Jurassic strata.

The survey supplemented by shallow boreholes and a deep borehole at Felixkirk, together with geophysical investigations, has resulted in a revision and modern synthesis of the district's stratigraphy and geological structure.

The Upper Carboniferous rocks, at outcrop, comprise deltaic and alluvial plain facies, deposited on the basinward margins of the Askrigg Block. Geophysical investigations suggest that Lower Carboniferous limestone forms a small structural high below Permian strata in the south-east of the district. The Carboniferous rocks are unconformably overlain by shallow-marine to continental Permian strata, including evaporite deposits, which, together with the succeeding, predominantly continental Triassic rocks, formed part of the gently subsiding East Midlands Shelf.

Initiation of the Cleveland Basin in late Triassic and Jurassic times resulted in a widespread transgression of the Tethys Ocean, manifested in the deposition of marine sediments throughout the Early Jurassic. The Felixkirk Borehole has provided a fully cored sequence of Lower Jurassic and Upper Triassic strata, and has produced new information about the sedimentation and biostratigraphy of these rocks in the west of the Cleveland Basin. Uplift of the Basin in Mid Jurassic times, associated with earth movements on the Mid-North Sea High, resulted in progradation of deltaic and paralic deposits from the north-west and north-east. This nonmarine episode was punctuated by brief marine incursions from the south and south-east which resulted in the deposition of important marker beds; the resurvey has resulted in a revision of the stratigraphy and palaeogeography of one of these marine units, the Eller Beck Formation. Renewed transgression of the epeiric sea in the late Mid Jurassic was followed by marine sedimentation throughout the Late Jurassic. Earth movements during this phase of sedimentation resulted in local unconformities. Inversion of the Cleveland Basin in Tertiary times caused uplift and subsequent erosion of post-Upper Jurassic strata, including the Chalk.

Shallow boreholes, together with field and geophysical investigations, have enabled a revision of the geological structure, including that of the complex Asenby–Coxwold Graben which crosses the southern part of the district.

Glacial ('Drift') deposits, the products of the Devensian glaciation, cover a large part of the district, particularly the lower ground. A synthesis of the sedimentation pattern during the advancing, maximum and waning stages of the ice sheet is presented.

Natural resources in the district are principally limestone, and sand and gravel, although brick clay, ironstone and coal were formerly worked in small amounts. Sand and gravel resources in the district have been re-evaluated. Landslipped ground, and cavities produced by the dissolution of Permian gypsum deposits, are potential risk factors in the district; their distribution and mode of origin are outlined.

Cover photograph
Corallian (Lower Calcareous Grit) escarpment at Roulston Scar.

View of the Middle and Upper Jurassic rocks forming the Hambleton Hills escarpment between Boltby Scar and Sneck Yate Bank; the middle and lower parts of the escarpment comprise landslip involving a series of rotational slips and mudflows, terminating above the cornfields (L 3039).

CONTENTS

FIGURES

PLATES

PREFACE

The area described in this memoir is an important agricultural region. It includes the cathedral town of Ripon and the market town of Thirsk, situated in the low-lying, largely drift-covered Vale of York. To the east the landscape is dominated by the prominent escarpment of the Hambleton Hills, and to the south-east by the Howardian Hills. These uplands include part of the North Yorkshire Moors National Park. Both amateur and professional geologists, and those interested in the countryside, will find much of interest in this account.

The survey of the district, supported by borehole and geophysical investigations, has enabled a substantial revision of the stratigraphy and structure of the Carboniferous, Permo-Triassic and Jurassic rocks. The deep, fully cored Felixkirk Borehole, in particular, has provided a wealth of new data, leading to a better understanding of the sedimentation and a refinement of the biostratigraphy of the rocks of late Triassic and early Jurassic age. The detailed study of the glacial landforms and sediments has increased understanding of the glacial processes and sedimentation in the district during the advance and retreat of the Devensian ice sheet, which moved southwards down the Vale of York during the last glacial period.

The natural resources, principally limestone and dolomite, and sand and gravel, have been reappraised. Limestone and dolomite are currently worked for aggregate and there is potential for further extraction; resources of sand and gravel have been shown to be less extensive than was previously thought. However, as demand rises from outside the district there may be increased pressure to exploit these limited resources. There are some important groundwater resources in the district. The potential risk factors associated with solution cavities in gypsum deposits have been identified.

Peter J Cook, DSc
Director

British Geological Survey
Keyworth
Nottingham NG12 5GG

September 1992

HISTORY OF SURVEY OF THE THIRSK SHEET

The primary six-inch geological survey of the district was made by G Barrow, A G Cameron, C Fox-Strangways and H H Howell between 1878 and 1880, and the results published in 1884 on Old Series one-inch Quarter Sheet 96SW as both solid and drift editions. A memoir, 'The geology of the country around Northallerton and Thirsk', jointly covering the Quarter Sheets 96NW and 96SW, which correspond to New Series Sheets 42 (Northallerton) and 52 (Thirsk) respectively, was published in 1886. A related memoir by C Fox-Strangways, 'The Jurassic rocks of Britain; Volume 1, Yorkshire', covering part of the district, was published in 1892.

The resurvey on the 1:10 560 scale was mostly carried out by Mr A C Benfield, Dr A H Cooper, Mr C G Godwin, Dr J H Powell and Mr A Thickpenny between 1978 and 1983; peripheral areas were surveyed by Mr H Johnson, Mr J G O Smart and Dr A A Wilson between 1975–1978. The work was funded in part by The Department of the Environment. Parts of the district are covered by sand and gravel assessment reports (Nos. 119, 135 and 143) of the BGS (formerly Institute of Geological Sciences) Mineral Assessment Unit.

Geological National Grid six-inch (1:10 560) maps included wholly, or in part, in Sheet 52 are listed below, together with the initials of the surveyors and the dates of the survey. Those maps marked * have been surveyed only in part.

Copies of these maps are available for public reference in the libraries of the British Geological Survey in Keyworth and Edinburgh. Photographic or dyeline prints may be purchased from BGS.

SE 27	NE	North Stainley	AAW,AHC	1975, 1978
	SE	Thieves Gill	HJ,JGOS,AAW,AHC	1975–78, 1977–80
SE 28	NE	Aiskew	JGOS,AHC	1975, 1978
	SE	Snape	JGOS,AHC	1975, 1978
SE 37	NW	Wath	AHC,JHP	1980–81
	NE	Baldersby	ACB,JHP	1980–81
	SW	Ripon	AHC	1987
	SE	Dishforth	CGG	1980
SE 38	NW	Gatenby	ACB	1979–80
	NE	South Otterington	ACB	1980
	SW	Pickhill	AHC	1981
	SE	Sand Hutton	ACB,AHC	1980, 1981
SE 47	NW	Dalton	ACB	1981–82
	NE	Hutton Sessay	ACB,AT	1980–83
	SW	Cundall	ACB,HJ	1977–78
	SE	Raskelf	ACB,JH	1977–79
SE 48	NW	Borrowby	JHP	1981
	NE	Kirby Knowle	JHP	1979–80
	SW	Thirsk	JHP	1981
	SE	Felixkirk	JHP	1981
SE 57	NW	Coxwold	AT,JHP	1979–81
	NE*	Ampleforth	JHP	1982
	SW	Oulston	ACB,JHP	1981–82
	SE*	Crayke	HJ,ACB,JHP	1978, 1981–84
SE 58	NW	Murton	JHP	1979–80
	NE*	Rivaulx Moor	JHP	1980
	SW	Cold Kirby	JHP	1979
	SE*	Ampleforth	JHP	1980

ACKNOWLEDGEMENTS

NOTES

This memoir was compiled by Dr J H Powell. Fossil identifications were provided by Dr B M Cox (late Jurassic macrofaunas), Dr H C Ivimey-Cook (early and mid Jurassic macrofaunas), Dr G Warrington (Triassic palynomorphs) and Dr I P Wilkinson (early Jurassic calcareous microfaunas). Mrs J M Allsop and Mr B C Chacksfield have contributed a geophysical assessment of the district, Dr D W Holliday a review of hydrocarbons potential and Mr R A Monkhouse an account of hydrogeology and water supply. The memoir was edited by Dr R W O'B Knox and Mr J Pattison.

Thanks are due to the various quarry and gravel pit operators in the district who allowed access to their excavations, to British Coal and British Gypsum for providing details of boreholes, and to the Yorkshire Region of the National Rivers Authority for providing licensed abstraction data.

Throughout the memoir the word 'district' refers to the area covered by the 1:50 000 Thirsk (52) Sheet.

National Grid references are given in square brackets unless otherwise stated; all lie within the 100 km square SE.

Bed thickness descriptions are based on the classification of Ingram (1954).

Geological sections are described in the text in descending order.

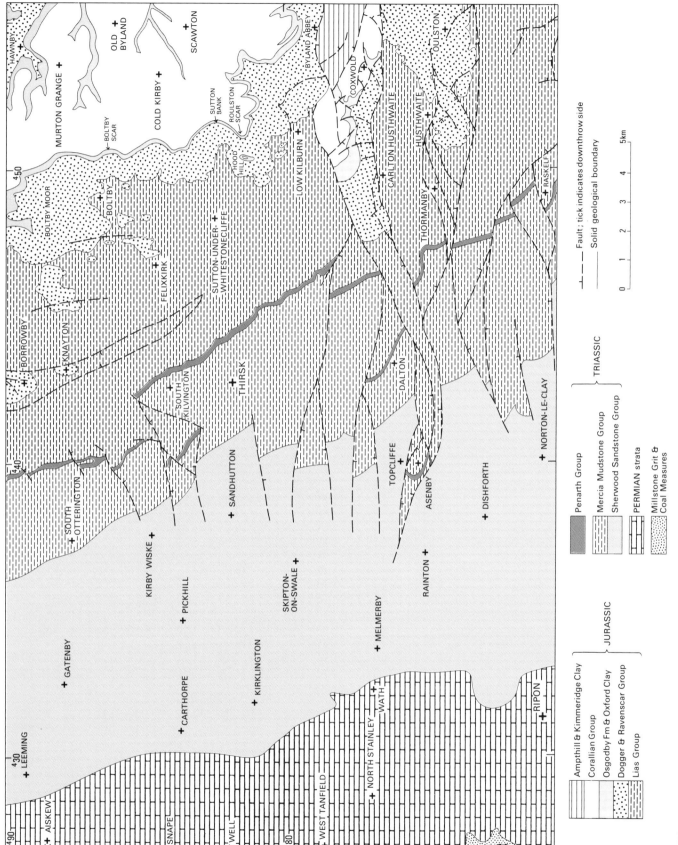

Figure 1 Sketch map of the solid geology of the Thirsk district.

ONE

Introduction

The district around Thirsk (Sheet 52) lies wholly in the county of North Yorkshire. It includes the northern part of the Vale of York together with the south-western part of the Hambleton Hills and the western extension of the Howardian Hills. Outside the major urban centres, Thirsk and Ripon, most of the district is given over to agriculture and is dominated by arable farming, although forestry is important in the Hambleton Hills. Industrial development, other than that peripheral to the towns, is restricted to the extraction of sand and gravel and the quarrying of Magnesian Limestone for aggregate.

PHYSIOGRAPHY

The topography of the district reflects the underlying geology (Figure 1) and two distinctive areas can be recognised. The lower-lying western and central area is underlain by Permian, Triassic and Lower Jurassic rocks concealed, for the most part, by an undulating blanket of drift deposits. Most of this area lies between 25 m and 60 m above OD but, near the western margin of the sheet, the Magnesian Limestones give rise to a belt of higher undulating land cut by the valley of the River Ure. Harder beds in the succeeding Sherwood Sandstone form subdued ridges to the east, some of which are followed by the old Roman Road and its modern successor, the A1.

The higher ground in the eastern part of the district is largely occupied by Middle and Upper Jurassic strata. In the north-east of this area, the ground rises steeply to over 340 m above OD to form the magnificent west-facing escarpment of the Hambleton Hills, formed predominantly of sandstone and limestone. In the extreme north-east, the easterly dip-slopes of these strata are deeply cut by the attractive wooded valleys of the River Rye and its tributaries. To the south, the escarpment swings eastward to overlook the highly faulted lower ground of the Coxwold–Gilling gap, partly excavated in Upper Jurassic mudstones, which, on the south, is bounded by the somewhat higher ground occupied by the Middle Jurassic rocks that form the western extension of the Howardian Hills.

GEOLOGICAL HISTORY

The oldest known rocks in the district are of Carboniferous age. Studies in the classical ground to the west, between Pateley Bridge and Settle, have shown that their sedimentation was controlled by differential movement of basement structural units (Marr, 1921; Leeder, 1982; Arthurton et al., 1988) that resulted in shallow-water sedimentation on the Askrigg 'Block', to the north of the Craven Fault system, and deeper-water sedimentation in the gently subsiding Craven Basin, to the south. This structural line, the Craven

Fault Belt, probably extended north-eastwards to the Thirsk district. Structural control became less pronounced during the Namurian, when the basin became infilled with clastic sediments resulting from the southerly progradation of rivers and deltas. Epeirogenic movements, sediment compaction and delta-switching resulted in cyclic sedimentation of fluviodeltaic sandstones, grey mudstones and siltstones, which were deposited in brackish and freshwater swamps and lagoons, and also the establishment of peat swamps, preserved as thin coals and rootlet beds, in the most stable parts of the basin. Comparison of strata seen at outcrop and proved in boreholes in the Thirsk district with corresponding beds in the adjacent Masham district (Wilson and Thompson, 1965; Institute of Geological Sciences, 1976) indicates that the former are of Namurian and early Westphalian age.

Hercynian earth movements at the end of Carboniferous times gave rise to faulting, folding and uplift. Subsequent arid-desert weathering resulted in the erosion of most of the Upper Carboniferous strata. During subsequent Permian times a major land-locked basin extended from eastern England across the North Sea to Central Europe (Ziegler, 1982; Glennie, 1983). The Thirsk district lay near the western margin of this basin, in tropical palaeolatitudes; thus the sub-Permian, Carboniferous sandstones show signs of subaerial erosion in a desert environment. In the late Permian, the topography was submerged by a westward transgression of the epicontinental Zechstein sea, caused by a eustatic rise in sea level (Smith, 1970a). This resulted in the deposition, locally, of finely laminated organic-rich mudstone and siltstone in a stagnant, anaerobic environment. Recurrent flooding of the basin followed by evaporation of its waters, possibly caused by glacioeustatic, sea-level fluctuations, produced the English Zechstein Cycles EZ1–EZ5 (Smith, 1970a). Where fully developed, individual cycles show an upward progression in evaporitic sedimentation of shallow-water carbonate-anhydrite-halite-sylvite. Halite and sylvinite deposits, however, are restricted to the deeper parts of the basin (Yorkshire coast), and towards the basin margins (Thirsk district) coeval mudstones were deposited in a lagoonal environment.

The junction between the uppermost evaporitic mudstones of Permian age and the overlying continental red-beds of the Sherwood Sandstone Group is gradational over a few metres and is probably diachronous throughout the district (Warrington, 1974b). This stratigraphical interval is unfossiliferous, but the Permian–Triassic boundary probably lies somewhere within the lower part of the Sherwood Sandstone Group (Smith et al., 1974). The Sherwood Sandstone Group consists mainly of red, cross-bedded sandstone, but includes dolomitic mudstone, siltstone and thin evaporites in the upper part. It was deposited in a hot, mainly arid, continental, predominantly fluvial environment as upward-fining cycles and, locally, as continental sabkha evaporites. Evidence from adjacent sheets suggests that the district lay at the distal end of a vast alluvial plain that extended north-wards from a source area in the south-south-west.

Around the margins of the North Sea Basin, the fluvial sedimentation represented by the Sherwood Sandstone Group was abruptly terminated by minor earth movements, followed by erosion (Smith, 1970a; Taylor et al., 1971). The succeeding Mercia Mudstone Group marks a change to predominantly argillaceous and evaporitic sedimentation in continental environments ranging from playa lake (Anderton et al., 1979) to coastal sabkhas bordering a hypersaline epeiric sea (Warrington, 1974a). The green-grey, dolomitic mudstones of the Blue Anchor Formation, which has a restricted fauna, reflect a change to a brackish, reducing, lagoonal environment.

Late in the Triassic, a widespread marine incursion introduced a shallow shelf-sea with anaerobic substrates, in which the brown, grey or black carbonaceous shales and thin bioturbated sandstones of the Westbury Formation were deposited. These organic-rich sediments contain an abundant, low-diversity fauna.

The Westbury Formation is succeeded by pale green, calcareous mudstones with a restricted brackish fauna, forming the Cotham Member of the Lilstock Formation, which represents a brief regressive phase. Together, these units make up the Penarth Group and were a precursor to the widespread marine conditions that prevailed during deposition of the Lias Group.

The Triassic–Jurassic boundary lies near the base of the Lias Group, which consists of a broad four-fold division comprising in upward sequence: deeper-water mudstone with thin intercalations of limestone and fine-grained sandstone; shallow-water, medium-grained, bioturbated sandstone; a condensed sequence of shallow-water, oolitic, berthierinitic ironstone; followed by deeper-water mudstone. Abundant benthic and nektic faunas indicate a connection with the Tethys Ocean, which extended eastwards over much of central and southern Europe, and the Middle East. Gentle folding and submarine erosion during the late Lower Jurassic resulted in erosion of late Toarcian sediments in the district. Consequently, the overlying Dogger Formation, at the base of the Middle Jurassic, rests unconformably on the Lias Group. It is lithologically heterogeneous and consists of phosphatic conglomerate, sandstone, shale, limestone and ironstone, which were deposited in small basins and on highs created by the irregular topography of the topmost Lias sediments. This episode was followed by regression of the sea and the southerly progradation of fluviodeltaic sediments, predominantly sandstones, derived from the Pennines or the Mid-North Sea High. Paralic, fluvial and fluviodeltaic sedimentation persisted throughout the deposition of most of the Middle Jurassic Ravenscar Group, but this pattern of sedimentation was interrupted by brief marine incursions from the south and south-east. The transgressions probably reflect epeiric sea-level fluctuations and are typified by sandstone, oolitic ironstone and peloidal, oolitic, and micritic limestones. Some of these transgressive marine units wedge out within the district, indicating that it lay at the western, shoreward limit of the incursions.

A more extensive marine transgression during Callovian times marked a return to marine sedimentation, which persisted to the end of Jurassic times. The Cleveland (Yorkshire) Basin was, however, subjected to periodic folding and erosion during the Callovian and early Oxfordian (Wright, 1983). Consequently, the marine siliciclastics comprising, in upward sequence, the Osgodby Formation, the Oxford Clay and the Lower Calcareous Grit are separated by both local and regional unconformities.

The Oxford Clay marks the base of the Upper Jurassic in this district and consists of calcareous siltstone and mudstone deposited in the offshore zone of a broad epeiric sea. The overlying Lower Calcareous Grit of the Corallian Group, a calcareous, locally oolitic sandstone rich in sponge spicules, reflects shallowing of the sea. During deposition of the succeeding Coralline Oolite Formation, mixed oolitic-carbonate and siliciclastic sediments were deposited throughout the district in warm, shallow-water shoal environments, locally with coral patch-reefs. A return to marine siliciclastic sedimentation, rich in sponge spicules, is indicated by the Upper Calcareous Grit, which passes gradationally upwards to deeper-water mudstone with carbonate concretions, deposited during the late Oxfordian. Basin subsidence, together with restricted oceanic circulation, resulted in the deposition of deep-water, organic-rich mudstones during the Kimmeridgian.

Rocks younger than the Upper Jurassic were removed by erosion following uplift and faulting during the Tertiary. Diagenetic studies (Hemingway and Riddler, 1982) suggest, however, that by late Cretaceous times the Jurassic Cleveland Basin was buried to about 2.5 km depth, when the 'Chalk Sea' covered the district, prior to basin inversion during the Tertiary.

The known glacial deposits of the district are the products of a single glaciation during the Devensian cold stage (about 18 000 to 10 000 years BP). As the ice sheet advanced southwards down the Vale of York, and later stagnated, it deposited a wide variety of sub- and englacial facies, such as till and glacial sand and gravel, in the form of eskers. Still-stands of ice during its retreat resulted in a progression of terminal moraines and the deposition of glacial-lake deposits. The ice sheet did not breach the main escarpment of the Hambleton Hills, but periglacial windblown (loess) deposits are present on the higher ground in this area, and the deeply incised tributaries of the River Rye were probably cut by streams flowing from the melting snowfields on the high ground. Near the western margin of the district, tills of a different character suggest a south-easterly advance of glaciers emanating from the Yorkshire Dales.

Late Pleistocene erosion has modified many of the glacial landforms, and glacial deposits have contributed to the river terrace and alluvial deposits. Scouring and erosion of the western-facing escarpment of the Hambleton Hills during the glaciation, and subsequent release of meltwater, have resulted in extensive cambering and landslipping in that area. Subsidence, due to groundwater dissolution of gypsum in the evaporitic Permian rocks of the Ripon area, is one example of currently active geological processes.

TWO

Carboniferous

Regional studies (Kent, 1966; Wills, 1973; Whittaker, 1985) suggest that throughout the district Permian strata rest unconformably on rocks of Carboniferous age (Figure 23b). The latter crop out, mainly below drift, in only three restricted areas on the western margin of the district. They are in effect extensions of the outcrop of Carboniferous strata in the neighbouring districts to the west (Masham (51) Sheet) and to the south (Harrogate (62) Sheet), which are documented in the appropriate Geological Survey maps and memoirs.

MILLSTONE GRIT

Wandley Gill Sandstone

The Millstone Grit strata represented at outcrop are of late Namurian age (Table 1). The oldest formation is the Wandley Gill Sandstone (Wilson and Thompson, 1965) which crops out, beneath drift, in a small area [2660 7075] in the south-western corner of the district. The BGS Winksley Borehole [2507 7151], drilled some 1800 m to the north-west, within the Masham district (Sheet 51), penetrated about 27 m of fine-grained sandstone with rootlet horizons and thin beds of mudstone, one with *Lingula* sp., (Institute of Geological Sciences, 1976). The formation immediately and conformably underlies the Gastrioceras cancellatum Marine Band and is therefore of Marsdenian age, and a probable correlative of the Huddersfield White Rock of the Harrogate district (Sheet 62). However, it is thought that only the highest beds of the Wandley Gill Sandstone correlate with the Huddersfield White Rock of the central Pennines and that lower beds correlate with other sandstones within the

Middle Grit Group there (I C Burgess, personal communication, 1984).

Laverton Shales

The beds above the Wandley Gill Sandstone comprise about 16 m of mudstone, the Laverton Shales (Wilson and Thompson, 1965). In the Winksley Borehole (Institute of Geological Sciences, 1976), the G. cancellatum Marine Band occurs near the base of these beds and the G. cumbriense Marine Band about 4 m higher, indicating a Yeadonian age (Table 1). Only the highest one or two metres of these mudstones crop out within the district beneath drift, south of Quarry House [2664 7787].

Laverton Sandstone

The overlying Laverton Sandstone, about 18 m thick, crops out south of West Tanfield. Its stratigraphical position above the G. cumbriense Marine Band, as proved in the Winksley Borehole, implies a Yeadonian age and a correlation with the Rough Rock of the central Pennines. It is mainly covered by drift, principally the alluvium of the River Ure, but 11 m of brown, thin- and medium-bedded, fine-grained sandstone are exposed in the river bank [2670 7798 to 2685 7804] near Quarry House. Further south, the Laverton Sandstone crops out, mainly below drift, in the valleys of Kex Beck and of the River Laver, south of Thieves Gill Farm [273 737] and west of Cow Myers [273 727]. Medium- and coarse-grained sandstone, 1.5 m thick, is exposed in the bank of the River Laver [2693 7208] near Galphay Mill, at the base of the steep slope formed by the Lower Magnesian Limestone.

Table 1
Stratigraphical framework of the Carboniferous rocks exposed near the western margin of the district, and probable correlation with the central Pennines. Based in part on Wilson and Thompson (1965) and Ramsbottom (1974).

Chronostratigraphy		Known marker bands	Lithostratigraphy		
Series	Stage	Thirsk – Masham		Central Pennines	
Westphalian	Westphalian A	*Lingula* band (Subcrenatum Marine Band?)	Winksley Shale	Lower Coal Measures (lower part)	Millstone Grit
Namurian	Yeadonian	G. cancellatum G. cumbriense	Laverton Sandstone	Rough Rock	
			Laverton Shales	unnamed mudstone	
	Marsdenian		Windley Gill Sandstone	Huddersfield White Rock and underlying beds	

LOWER COAL MEASURES

Winksley Shale

In the Winksley Borehole and in the nearby exposures in the River Laver at Winksley Banks, the Laverton Sandstone is succeeded by a thin silty mudstone, passing up to a seatearth and a thin coal, overlain by 15 m of mudstone with three *Lingula* bands; these beds are referred to the Winksley Shale (Wilson and Thompson, 1965). The lowest of the *Lingula* bands may be equivalent to the Subcrenatum Marine Band, which marks the base of the Westphalian. Within the district, it is estimated that some 7 m of these Westphalian mudstones, referred to the Winksley Shale, are present in the valleys of Kex Beck and the River Laver, where they are entirely covered by drift.

CARBONIFEROUS ROCKS AT DEPTH

Carboniferous rocks have been recorded in a number of boreholes which have penetrated the overlying Permian rocks. The majority are located up to 2.5 km east of the Carboniferous outcrop in the area south-west and south of North Stainley. A borehole at Musterfield Farm [2713 7608] (Appendix 2) proved, beneath the Lower Magnesian Limestone (Cadeby Formation), about 87 m of fine- and coarse-grained sandstones with interbedded shales, three of which contained *Lingula* sp. and another which yielded *Myalina* sp. The stratigraphical designation of these beds is uncertain but they may be equivalent, in part, to the Laverton Sandstone and the overlying Winksley Shale (A A Wilson personal communication 1983).

Slightly further east, water boreholes at New Zealand Farm [2752 7503], Potgate Farm [2778 7552] and Stainley Hall [2864 7640] all proved, beneath the Lower Magnesian Limestone, sandstones and shales, clearly of Carboniferous age but otherwise unspecified. Near Wood Farm, a water borehole [2878 7531] (Appendix 1) penetrated about 46 m of interbedded sandstone and shale, in which one shale bed yielded *Lingula* sp.; a thin bed of shelly, crinoidal limestone may represent the Cayton Gill Shell Bed of Kinderscoutian age.

The Aiskew Bank Farm Borehole [2667 8888], located, in the north-east corner of the adjoining Masham district, proved a Carboniferous sequence (Appendix 2) including, in descending order, the Lower Follifoot Grit, the Colsterdale Marine Beds and the Red Scar Grit (of Arnsbergian age). Ten kilometres to the south-east, the British Coal Kirklington Borehole [3287 8091] (Appendix 2) proved the same sequence. Five kilometres east of here, at Sandhutton, another British Coal borehole [3798 8157] proved Carboniferous cherts, limestones and sandstones from 387 to 417 m depth. These beds are probably the equivalent of the stratigraphically lower Richmond or Crow cherts (of Pendleian age). It appears therefore that a Carboniferous sequence, similar to that of the Masham district, extends eastwards beneath the district. It is likely, however, that the gentle south-easterly dip of the Masham Carboniferous succession does not extend far beneath the Permian cover of the district, because gentle folding or faulting must bring the Richmond Chert sequence back up at Sandhutton. Three kilometres south of the district, the Ellenthorpe Borehole (Falcon and Kent, 1960), which is located on the projected axial trace of the Harrogate Anticline, proved Carboniferous strata of Dinantian age (A R E Strank, personal communication, 1984), suggesting that the anticline may become more strongly deformed towards the southern margin of the district.

THREE

Permian

The Permian rocks of Yorkshire were first shown by William Smith's map of Yorkshire (1821) on which the Yellow or Magnesian Limestone, separated by red clay and gypsum from the overlying Knottingley Limestone were delineated. This map was improved by Sedgwick (1829) who also published a detailed description of the Permian strata. Sedgwick divided the sequence into Magnesian Limestone, Lower Red-marl and Gypsum, and Upper Slaty Limestone. For the adjacent Harrogate area this classification was refined by the Geological Survey (Geological Survey of Great Britain, 1874; Fox-Strangways, 1908) to Lower Magnesian Limestone, Middle Marls, Upper Magnesian Limestone and Upper Marls. However, in the Thirsk district, where there is less exposure, the sequence was mapped and described as Magnesian Limestone, undivided (Geological Survey of Great Britain, 1884; Fox-Strangways et al., 1886).

The traditional fourfold subdivision of the Permian used for the Harrogate (62) Sheet has remained almost unchanged (Table 2; British Geological Survey, 1987) and is retained, for consistency, in this Memoir. However, it does not strictly comply with modern formal stratigraphical guidelines (Hedberg, 1976) and has been revised by Smith et al. (1986). The new formal stratigraphical names are shown in parentheses (Table 2, and below), but are not otherwise used here.

Full details of measured sections in the district are given by Cooper (1987); condensed logs of the more important are included in this description.

The climax (Asturian phase) of the Hercynian earth movements, at the end of Carboniferous times, caused faulting and folding, which resulted in the formation of positive structures, such as the Harrogate Anticline to the south of the district. During subsequent Permian times, a major land-locked basin extended from eastern England across the North Sea to eastern Europe (Ziegler, 1982; Glennie, 1983). The district lay near the western margin of this basin, in tropical palaeolatitudes.

Newly uplifted areas were subjected to intense, mainly subaerial erosion in a desert environment, which peneplaned much of the district but left some residual steep-sided hills. This irregular relief was subsequently buried by the carbonate deposits of the Lower Magnesian Limestone. The unconformity at the base of the Lower Magnesian Limestone has been proved in several boreholes (Appendix 2) and is poorly exposed in the banks of the River Ure [2694 7798] and River Laver [2674 7192; 2695 7208], where Carboniferous sandstones commonly show signs of leaching and red-brown staining associated with subaerial erosion.

During late Permian times, the depositional basin underwent a series of flooding and evaporation cycles, possibly caused by glacioeustatic sea-level changes, giving rise to Zechstein Cycles EZ1–EZ5 (Smith, 1970b, 1989) (Table 2). Where fully developed, individual cycles show an upward progression in evaporitic sedimentation through carbonate-

anhydrite-halite-sylvite, reflecting the progressive crystallisation of minerals with increasing solubility. The carbonate and anhydrite phases are best developed near the margins of the basin and those of the EZ1 and EZ3 cycles are generally well preserved in the district. Halite and sylvinite deposits, however, are restricted to the more central parts of the basin, around the Yorkshire coast and further east (Smith, 1974a); westwards, their lateral equivalents, at outcrop, are the red-brown, semi-terrigenous mudstones of the Middle Marl (Edlington Formation) (EZ1–2) and the Upper Marl (Roxby Formation) (EZ3–5). The boundaries of the cycles are not necessarily coincident with the formational boundaries (Table 2).

BASAL BRECCIA

Local pockets of breccia and conglomerate overlie the Carboniferous sequence unconformably; these have not been distinguished separately on the map from the overlying Lower Magnesian Limestone, but are shown on the vertical section. The Aiskew Bank Farm Borehole [2667 8888] (Pattison, 1978; Appendix 2) proved 3.95 m of these deposits, comprising Carboniferous limestone fragments with a ferruginous patina (desert varnish) cemented by dolomitic limestone. The Kirklington Borehole [3287 8091] and the Sleningford Mill Borehole [2778 7841] (Bridge and Murray, 1983) penetrated 0.47 m and 0.3 m respectively of similar deposits (Appendix 2). The Basal Breccia may have been deposited coevally with the aeolian Basal Permian Sands, which are absent in the district, but which have been proved in the Harrogate area to the south (Cooper and Burgess, in press). Leaching and red staining of the sandstone below the unconformity and the desert varnish developed on the sandstone clasts, together suggest subaerial erosion in an arid environment. Transgression by the late Permian (Zechstein) sea resulted in subsequent cementation of the breccia and conglomerate by marine carbonates.

MARL SLATE (MARL SLATE FORMATION) (EZ1)

A eustatic rise in sea level during the late Permian, representing the early phase of the EZ1 cycle, resulted in a rapid marine transgression over the intracontinental basin. In the district, the Marl Slate, a finely laminated, carbonaceous, calcareous siltstone, up to a few metres thick, was deposited locally in a stagnant, semi-euxinic sea. These beds have not been differentiated from the Lower Magnesian Limestone at outcrop, but they have been suggested in boreholes (Appendix 2) at Aiskew Bank Farm [2667 8888] (Pattison, 1978) and Sleningford Mill [2778 7841] (Bridge and Murray, 1983) where they are 0.1 m and 0.86 m thick respectively. Similar lithologies also occur at the base of the Lower

Table 2 Stratigraphical framework and nomenclature of the Permian strata in the district and their relationship to coeval strata to the east. Formalised names are shown in parentheses (Smith et al., 1986); thicknesses in metres.

Symbol on map	Sequence at outcrop	Sequence at depth, and east of district		English Zechstein Cycle
		Saliferous Marl (Roxby Formation)		
		Top Anhydrite (Little Beck Formation)		EZ5
		(Sleights Siltstone Formation)		
		Upper Halite and Potash (Sneaton (Halite) Formation)		
UPM	UPPER MARL (Roxby Formation) (10–18 m)	UPPER MARL (Roxby Formation) (30–40 m)	Upper Anhydrite (Sherburn (Anhydrite) Formation)	ZEZ4
		(Upgang Formation)		
		(Carnallitic Marl Formation)		
		Middle Halite and Potash (Boulby (Halite) Formation)		
	—Evaporites dissolved away at outcrop—	Billingham Main Anhydrite (Billingham (Anhydrite) Formation		EZ3
UML	UPPER MAGNESIAN LIMESTONE (Brotherton Formation) (8–12 m)	UPPER MAGNESIAN LIMESTONE (Brotherton Formation) (21–28 m)		
		(Fordon (Evaporite) Formation)		
MPM	MIDDLE MARL (Edlington Formation) (20–50 m)	MIDDLE MARL (Edlington Formation) (∿70 m)	Anhydrite (in Fordon Formation)	EZ2
		(Kirkham Abbey Formation)		
	—Evaporites dissolved away at outcrop—	Hayton Anhydrite (Hayton Formation)		
LML	LOWER MAGNESIAN LIMESTONE (Cadeby Formation) (40–65 m)	LOWER MAGNESIAN LIMESTONE (Cadeby Formation) (95 m)		EZ1
	MARL SLATE (Marl Slate Formation) (0–1 m)	MARL SLATE (Marl Slate Formation)		
	BASAL BRECCIA (0–4 m)	BASAL PERMIAN SANDS		
	Permian strata unconformable on Carboniferous strata			

Magnesian Limestone in the Wood Farm Borehole [2878 7531] (Appendix 2).

LOWER MAGNESIAN LIMESTONE (CADEBY FORMATION) (EZ1)

The Lower Magnesian Limestone represents the carbonate phase of the first (EZ1) cycle in the Zechstein basin (Table 2). Because the district was marginal to this basin, sedimentation was laterally variable, as deposition gradually overwhelmed the undulating topography. The formation ranges in thickness from 40 to 65 m at outcrop, but thickens eastwards (downdip) to 95 m. Further east, outside the district, it thickens even more towards a buried reef which marks the edge of the carbonate platform (Smith, 1970b; Taylor and Colter, 1975).

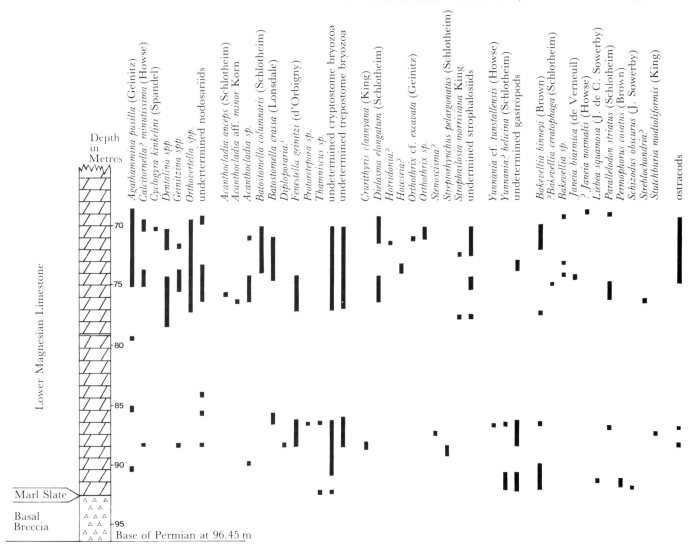

Table 3   Vertical distribution of macrofossils and microfossils recognised in hand-specimens from the Lower Limestone of the Aiskew Bank Farm Borehole (after Pattison, 1978).

The formation consists largely of dolomite and calcitic dolomite, which resulted from a complex diagenetic history (Clark, 1980; Fuzesy, 1980; Harwood, 1980, 1986; Kaldi, 1980a, b; Kaldi and Gidman, 1982). Initial dolomitisation and subsequent alteration have generally destroyed most of the fine sedimentary textures and sedimentary structures. At the extreme, the rock was reduced to a porous, vuggy dolomite. Dolomitised rock is patchy within individual exposures, and forms amorphous masses within otherwise well-bedded sequences.

The Lower Magnesian Limestone is moderately fossiliferous. The Aiskew Bank Farm Borehole [2667 8888] cored a fairly complete section through the formation and the distribution of fauna within it is shown in Table 3.

In northern England, south of Ripon, the Lower Magnesian Limestone is generally subdivided into two formal lithostratigraphical units, in upward sequence, the 'Lower Subdivision' (Wetherby Member), and the 'Upper Subdivision' (Sprotbrough Member); these are separated by the thin Hampole Beds (Smith et al., 1986). However, in the district, this lithological distinction is less pronounced; the lower and upper subdivisions can only be recognised informally (Cooper, 1987), mainly in the south. These units are not shown separately on the map, but may be tentatively recognised in some well-exposed sections and a few boreholes; they are described sequentially, below.

The lower unit is 14 to 34 m thick; its lower part consists of interbedded carbonate mudstone, locally algal-laminated, and shelly dolomite. Subordinate lithologies include thin mudstone partings which are locally pyritic and carbonaceous; oncolitic dolomite with a glauconitic matrix also occurs. The carbonate lithofacies are laterally variable throughout the district (Figure 2) but there is an overall upwards decrease in abundance of shelly, benthic fauna (Cooper, 1987). Coquinoid dolomites with an abundant foraminiferal, bryozoan and bivalve fauna (Pattison, 1978;

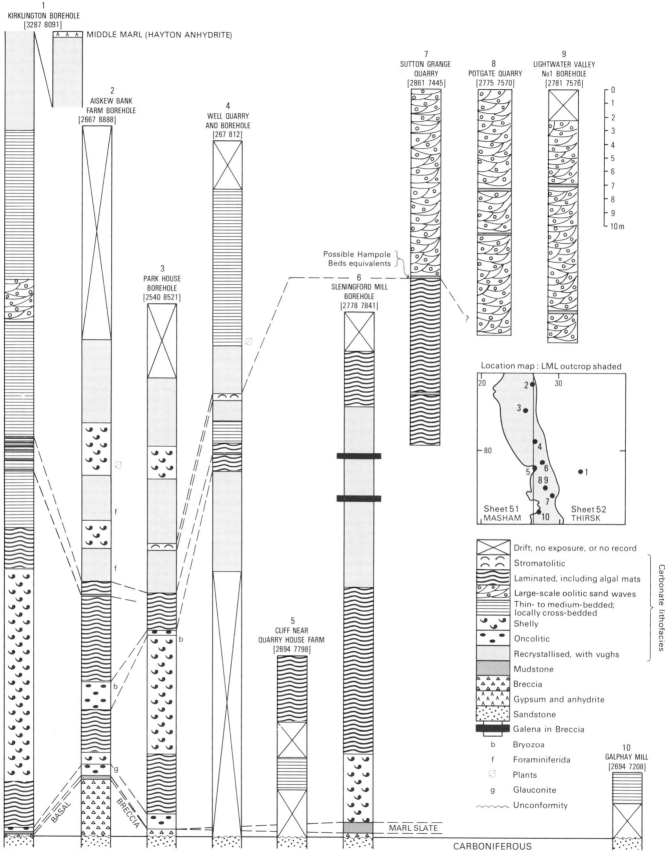

Figure 2 Lithofacies of the Lower Magnesian Limestone (Cadeby Formation) in the Thirsk district and the adjoining Masham district.

Table 3) were proved, low in the sequence, in boreholes at Aiskew Bank Farm [2667 8888] (Pattison, 1978; Appendix 2), and Park House [2540 8521], both in the Masham (51) district, and at Sleningford Mill [2778 7841] (Bridge and Murray, 1983) and Kirklington [3287 8091] in the Thirsk district; oncolitic overgrowths and glauconite peloids are locally common in the first two boreholes. These carbonates are interbedded with dark grey, pyritic, carbonaceous, laminated mudstone beds (up to 0.1 m thick). At Quarry House [2694 7798] and Galphay Mill [2694 7208], however, the shelly fauna is absent, and the lowermost beds are represented by finely laminated to thin-bedded dolomites with traces of cross-bedding and numerous mudstone partings.

The upper part of the lower unit is a poorly fossiliferous dolomite with relic ooliths; it ranges from laminated and thin bedded (Park House and Aiskew Bank Farm boreholes), to medium and thick bedded (Sleningford Mill Borehole), and to thick bedded and structureless (Well Quarry [267 812]). Channel structures with erosive scours and ooliths are present in coeval strata near West Tanfield [2694 7798]. The characteristics outlined above suggest deposition in the intertidal to shallow subtidal zone of a semi-restricted lagoon, at the shoreward margin of a broad carbonate platform.

South of the district, the lower and upper members of the Lower Magnesian Limestone are separated by impersistent, thin (0.03 to 0.6 m) mudstones and fenestral dolomites, the Hampole Beds (Smith, 1968). In the district they are tentatively recognised (Smith, 1968) at Sutton Grange Quarry [2861 7445], where (algal?) laminated dolomite is overlain by a thin (0.1 m) bed of clay, possibly equivalent to the Hampole Beds, which is succeeded by 15 m of dolomite with poorly developed, large-scale cross-bedded facies typical of the 'Upper Subdivision' (Sprotbrough Member). A comparable mudstone bed is present at a similar stratigraphical level at Potgate Quarry [2775 7570], and also at Well Quarry [267 812], to the north, where the possible equivalent of the Hampole Beds may be represented by, in upward sequence, laminated dolomite, thin clay, and thin-bedded, stromatolitic dolomite (4 m. thick). Boreholes at Park House and Aiskew Bank Farm, just to the north-west of the district (Figure 2), proved distinctive laminated beds associated with mudstone partings at a similar stratigraphical level, which may also equate with the Hampole Beds. The depositional environment of the Hampole Beds has been interpreted as intertidal or supratidal, probably marking a period of subaerial emergence in the area south of Ripon during deposition of the Lower Magnesian Limestone sequence (Smith 1968). This facies is restricted to a fairly narrow intertidal zone, and the equivalent beds in the Thirsk district may represent a coeval, but slightly deeper-water facies.

The upper part of the Lower Magnesian Limestone ranges from 18 to 33 m in thickness, and consists, for the most part (Figure 2), of evenly bedded, commonly oolitic dolomite, locally with shell fragments; dome-shaped ?stromatolites (10 to 30 cm diameter) are present low in the sequence at Well Quarry and in the Park House Borehole. Bedforms comprise cross-stratification ranging from cross-lamination (0.1 m sets) to large-scale cross-bedding (3 to 10 m sets) resulting from the migration of subaqueous dunes or sand-waves (Smith, 1974a,b; Cooper, 1987). These bed-

forms, seen at Sutton Grange [2861 7445] and Potgate [2775 7570] quarries, are typical of the 'Upper Subdivision' (Sprotbrough Member) to the south of the district (Kaldi, 1980a). At East Tanfield [2900 7765] the upper part of the sequence consists of large-scale, cross-bedded, channelled, oolitic dolomite. Similar oolitic dolomite is present at Sutton Grange Quarry [285 745], but here the fine texture has largely been destroyed by dolomitisation. These lithofacies suggest deposition in an intertidal to subtidal lagoon, possibly protected by an offshore oolite bank, represented by the oolitic facies at Sutton Grange Quarry.

Details

Aiskew Bank Farm Borehole

Situated in the north-eastern corner of the Masham (51) district, adjacent to the north-western corner of the Thirsk district (Figure 2), this borehole [2667 8888] proved most of the Lower Magnesian Limestone, the Basal Breccia, and its unconformable relationship with the underlying Carboniferous sequence. Lithological details of the borehole are given in Appendix 3 and palaeontological data (Pattison, 1978) are shown in Table 3.

Well Quarry

Well Quarry [267 812] showed the most northerly major exposure of the Lower Magnesian Limestone in the district (Figure 2). A composite section along the south face of the quarry [2692 8095 to 2684 8093] exposed the following sequence:

	Thickness m
Dolomite, dark grey to buff, thin-bedded, with sporadic shells; vuggy in part; coal fragments along one bedding plane	10.90
Clay, brown	0.01
Dolomite, buff and grey-buff, finely crystalline, vuggy in part; stromatolitic laminae at base	4.70
Dolomite, buff, thin- to very thin-bedded, with abundant vughs in places; clay covered bedding planes near top	2.90
Dolomite, buff, massive	0.70
Dolomite, buff, thin- to thick-bedded, with clay partings and large vertical vughs	7.60

Further details of the sequence are given by Bridge and Murray (1983).

In the quarry, Harwood (1981, 1986) inferred localised penecontemporaneous hydraulic fracturing of the dolomitic limestone with diagenitic baryte deposited around the breccia.

Well Quarry Borehole [2673 8128] (Appendix 2), with an approximate surface elevation of 80 m above OD proved 25.3 m of limestone on 5.8 m of "marl" (Lower Magnesian Limestone) resting on Carboniferous shale and sandstone. However, a borehole at Mowbray Hill [2600 8123], about 800 m west of here (just within the Masham district), proved 41.6 m of Lower Magnesian Limestone resting on Carboniferous strata. A further borehole, 1300 m to the south-south-west at North Tanfield Farm [2609 8010] (also in the Masham district), proved 9.1 m of glacial deposits, on 54.3 m of limestone and 6.7 m of shale and limestone, overlying Carboniferous shale and sandstone. The apparently thin sequence of limestone proved at Well Quarry results from erosion of the limestone dip slope, which is incised and oversteepened from Well, southwards to East Tanfield.

Kirklington Borehole

Six kilometres east of Well Quarry the full 63.56 m thickness of the Lower Magnesian Limestone was penetrated in the Kirklington Borehole [3287 8091] (Appendix 2). This proved a basal (algal?) laminated unit, 2.93 m thick, overlain by 15.75 m of shelly and bryozoan-rich limestone, followed by ripple-marked and cross-bedded dolomite and limestone with sparse relict ooliths (Figure 2).

Tanfield Mill and Sleningford Mill

Near West Tanfield the Lower Magnesian Limestone is exposed in the banks and bed of the River Ure from Tanfield Mill [2759 7864] to Sleningford Mill [2820 7836]. Here the bedding is subhorizontal with several open monoclinal flexures dipping 3 to 5° to the south-east. About 12 m thickness of buff, thin- to medium-bedded dolomitic limestone are exposed. The rock is fine- to medium-grained crystalline with scattered shell fragments and relict ooliths. Vughs, scattered throughout the sequence, are especially common upstream of Sleningford Mill [2783 7846] where they reach 0.1 m across and contain well-developed dolomite crystals up to 1.5 cm long. Near this locality, Lamming and Robertson (1968) recorded an east–west-trending vein of galena with associated baryte.

Sleningford Mill Borehole

The Sleningford Mill Borehole [2778 7841] proved 34.2 m of dolomitic limestone containing some mineralised breccia with galena; this passes down to mudstone and conglomerate, which rest unconformably on Carboniferous strata; details are given in Appendix 2 and Figure 2.

Quarry south of West Tanfield

Situated 0.5 km south of West Tanfield [2707 7827] this small disused quarry exposes a succession below that of Sleningford Mill and above that of Quarry House, nearby. The following sequence is present:

	Thickness m
Dolomite, buff-grey, not accessible; thin- to medium-bedded, laterally wedging out; vuggy	1.30
Dolomite, pale buff-grey weathering to buff, hard and microcrystalline to finely crystalline; thin- to medium-bedded; laterally wedging out; sparse vughs	1.73
Dolomite, grey-buff to buff, microcrystalline, hard and splintery; scattered large and small vughs	0.24
Dolomite buff and yellow-buff, microcrystalline, with numerous small vughs; thin- and very thin-bedded, with a few beds wedging out	0.42
Dolomite, buff, microcrystalline to finely crystalline, with small ooliths in places; medium- and thick-bedded, locally thin-bedded; laterally wedging out, in part; locally vuggy	2.05

Near Quarry House Farm

A natural cliff section [2694 7798] adjacent to the River Ure, 250 m south-east of Quarry House Farm, exposes 10 m of Lower Magnesian Limestone near the base of the formation. The lowest part of the Permian sequence is not exposed here, but the presence of the Carboniferous Laverton Sandstone in the river bed, 100 m to the west, suggests that the basal unconformity is between 2 and 5 m below the following measured section (see also Figure 2):

	Thickness m
Loose dolomitic limestone fragments	2.00
Dolomite, brown-buff, microcrystalline to very finely crystalline, with small dolomite-lined vughs; thinly bedded, becoming laminated towards the top; the bedding surfaces are uneven and beds thin slightly in places	1.15
Dolomite, brown-buff, microcrystalline, with streaks of crystalline dolomite; thick-bedded, splitting into thin and medium beds; faint parallel lamination at the base	0.53
Dolomite, buff, microcrystalline, laminated at top, becoming very thinly bedded at the base; persistent (algal) lamination; sparse small vughs	0.47
Dolomite, buff, very finely crystalline, occurring as one medium homogeneous bed with parallel banding in the bottom 0.03 m	0.24
Dolomite, yellow-buff, microcrystalline, laminated to very thinly bedded in regular, but uneven (possibly algal) laminae; scattered small vughs	0.45
Clay, dolomitic, purplish grey-brown with faint banding and forming an impersistant bed with an uneven base and top	0 – 0.05
Dolomite, yellow-buff, microcrystalline, massive, with slight banding in the bottom 0.1 m and scattered small vughs; channelled base	0.25
Dolomite, buff, microcrystalline to very finely crystalline, thickly laminated to very thinly bedded with undulating, but regular laminae and a few beds which wedge out	1.55 – 1.80
No exposure	2.60
Dolomite, grey-buff, microcrystalline, porcellanous and very finely crystalline; slightly uneven beds; thin and very thinly bedded with laminated partings and traces of cross-lamination	1.05
No exposure	0.40
Dolomite, yellow-buff, microcrystalline, but weathered and slightly earthy; regularly bedded in thin and very thin beds	0.80
Dolomite, yellow-buff (exposed below water of River Ure)	0.30

East Tanfield

At East Tanfield the River Ure has cut a channel in the upper part of the Lower Magnesian Limestone. The section on the south bank [2909 7762 to 2898 7764] is:

	Thickness m
Alluvium, no exposure	2.00
Clay (till), buff-brown, with a few pebbles and streaks of buff-coloured dolomitic limestone; uneven convolute basal contact	0.03 – 0.7
Dolomite, buff to buff-brown, microcrystalline to porcellanous, vuggy	1.27
Dolomite, buff to brown-buff, coarsely crystalline and porous, with probable ooliths; massive bed with cross-bedding in sets 0.01 to 0.05 thick; the cross-bedding dips 22° at N016°	1.13
Dolomite, buff to pale buff, microcrystalline to coarsely crystalline, with scattered relict ooliths; vuggy in part; thin- to medium-bedded	3.33

Dolomite, buff, porous, vuggy, microcrystalline, with scattered ooliths; thin- to medium-bedded with cross-stratified channel-fill at base; channels up to 15 m wide and 0.6 m deep   3.02

Potgate Quarry

During the resurvey of the area (1981–83) Potgate Quarry [2775 7570] was being worked for roadstone and road base material. A composite section of the Lower Magnesian Limestone sequence exposed at that time is as follows (see also Figure 2):

	Thickness m
Top of section, thin glacial till stripped off	
Dolomite, buff, microcrystalline to finely crystalline, very thickly bedded, with numerous vughs and a streaky texture	1.75
Clay, buff-brown, hard and compact	0.02
Dolomite, buff, grey-buff and orange-buff, microcrystalline to finely crystalline, thin- to thick-bedded, with abundant vughs	4.03
Clay, buff-brown; an uneven bed which pinches and swells	0.03
Dolomite, similar to beds above	1.25
Clay, brown, blocky, with variable thickness; rests on an uneven pot-marked surface	0.05–0.20
Dolomite, similar to beds above but with sparse clay partings	3.25
Clay, brown, on an erosive surface	0.03
Dolomite, grey and buff, microcrystalline to very finely crystalline; locally vuggy; occasional clay laminae; dark carbonaceous partings (0.01 m thick) in basal 4.90 m; thin- to thick-bedded	7.32

A nearby water borehole at Musterfield [2713 7608] (Appendix 2) proved 29.9 m of Lower Magnesian Limestone overlying Carboniferous strata. Another water borehole near Potgate Farm [2778 7553] (Appendix 1) proved the Lower Magnesian Limestone to be at least 53 m thick. A little further east near Wood Farm [2888 7531] (Appendix 2) the same sequence is at least 65.2 m thick.

Sutton Grange Quarry

This quarry near Sutton Grange [2861 7445] works the Lower Magnesian Limestone for agricultural lime and roadbase material. The rock is variable in quality, and some of the higher parts of the quarry expose leached dolomite which is soft and friable. A similar lithology was also recorded nearby in BGS Spigot's Well Borehole [2969 7399] which was abandoned at a depth of 23.19 m, proving only poorly cemented dolomitic sand. At Sutton Grange Quarry a section through the least altered part of the sequence gave the following sequence (see also Figure 2):

	Thickness m
Top of quarry, thin soil and weathered dolomitic limestone	
Dolomite, buff-grey, fine-grained to microcrystalline, with relict ooliths?; thin- to medium-bedded, with undulating bedding planes and stylolitic contacts; some pinching out of beds and some traces of large-scale cross-bedding; in the lower part of the unit numerous grey hard laminae are present; small vughs are common throughout; massive, uneven, recrystallised bed at base	13.48

Clay, brown and blocky	0–0.10
Dolomite, buff, fine-grained, crystalline, thin-bedded to massive; algal-laminated, with scattered stylolitic bedding planes coated with bituminous residues and clay; small vughs throughout upper part	8.60
Clay, brown and blocky	0–0.08
Dolomite, buff, microcrystalline to finely crystalline, unevenly laminated or thinly bedded, with highly irregular and sporadically stylolitic bedding planes; irregular cavities and elongate crystal-filled nodules (probably after bioturbation); numerous clay partings	2.95

Thieves Gill House

A small disused quarry at the side of the Thieves Gill glacial drainage channel [2741 7397] exposed the following sequence of Lower Magnesian Limestone:

	Thickness m
Dolomite, buff and white-buff, microcrystalline and porcellanous; thin-, medium- and thick-bedded; stylolitic contacts; small vughs mainly in the thin and very thin beds. The rock is slightly folded into an anticline, probably as a result of cambering	5.00

A nearby borehole at Thieves Gill House [2735 7399] proved 1.21 m of drift on Lower Magnesian Limestone to 31.08 m, resting on red sandstone to 35.57 m.

Birkby Wood and Mill Bank quarries

Disused quarries at Birkby Wood [2720 7240] and Mill Bank [2702 7204] both expose similar facies of the Lower Magnesian Limestone, about 12 m above the base of the formation. The sequence at Birkby Wood is as follows:

	Thickness m
Top of section: feather edge of brown sandy clay (till) with pebbles and cobbles mainly of Carboniferous sandstone plus abundant Magnesian Limestone fragments	
Dolomite, beige-buff, hard and microcrystalline; thin- and very thinly bedded in uneven beds with stylolitic contacts; the beds are brecciated in places with a secondary cement of calcite around angular dolomite fragments; aggregate of colourless to pale yellow dolomite crystals in basal 2.0 m	3.15
Dolomite, grey-buff, hard, mainly microcrystalline, vuggy in places; the bottom 0.4 m of the exposure is yellow-buff, soft and porous; thin- to medium-bedded, but beds coalesce to form thick units; the bedding contacts are slightly stylolitic	2.40

Galphay Mill

At Galphay Mill [2694 7208] a section in the south bank of the River Laver exposes strata close to the basal Lower Magnesian Limestone unconformity; the following sequence (also shown in Figure 2) is present:

	Thickness m
Dolomite, buff-grey to grey, hard, splintery, microcrystalline, thin- to medium-bedded, with dolomitic mudstone partings; slight cambering	

towards the river	2.20

No exposure; concealed unconformity with the
Carboniferous strata ... 2.50

LAVERTON SANDSTONE (NAMURIAN)
Sandstone, yellow-buff, medium- to coarse-grained,
consisting mainly of subangular quartz grains with
white-weathered feldspars and a little mica. The
sandstone is thin to medium bedded and dips about
7° at N114° ... 1.50

MIDDLE MARL (EDLINGTON FORMATION), INCLUDING THE ?HAYTON ANHYDRITE (EZ1–2)

The Middle Marl crops out in a belt of low ground to the east of the Lower Magnesian Limestone escarpment. Where the Middle Marl outcrop is drift-free it weathers to produce a heavy, red-brown clay soil; this, taken together with its topo-

graphic expression as a slack between the Lower and Upper Magnesian limestones, is commonly the only evidence for its presence. However, the formation is poorly exposed along the Ure Valley between Ripon [3129 7336] and Ripon Parks [3086 7515] where small exposures of red-brown silty mudstone are present. At outcrop the Middle Marl is generally between 15 and 20 m thick, but in places it thins to 10 m due to slight cambering of the overlying Upper Magnesian Limestone. Boreholes show that, downdip from the outcrop, it ranges in thickness from 20 to 50 m, with a maximum of 70 m in the north of the district (Figure 3a). Most of this variation is due to the presence or absence (as a result of near-surface dissolution) of the underlying ?Hayton Anhydrite. This anhydrite does not form a mappable feature at outcrop and is included here within the Middle Marl (Edlington Formation).

The ?Hayton Anhydrite (Hayton Formation) is up to 35 m thick. In the Kirklington Borehole [3287 8091] (Appendix 2) it is 29 m thick and typically comprises bluish grey

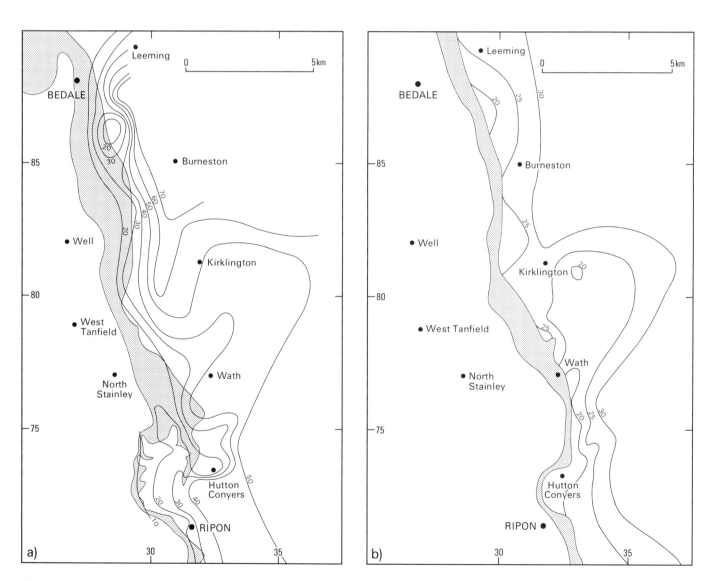

Figure 3 Isopachyte map for a) the Middle Marl (Edlington Formation) and b) the Upper Marl (Roxby Formation) in the Thirsk and adjoining Masham districts.

anhydrite with a slight nodular ('chicken-wire') texture picked out by buff-coloured dolomite; it forms the anhydrite phase of the lowest Zechstein cycle (EZ1) (Table 2). Although probably originally deposited as gypsum in a hypersaline lagoon environment (Smith, 1989), calcium sulphate was altered to the anhydrous phase (anhydrite) during subsequent burial and diagenesis. However, anhydrite is metastable, hydrating to gypsum if subsequent uplift brings it into contact with groundwater at depths less than 1000 m (Mossop and Shearman, 1973). Consequently, the Hayton Anhydrite passes laterally westwards, updip, into an irregular belt of secondary gypsum running subparallel to the Middle Marl outcrop. On continued contact with passing groundwater the gypsum partially, or fully, dissolves away, resulting in cave systems and causing the overlying strata to founder (Smith, 1972; James et al., 1981; Cooper, 1986, 1988, 1989) (see also p.15). The buried surface of this gypsum has a rugged karst morphology.

At Ripon Parks [3083 7517] (see details and Plate 1) the gypsum in the Middle Marl (possibly equivalent to the Hayton Anhydrite) is exposed in the west bank of the River Ure (Kendall and Wroot, 1924; Forbes, 1958; James et al., 1981). Here 7.1 m of massive, grey, alabastrine gypsum and porphyroblastic gypsum (probably equivalent to the upper part of the Hayton Anhydrite) are overlain by 2.83 m of interbedded gypsum and mudstone; this is capped by 3.73 m of mudstone with subordinate fibrous gypsum veins. This sequence, along with exposures immediately north along the River Ure [3075 7566], exhibits a series of tight folds, including one recumbent anticline (Plate 1). These folds probably formed by lateral pressure resulting from an increase in volume (c.63 per cent) during the hydration of anhydrite to gypsum (Mossop and Shearman, 1973).

Overlying the supposed Hayton Anhydrite there is a thin sequence of lenticular dolomitic limestone, possibly the Kirkham Abbey Formation (Smith et al., 1974), which forms the carbonate phase of the second Zechstein cycle (EZ2). This formation, which varies from 0 to 4 m thick, is tentatively recognised at Ripon Parks (James et al., 1981) and in boreholes, mainly in the east of the district. However, it does not form a mappable feature and is included in the Middle Marl (Edlington Formation) in this account.

The upper 20 m of the Middle Marl formation consists predominantly of laminated to thin-bedded, mainly red-brown siltstone and mudstone with sporadic thin gypsum and anhydrite beds. These beds are the semi-terrigenous, lateral equivalents of the Fordon Evaporites (Stewart, 1963; Taylor and Colter, 1975; Colter and Reed, 1980; Smith, 1980), the halite phase of the EZ2 cycle, which are confined to the more central part of the Zechstein basin, further east.

Details

Kirklington Borehole

Details of the Middle Marl, including the Kirkham Abbey Formation and the Hayton Anhydrite, are given in Appendix 2.

Ripon Parks

On the west bank of the River Ure at Ripon Parks, the Middle Marl is exposed for a distance of nearly 600 m [3075 7571 to 3088 7513] as a series of folds which range from open folds in the massive gypsum to disharmonic tight and recumbent folds in the interbedded gypsum and mudstone (Plate 1). These folds have variable trends, with both approximately ENE–WSW and NW–SE fold axes.

The sequence is illustrated by Kendall and Wroot (1924), Forbes (1958) and James et al., (1981); further details are given by Cooper (1987). The sequence exposed at the southern end of the Ripon Parks section is:

Plate 1   Marl interbedded with gypsum showing contorted bedding and folding possibly resulting from an increase in volume associated with the hydration of anhydrite to gypsum. Middle Marl, Ripon Parks (A7550).

	Thickness m
Clay, sandy, reddish brown, with pebbles, cobbles and boulders (till)	1.00
Mudstone, pinkish brown and grey, gypsiferous, with numerous thin beds of gypsiferous dolomite and calcareous mudstone; numerous fibrous veins	3.73
Mudstone, grey, calcareous and gypsiferous, with abundant nodules of both pink and white gypsum and sporadic thin beds of grey and pinkish grey gypsum, especially near base; abundant fibrous gypsum veins	2.83
Gypsum, grey and white, massive, banded; mainly alabastrine, but with scattered porphyroblasts and numerous thin beds of porphyroblastic gypsum; interbedded grey, muddy gypsum and mudstone in the bottom 2 m; numerous concordant and cross-cutting fibrous gypsum veins with concentrations of porphyroblastic gypsum adjacent to them	7.10

This section in the massive gypsum is being actively dissolved by the River Ure. During the resurvey of the area part of the cliff had collapsed and the large gypsum blocks that fell into the river dissolved in little more than one year (James et al., 1981). When the section was revisited in June 1989 the massive gypsum cliff was undercut to a depth of between 4 and 5 m.

The only other exposure of the gypsum was 300 m west of the river section [3050 7511]. Here, adjacent to a subsidence hollow, 5 m of gypsiferous beds are poorly exposed. The red-brown, grey and white, laminated to thin-bedded gypsum ranges in texture from alabastrine to coarsely crystalline, porphyroblastic and fibrous. The beds dip in numerous directions at up to 60°, suggesting folding similar to that seen adjacent to the River Ure.

UPPER MAGNESIAN LIMESTONE (BROTHERTON FORMATION) (EZ3)

The Upper Magnesian Limestone forms a low, mainly drift-covered escarpment, east of and subparallel to the Lower Magnesian Limestone and Middle Marl. It is exposed in a few quarries and natural exposures, but much of the outcrop has been mapped from the distribution of lithologically and faunally distinctive soil brash. The formation consists of thin-bedded, whitish grey or pinkish grey, porcellanous calcitic dolomite and dolomitic limestone, which is commonly cross-bedded and which produces a fetid smell when broken. Typical exposures (see details) are found near Ripon [3108 7332], Nunwick [3184 7473] and Ripon Parks [3090 7513]. At Chapel Hill [2930 7925] an atypical lithology is exposed, comprising yellow-buff, thin-bedded, fine- to coarse-crystalline dolomite and calcitic dolomite; late diagenetic dolomitisation and recrystallisation has destroyed all the fine textural details.

The Upper Magnesian Limestone forms the carbonate phase of the third Zechstein cycle (EZ3), and represents a renewed marine incursion which flooded the flat, coastal sabkha plain of the Middle Marl. Consequently, the formation is laterally persistent and relatively uniform in thickness, ranging from 8 to 12 m at outcrop. Boreholes in the east of the district indicate that it thickens downdip to between 21 and 28 m. The restricted and distinctive fauna includes the bivalves *Liebea squamosa* and *Schizodous obscurus*. The formation also contains the alga *Calcinema permiana*

which is almost restricted to, and diagnostic of the EZ3 third cycle carbonate (Pattison et al., 1973). The alga takes the form of sinuous, thread-like tubes 0.5 to 1.0 mm in diameter and is locally so abundant that it forms small lag deposits and thin ripple-marked beds.

At and near the outcrop, foundering of the Upper Magnesian Limestone, caused by the dissolution of gypsum (including the equivalent of the Hayton Anhydrite) in the Middle Marl, is a common phenomenon (Smith, 1972; Cooper, 1986). Exposures of the Limestone therefore often have steeper, and directionally more variable dips than the underlying Lower Magnesian Limestone; local cambering of the mudstones of the Middle Marl also affects the dip. Dips of 10° in Chapel Hill Quarry [2930 7925] are the result of foundering; cambering and foundering elsewhere locally produce dips of up to 30° in all directions, such as those seen at Ripon Parks (see details). Localised angular, open folds, with a wavelength of a few metres, are also produced by this mechanism.

Details

Kirklington Borehole

In this borehole [3287 8091] the Upper Magnesian Limestone is 9.70 m thick (see Appendix 2 for detail).

Chapel Hill

In the disused quarry at Chapel Hill [2933 7922] atypical dolomitised Upper Magnesian Limestone is exposed. The quarry shows 2.2 to 2.5 m of buff to yellow, finely to coarsely crystalline, porous dolomite with numerous dolomite-lined vughs. The beds are uneven, mainly thin and very thin bedded, and they weather to a rubbly state. The strata dip unevenly 6 to 10° to the NE, E and SE.

Ripon Parks

Immediately south of the Ripon Parks gypsum section, the Upper Magnesian Limestone is exposed on the west bank of the River Ure [3090 7513]. The limestone sequence here dips steeply, between 32° and 56° WSW; this is due to foundering after dissolution of gypsum in the Middle Marl. The following sequence is present:

	Thickness m
GLACIAL TILL	
Clay, sandy, red-brown, becoming grey at base, with abundant pebbles, cobbles and boulders of Carboniferous sandstone and limestone, plus a few Magnesian Limestone fragments	5.80
UPPER MARL	
Mudstone, brownish red with grey streaks	0.52
UPPER MAGNESIAN LIMESTONE	
Dolomitic limestone, buff and grey, crystalline to porcellanous, with small vughs; thin- to medium-bedded; beds well-laminated in places	5.35
Dolomitic limestone, grey, microcrystalline to finely crystalline, with a few vughs; laminated in thin and medium beds; abundant remains of *Calcinema* sp.	2.40
Dolomitic limestone, buff and grey, very finely crystalline to microcrystalline, thin- and medium-bedded, laminated in places	2.96

Hall Garth Ponds, Nunwick

A subsidence hollow [3184 7472], measuring about 25 × 35 m in width, and reported to be 7 m deep, formed at Hall Garth Ponds, in about 1940, by subsidence after the dissolution of gypsum (equivalent to the ?Hayton Anhydrite) in the Middle Marl (Cooper, 1986). Approximately 2 m of buff-coloured, thin-bedded dolomitic limestone is exposed above the water level. In an adjacent subsidence hollow [SE 3187 7474], 0.4 m of buff-coloured dolomitic limestone with *Calcinema* sp. is present.

Ripon Parks Farm

Near Ripon Parks Farm two exposures [3129 7390; 3141 7384] of the Upper Magnesian Limestone are present; they show 2.0 m and 3.5 m of the sequence respectively. Both comprise buff-grey, thin-bedded, microcrystalline to porcellanous, vuggy, commonly cross-laminated dolomitic limestone, with abundant remains of *Calcinema* sp. The dip is variable due to foundering caused by dissolution of gypsum in the underlying sequence.

Spring Hill

At Spring Hill the Upper Magnesian Limestone is exposed in the sides of two subsidence hollows. The first [3108 7332] is about 10 m deep; it has about 2 to 5 m of buff, thin- to very thin-bedded dolomitic limestone exposed in its sides. The other hollow [3122 7328] is reported to have formed on May 21st 1870; it is about 10 m deep and 20 m in diameter (Cooper, 1986). The upper part of the hole exposes 1.5 m of till underlain by 3.0 m of buff, thin-bedded porcellanous dolomitic limestone.

Low Common

Near Low Common [3107 7262] 1 to 3 m of sandy till overlie up to 2.5 m of grey-buff, thin- to very thin-bedded, microcrystalline, dolomitic limestone with small vughs, dipping about 10° to the south. The ground south of here has numerous enclosed subsidence hollows. Site investigations in the vicinity have shown that much of the Upper Magnesian Limestone is partially foundered. Apart from obvious subsidence hollows, there are also subsided areas in the Upper Magnesian Limestone filled with glacial till, and others filled with plugs of Upper Marl and Sherwood Sandstone. The latter have dropped down from the overlying strata (now removed by erosion) into the Upper Magnesian Limestone.

UPPER MARL (ROXBY FORMATION) (EZ3–5)

The Upper Marl is not generally exposed in this district, but is present in a tract of low, drift-covered ground sandwiched between the escarpments of the Upper Magnesian Limestone and the Sherwood Sandstone Group. However, at Ripon Golf Course [3098 7292] up to 3 m of red mudstone is exposed in a small outlier of the formation. In boreholes near the outcrop the Upper Marl is typified by brownish red, silty mudstone, commonly with green reduction spots and numerous beds of gypsum.

At outcrop, the formation is between 10 and 18 m thick, but downdip it thickens to between 30 and 40 m in the east of the district (Figure 3b). Much of this increase in thickness is due to the presence of interbedded EZ3 cycle evaporites, mainly the Billingham Main Anhydrite (Billingham Formation) in the lower part of the formation. Higher in the sequence, thin fourth and fifth cycle evaporites including the

Upper Anhydrite (Sherburn Formation) and Top Anhydrite (Little Beck Formation) (Table 2) are also present. The Upper Marl thus includes an interval from the upper part of EZ3 to the top of EZ5. It comprises the terrigenous and semi-terrigenous equivalents of the anhydritic halite and sylvinite sequences which were deposited, coevally, further east in the more central parts of the Zechstein basin. These basinward sequences are overlain by the Saliferous Marl (Smith, 1974a), now also termed the Roxby Formation (Smith et al., 1986) (Table 2).

The anhydrite/gypsum beds in the Upper Marl are commonly banded, with traces of dolomite, and probably formed as widespread lagoonal deposits subsequent to deposition of the Upper Magnesian Limestone on a marine carbonate platform. Like the anhydrite in the Middle Marl, these evaporite beds pass westwards, updip, into zones of secondary gypsum, which in turn pass into dissolution zones, with the result that the formation thins and the overlying beds are commonly foundered (see p.20); this subsidence also affects the overlying Sherwood Sandstone Group (Smith, 1972; Cooper, 1986).

The junction between the Upper Marl and the overlying Sherwood Sandstone Group is an interbedded gradation over a few metres as the lithology becomes more arenaceous upwards. The contact is probably diachronous and at outcrop, near the western margin of the basin, it marks a transition to completely terrigenous sedimentation. This part of the sequence is unfossiliferous, but in the district the boundary between the Permian and Triassic is thought to lie within the lower part of the Sherwood Sandstone Group (Smith et al., 1974). However, to the east of the district, in the main North Sea basin, the boundary is probably within the Saliferous Marl (Roxby Formation) (Pattison et al., 1973, p.223; Warrington et al., 1980; Smith et al., 1986).

Details

Kirklington Borehole

This borehole [3287 8091] (Appendix 2) proved the only detailed section through the Upper Marl in the district. It is 27.12 m thick and consists of 9.30 m of anhydrite (Billingham Main Anhydrite) overlain, in upward sequence, by gypsiferous siltstone, sandstone and siltstone.

SUBSIDENCE CAUSED BY THE DISSOLUTION OF GYPSUM

In areas of the Thirsk district where there is a considerable groundwater flow through the Permian gypsum beds, the gypsum has partially dissolved (James et al., 1981) and a continually evolving cave system has developed. The caverns periodically collapse to form subsidence hollows and foundered strata at the surface (Plate 2). Subsidence occurs in a tract up to 3 km wide, extending from Ripon northwards to east of Bedale; the area in which subsidence might occur is shown as an inset diagram on the 1:50 000 map. The subsidence belt is limited to the west by the edge of the gypsum beds, and to the east by the downdip transition to anhydrite. The area between Nosterfield, Ripon and Bishop Monkton has suffered about 40 instances of subsidence in the past 150 years; further details are given by Cooper (1986).

Over much of the gypsum belt the subsidence hollows are randomly distributed. However, in the Ripon area the water flow in the gypsiferous beds is mainly phreatic and it is likely that the caverns, which ultimately collapse to form subsidence hollows, are located at the intersections of joints (Cooper, 1986). Joint measurements in the Lower Magnesian Limestone and Sherwood Sandstone Group of the Ripon area (Figure 4b) indicate that there are two major sets, approximately at right angles. Thus there is a linear or grid-like pattern of subsidence hollows. The same is true of hollows near Hutton Conyers, Ure Bank and Sharow. (Figure 4a). In these areas individual hollows have an elliptical or elongate form, the trend of which is approximately parallel to the regional joint pattern, suggesting that the distribution of subsidence hollows is largely controlled by the orientation of the major joint set. This supports studies in Germany (Ströbel, 1973) which show a similar relationship between hollows and joint pattern.

The long-term future for the actively subsiding areas is continuing subsidence, but it is currently impossible to predict which places are likely to be affected. However, in areas where the subsidence hollows have a regular grid-like or linear arrangement controlled by jointing, it is likely that the ground on lines between hollows is most at risk. The more numerous and closer-spaced the hollows, the greater likelihood there is of other hollows developing along that line. Land immediately next to an existing single subsidence hollow is also at risk because many of the hollows occur in groups of two or three. These groups of hollows are presumably caused by the collapse of a large cavern, forcing the dissolution to continue in adjacent ground.

Where a subsidence hollow develops, the best remedial action is to fill it with inert material. This will help prevent the sides from slipping and migrating outwards, thus stopping the hollow from becoming a large conical depression.

However, further subsidence of the fill in hollows has occurred in several places. Filling the hollow with toxic refuse should be avoided because pollution of groundwater and local springs may occur. Disposal of surface water into hollows is also unwise as it may cause further subsidence. The effects of water abstraction from the gypsiferous formations is not known, but removal of large quantities of water with a high sulphate content may increase groundwater flow rates and accelerate the subsurface dissolution of gypsum, exacerbating the subsidence.

For very expensive structures, detailed site investigation before construction is the only certain way to determine the stability of the ground. Such an investigation should involve drilling boreholes down to the Lower Magnesian Limestone (20–130 m) to determine the state of the gypsum beds, the presence or absence of cavities, and the hydrogeological conditions in the adjacent strata.

Details

The most subsidence-prone area in the gypsum belt is centred around Ripon and extends northwards to North Stainley. This is probably due to the local hydrological conditions caused by a deep, drift-filled buried valley (Figure 21, and rockhead contour map, Sheet 52) intersecting the Permian and Triassic strata. The outcrop of the Lower and Upper Magnesian limestones, in particular, act as a catchment area for water which moves downdip towards the buried valley and dissolves the gypsum beds. Similar hydrological conditions occur at Snape Mires [285 860] in the north of the district. Evidence for this water movement comes from the calcareous tufa around numerous springs at Snape Mires, from calcareous tufa-cemented gravels in the buried valley system near Ripon (Abraham, 1981; Morigi and James, 1984) and from sulphate-saturated groundwater found in boreholes near Ripon Race Course (Cooper, 1986).

The form of a subsidence hollow depends upon whether there is solid competent rock or a substantial thickness of unconsolidated (usually glacial) deposits at the surface. The former case results in

Plate 2 Subsidence hollows formed after the dissolution of Permian gypsum. Hutton Conyers, near Ripon (L3026).

the development of steep-sided cylindrical shafts, and the latter in conical depressions.

A subsidence hollow developed in solid rock appeared near Ripon Railway Station [3186 7260] in July, 1834 (Tute, 1868, 1870; Harrison, 1892). This hole is still open and has the form of a cylinder about 14 m in diameter and 15 m deep, with red sandstone (Sherwood Sandstone Group) exposed in the sides. A similar collapse occurred during 1860, breaching the Upper Magnesian Limestone at Ripon Parks [3122 7328] (Tute, 1868, 1870), and another about 30 m in diameter affected the same formation at Hall Garth Ponds [3184 7472] during 1939.

Throughout much of the Ripon area, thick drift deposits, locally in excess of 20 m, blanket the bedrock. Initially, the subsidence hollows in these areas have a near cylindrical form, but the sides rapidly degrade to produce a conical depression, as in Corkscrew Pits [3199 7315]. A small, actively subsiding hollow nearby [3194 7316] has been repeatedly artificially filled and is only about 1.5 m deep; support given by the infill has preserved the near-vertical sides of the hollow (Plate 2). A subsidence hollow [3170 7192] at Magdalen Road started as a slight downwarp which damaged two garages standing on the site. After further collapse and the development of tension gashes and slipping at the margins, the hole was infilled, thereby effectively controlling its diameter.

At Snape Mires [285 860], east of Bedale, almost complete dissolution of the Permian gypsum, as proved by boreholes, has resulted in a large bedrock depression about 28 sq km in area (Figure 5); bedrock levels are as much as 25 m below ground level. A fluvioglacial terrace deposit which once covered the area has subsided and the depression is filled with laminated clay, mainly of late- and postglacial age. Similar lacustrine deposits elsewhere in the Vale of York have a flat morphology, but at Snape Mires the surface undulates rapidly, with differences in elevation of up to 6 m. Between Rough Plantation [2835 8525] and Flood Bridge [2857 8752], the undulations take the form of ridges and elongate hollows up to 1 km long. These features have an approximate north–south or east–west orientation (Figure 5) and several turn through right angles. The probable sequence of events resulting in this morphology is shown in Figure 5. The orientations of these subsidence ridges and hollows closely approximates to the joint directions found in the Permian rocks to the south-west (Figure 4). It is likely, therefore, that the ridges represent the initial collapse of a joint-controlled cave system in the underlying gypsum (the pattern of which has been preserved by the drift infill), whereas the hollows mark the sites of the almost complete dissolution of the remaining gypsum. Similar joint-controlled subsidence troughs are recorded from the gypsum plain in Texas (Olive, 1957).

SULPHATE-RICH GROUNDWATER

The subsurface dissolution of gypsum (see above) results in sulphate-rich groundwater being present in the bedrock. This water commonly issues from springs and is also present in the drift deposits, such as at Ripon Race Course and Snape Mires (Cooper, 1986). This groundwater has the potential to harm buried concrete. The area most likely to be affected is similar to that prone to subsidence caused by gypsum dissolution (see inset diagram on the 1:50 000 map).

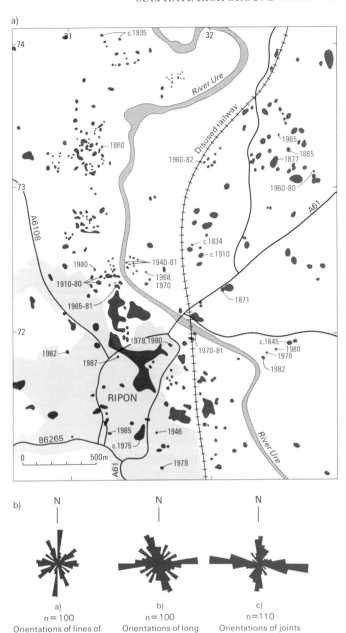

Figure 4 a) Map showing post-Devensian subsidence hollows (brown) in the Ripon area with the dates of recent subsidences where known (after Cooper, 1989). b) Rose diagrams showing the relationships between the orientations of lines of hollows, long axes of individual hollows and joints in the Ripon area (after Cooper, 1986).

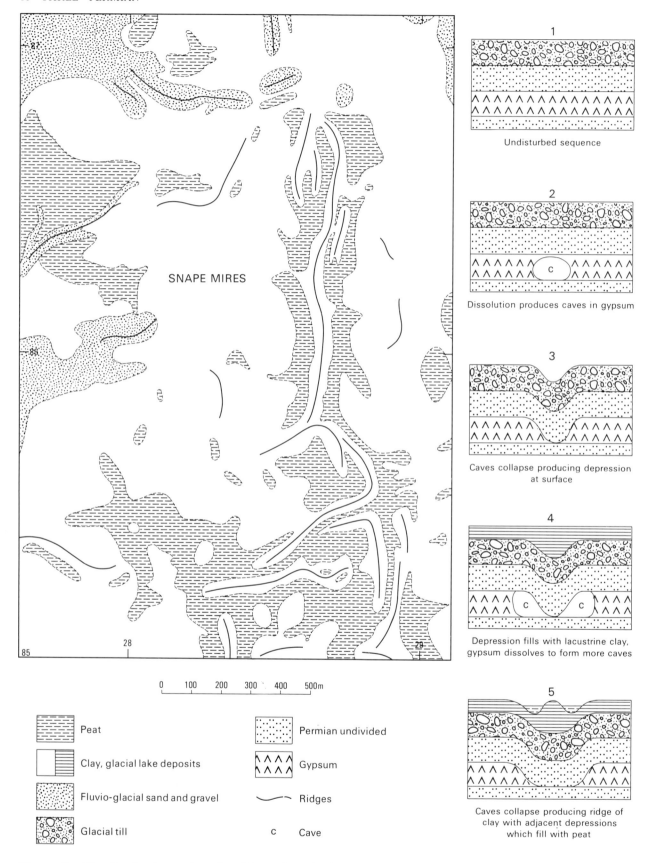

Peat

Clay, glacial lake deposits

Fluvio-glacial sand and gravel

Glacial till

Permian undivided

Gypsum

Ridges

c   Cave

1
Undisturbed sequence

2
Dissolution produces caves in gypsum

3
Caves collapse producing depression
at surface

4
Depression fills with lacustrine clay,
gypsum dissolves to form more caves

5
Caves collapse producing ridge of
clay with adjacent depressions
which fill with peat

Figure 5   The distribution and mode of formation of subsidence ridges in Snape Mires, near Bedale, North Yorkshire. After Cooper (1986).

FOUR

Triassic

During most of the Triassic period, the western part of the North Sea Basin, including the Thirsk district, was the site of continental red-bed sedimentation. A thick sequence of mainly red sandstones was followed by a succession of variably red, brown and green dolomitic mudstones and silt-stones (formerly known as 'marls'), with evaporites. Towards the end of the Triassic a widespread marine transgression led to the deposition of black shales, greenish, calcareous mudstones and dark grey mudstones with thin limestones. Beds in the Lias Group, below the lowest occurrence of *Psiloceras*, are considered to be Triassic (Cope et al., 1980; Warrington et al., 1980) but are, for convenience, described with the remainder of the Lias (chapter five).

The terrigenous Triassic sediments of Britain were traditionally divided into the 'Bunter' and the overlying 'Keuper'; names adopted from the Triassic of Germany (Sedgwick, 1829) for the predominantly arenaceous and argillaceous beds respectively. However, on the one-inch geological map of the district (Geological Survey of Great Britain, 1884), the lower red sandstones were classified as Keuper Sandstone, and the overlying 'marls' as Keuper Marl. In the accompanying memoir (Fox-Strangways et al., 1886), it was explained that, although the lower sandy beds in the ground to the south had been allocated to the Bunter Sandstone, this formation appeared to die out northwards and could not be recognised in the Thirsk district.

Later workers recognised that the arenaceous unit could not be subdivided and they adopted the term Bunter Sandstone. However, Warrington et al. (1980) concluded that the traditional subdivisions were significantly different in terms of age and facies from the European units with which they were believed to correspond, and that the nomenclature was inconsistent with modern stratigraphical usage. Their formalised lithostratigraphical terms are adopted here; thus the arenaceous beds (Keuper and Bunter Sandstone) have been assigned to the Sherwood Sandstone Group, the overlying marls (Keuper Marl) to the Mercia Mudstone Group, and the marine shales and calcareous mudstones (Rhaetic Beds) to the Penarth Group (Table 4). The Sherwood Sandstone and Mercia Mudstone groups are poorly exposed in the district and it has not been found practicable to subdivide them into the formations that have been recognised in south Yorkshire and central England (Warrington et al., 1980).

The uppermost brackish and marine beds of the Triassic were formerly referred to the Rhaetic, but now constitute the Penarth Group (Warrington et al., 1980); palaeontological evidence has confirmed the Triassic age of these beds (Warrington, 1974b).

SHERWOOD SANDSTONE GROUP

The Sherwood Sandstone Group, approximately 300 m thick, consists mainly of poorly to moderately cemented, un-fossiliferous, fine- to medium-grained sandstones, mainly brick-red but also grey, yellow and mottled. In general they are medium to thick bedded and commonly cross-stratified; small-scale ripple cross-lamination is only rarely present. Clasts consist mainly of quartz but also include feldspars, rock fragments and micas; ilmenite and zircon are the dominant heavy minerals (Smithson, 1931). Mudstone-flake breccias are common, but there is no evidence for the presence of the coarse-grained pebbly facies which is prominent to the south, between Doncaster and Nottingham (Warrington, 1974b). Thin beds of red siltstone and mudstone occur throughout the group, but are most common near the gradational base with the underlying Permian Upper Marl. Typically they form the tops of upward-fining cycles, 1 to 2 m thick, which commence with an erosively based, mudstone-flake breccia, and pass up to cross-stratified sandstone, commonly with mudstone flakes, which in turn is overlain by siltstone and mudstone showing sporadic evidence of subaerial exposure such as mudcracks and pseudomorphs after gypsum.

These characteristics suggest deposition in a predominantly fluvial environment, in the distal region of a vast alluvial plain of low relief that extended from the south-west. Oxidising conditions and the evaporation of shallow, ephemeral lakes indicate a semiarid climate. Regional facies distribution (Warrington, 1974b) and palaeocurrent data from adjacent areas point to a north-eastward sediment dispersal.

The Sherwood Sandstone Group is concealed by drift over most of the outcrop, but considerable information is available from boreholes which have been drilled to exploit its potential as an aquifer. However, the lower beds are sporadically exposed on the crests and flanks of mainly north-north-west-trending ridges which extend from Leeming to south and west of Dishforth; these may represent the scarp features of slightly more resistant horizons.

Details

Gatenby to Ripon

The sandstones mainly appear as field brash, but disused quarries near Gatenby [3115 8731] and near Burneston [3078 8605], now filled in, formerly exposed a few metres of red, micaceous sandstone. Further south, small exposures, up to 1 m thick, of red, fine-grained, thinly bedded, micaceous sandstone are still visible in old quarries [345 788; 343 758], north-east and south-east of Melmerby respectively. The Sherwood Sandstone is more extensively exposed along the southern bank of the River Swale, south-east of Baldersby St James, where outcrops [3712 7686; 3765 7669] and an old quarry [3769 7668] reveal up to 2.5 m of thin- to thick-bedded, red, fine- to medium-grained, micaceous sandstone, cross-laminated and cross-bedded in part.

North-east of Ripon, about 5 m of soft, red, fine-grained sandstone are exposed in the old railway cutting [3180 7292], 600 m north of the former Ripon Station. Between Hutton Conyers and Sharrow, up to 20 m of similar, commonly cross-stratified sand-

Table 4
Stratigraphical framework of the Triassic strata in the district, comparing the previous nomenclature with that of the present.

Period	Stage	Lithostratigraphy			
		Primary survey (Fox-Strangways et al., 1886)	Warrington (1974b)	Present nomenclature (after Warrington et al., 1980)	
Jurassic	Hettangian	Lower Lias	Lower Lias	Lias Group	Redcar Mudstone Formation†
c	Rhaetian	Rhaetian	Black Shale	Rhaetic	Penarth Group	Lilstock Formation (Cotham Member)* / Westbury Formation
I		beds	Tea Green Marl	Tea Green Marl		Blue Anchor Formation
s	— — ? — — Norian — ? — —				
s	Carnian	Keuper	Keuper	Mercia Mudstone Group	
A	— — ? — Ladinian	Marl	Marl		
I	— ? — — Anisian				
R	— — ? —				
T	Scythian	Keuper Sandstone	Bunter Sandstone	Sherwood Sandstone Group	
		— — — — ? — —	— — — — ? — —	— — — — —	
Permian ?pre-Scythian		Upper	Marls	Roxby Formation	

* only the Cotham Member is represented in this area
† the basal c.10 m of the Lias Group is of Rhaetian age.

stone are seen in the sides of numerous subsidence hollows [e.g. 3186 7260; 3243 7316] caused by the dissolution of gypsum beds in the underlying Permian Upper Marl (see chapter three). A disused roadside quarry [3208 7236], north-east of Ripon, exposes about 8 m of red-brown, thick-bedded sandstone with 0.10 to 0.50 m-thick trough cross-bedded sets; foresets are accentuated by clay laminae, and mud-flake conglomerates, with clasts up to 0.15 m across, are common at the base of some sets and in erosional scours. East of Hutton Conyers, up to 2 m of soft, red, fine-grained sandstone are exposed as soil brash on hill-tops and in small disused quarries, the best exposed of which are located near Lawson's Barn [3404 7355] and north-east of Blois Hall [3495 7293].

Rainton area

The most extensive quarries in the Sherwood Sandstone of the district straddle the A1 road, south-west of Rainton. To the west of the road, King Quarry [360 743] formerly exposed red and white sandstone, but is now completely filled in. To the east, Rainton Quarry [364 744] still exposes some 7 m of yellowish brown sandstone beneath which the Primary Survey recorded about 0.8 m of "flaggy shale".

MERCIA MUDSTONE GROUP

Around the margins of the North Sea basin, the fluvial sedimentation of the Sherwood Sandstone Group was abruptly terminated by minor earth movements, followed by erosion. The strata of the succeeding Mercia Mudstone Group are predominantly argillaceous and evaporitic.

Within the district, the base of the Mercia Mudstone is completely masked by drift and there is no field evidence for the erosional unconformity which has been identified both to the north (Smith, 1970a; Taylor et al., 1971), and to the south (Edwards, 1951; Smith and Warrington, 1971). Borehole records, however, testify to the abruptness of the change from sandstone to mudstone.

The Mercia Mudstone, about 190 m thick, consists mainly of dolomitic mudstone and silty mudstone, commonly brown, red-brown, or red, but with thin bands and patches of green. The mudstones are generally blocky, but may be finely interlaminated with well-sorted siltstones. Clay minerals include illite, chlorite and montmorillonite (Davis, 1967; Edwards, 1967). Thin beds of hard, grey-green siltstone and very fine-grained sandstone, cross-laminated in part, are present sporadically throughout the sequence. Gypsum and, at depth, anhydrite occur as beds up to 1 to 2 m thick, and also as nodules and ramifying veins. Lack of exposure has precluded the mapping of these evaporitic beds within the district. Borehole records (see details), however, indicate that they are concentrated at three levels, near the base, middle and top of the group, as they are further south (Smith et al., 1973) and east (Whittaker et al., 1985).

Regional studies (Warrington, 1974b) suggest that the uppermost unit of the Mercia Mudstone Group, the Blue Anchor Formation (formerly the Tea Green Marl), comprising 10 m of grey-green dolomitic mudstones and siltstones, should be present in the district. A few exposures of similar lithologies confirm the presence of the unit but they are insufficient to delimit its extent as a mappable unit.

The Mercia Mudstone has yielded no fauna. However, a number of borehole samples have been processed for palynomorphs, which have provided evidence for the presence of the Anisian, Ladinian and Carnian or Norian stages of the Triassic (Table 4).

The predominantly red colour and argillaceous nature of the rocks, the absence of fauna and the presence of evaporites suggest deposition under oxidising conditions in environments ranging from highly saline lagoonal or lacustrine, with periodic desiccation, to fluvial, with infrequent flash floods bringing coarser-grained clastics into the basin. Some workers have drawn parallels with playa lakes (Glennie and Evans, 1976; Arthurton, 1980); others, pointing to the presence of a marine carbonate and halite facies in a probable correlative (the Muschelkalk) further east in the North Sea Basin (Warrington, 1974b), advocate a hypersaline, epeiric sea fringed by sabkhas.

The grey-green colour of the highest beds, equivalent to the Blue Anchor Formation, suggests deposition under more reducing conditions, although in other respects they are lithologically similar to the underlying red-beds. They were probably deposited, subaqueously, in coastal lagoons (salinas), although, elsewhere in eastern England, the presence of fish scales (Elliott, 1961) suggests a local marine influence. The deposits represent a transition to the overlying fully marine Westbury Formation of the Penarth Group, which formed during a widespread marine transgression.

Details

South Otterington to Kilvington

Exposures of the Mercia Mudstone Group within the district are limited by thick drift cover. However, in the north, soil brash comprising variegated red, red-brown and grey-green mudstone with silty fragments occurs in areas of thinner drift east of South Otterington and at a number of localities below the feature formed by the Penarth Group, which runs south from the northern margin of the district [398 897] to Big Wood [407 851], west of North Kilvington. A borehole at Summer Carr [3979 8881] and several boreholes around Beal House [3969 8663] proved gypsum bands and nodules in the uppermost 50 m of the group. Near Thiefhole [3962 8885] and south of Thirsk Bank [3975 8800], north-east and south-east of Thornton le Moor respectively, soils contain fragments of hard, probably dolomitic, grey-green siltstone. Further south, a similar lithology is exposed in a stream section [4070 8508] at Big Wood, whilst "Tea-green Marl" was recorded in a small opening [3982

8414], no longer visible, near Able Grange (Fox-Strangways et al., 1886). Grey-green siltstones with pseudomorphs after halite have been observed in a ditch [4297 8405] near South Kilvington. All these localities are high in the Mercia Mudstone and indicate the presence of the Blue Anchor Formation.

Thirsk

Between South Kilvington and the Asenby-Coxwold Graben, the outcrop of the Mercia Mudstone is extensively drift covered and is known only from boreholes drilled for water supply, site investigation and bulk mineral assessment (Morigi and James, 1984). The deepest is that at the former Marrs Brewery, Thirsk [4283 8199]. The lithology is described in full by Fox-Strangways et al., (1886, p.10) but, in summary, it proved 76.8 m of red and grey mudstones with two gypsiferous horizons, the higher, 28.8 m thick, and the lower 5.5 m thick, respectively to 36.6 m and 3.5 m above the base of the group. Sparse miospore assemblages recovered from boreholes at Sowerby Parks [4399 7865] and near Gristhwaite Farm [4272 7858] indicate middle to late Triassic, possibly Ladinian and Ladinian or Carnian ages respectively (Figure 6; localities 1, 2).

At Stockhill Green, south-east of Thirsk, the drift is thinner; here grey-green mudstone fragments occur as soil brash on a prominent ridge [4588 7856], and 1.3 m of grey-green mudstone and siltstone were exposed beneath drift in excavations for an irrigation reservoir [4623 7856]. The Penarth Group crops out nearby, and it is likely that both localities lie within the Blue Anchor Formation. South of Thirsk, many of the extensive series of mineral assessment boreholes drilled in the Dalton area (Morigi and James, 1984) penetrated variegated red and green mudstone, grey-green siltstone and very fine-grained sandstone. Boreholes near Paradise Farm [4281 7747] and west of Dalton [4211 7644] yielded miospores indicative of middle Triassic (Anisian–Ladinian) ages (Figure 6; localities 3, 4).

Asenby to Sessay

The presence of the Mercia Mudstone Group subcrop within the westward extension of the main Asenby–Coxwold Graben is established by a borehole at Baldersby Park [3841 7577], which proved marl and gypsum below thick drift deposits. Boreholes to the north-east of Asenby [4027 7556; 4028 7556] yielded miospores, including *Perotrilites minor*, indicative of an Anisian (middle Triassic) age (Figure 6; locality 5). South of the principal faults, the group is again obscured beneath thick drift and is known mainly from boreholes (Morigi and James, 1984). In the past, domestic water supplies were often obtained from wells sunk to gypsum horizons. Thus a well at Sessay Rectory [4616 7512] proved gypsum high in the succession (Fox-Strangways et al., 1886). At Little Sessay degraded excavations [467 746] testify to the working of this gypsum horizon beneath thin drift and, slightly further east [471 746], soil brash of yellowish green, khaki and red mudstone occurs. To the south, in a separate fault block, boreholes at Crakehill Farm [4403 7428] and Sessay Park [4540 7429] proved gypsum beds at lower horizons, while south-west of Clark Wood [445 741], soil brash of "green marl" was formerly seen (Fox-Strangways et al., 1886). A nearby borehole [4461 7468] yielded miospores indicative of a middle Triassic (Anisian–?Ladinian) age with an acanthomorph acritarch; if in situ the latter is indicative of a subaqueous depositional environment connected to a marine source (Figure 6; locality 6).

Cundall to Raskelf

In the south of the district, gypsum beds in the lowest 20 to 30 m of the Mercia Mudstone Group were proved in boreholes at Cundall [4242 7263] and north-east of Brafferton [4513 7071]. A borehole near Fawdington House [4381 7212] yielded a rich miospore

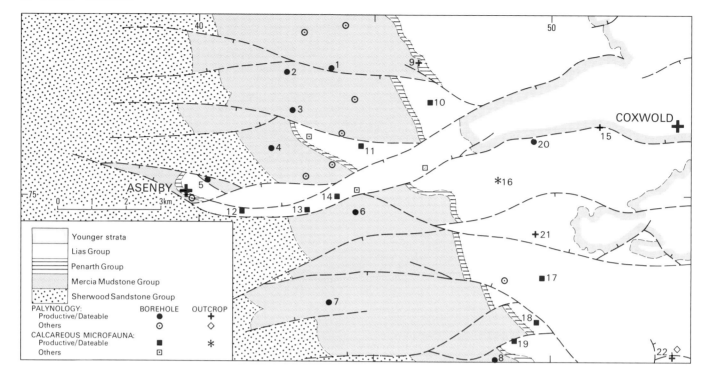

Figure 6 Sites of micropalaeontological investigations of the Mercia Mudstone, Penarth and Lias groups south and south-east of Thirsk (see relevant chapters for details of age assignments: 1–9, Triassic; 10–22, Jurassic).

assemblage, including *Perotrilites minor*, that is indicative of an Anisian (middle Triassic) age (Figure 6; locality 7).

North and west of Raskelf, the drift-covered outcrop is defined by boreholes, the most southerly of which, south-west of Raskelf Church [4846 7052], proved red-brown and pale green mudstone that yielded a sparse miospore assemblage indicative of a late Triassic (Carnian or Norian) age (Figure 6; locality 8) with tasmanitid algae indicative of a subaqueous depositional environment connected to a marine source.

PENARTH GROUP

A break in sedimentation after deposition of the Blue Anchor Formation was followed by deposition of the Penarth Group during a widespread marine transgression. The group (Table 4) is divided, on evidence outside this district, into the Westbury Formation, below, and the Lilstock Formation, above (Warrington, 1974b; Warrington et al., 1980).

The **Westbury Formation**, penetrated in the Felixkirk Borehole (Figure 8; Powell, *in* Institute of Geological Sciences, 1983; Ivimey-Cook and Powell, 1991) consists of about 5 m of brown, dark grey or black, organic-rich bioturbated, fissile mudstone with thin beds and laminae of pale grey, fine-grained, rippled pyritic sandstone and siltstone; convolute laminae and contorted slump balls are also present. The fauna (Appendix 2; Ivimey-Cook and Powell, 1991) comprises abundant bivalves including *Eotrapezium* spp. and *Rhaetavicula contorta*. These, together with palynomorphs (Figure 7 and Benfield and Warrington, 1988), indicate a latest Triassic (Rhaetian) age for the Westbury Formation. The high organic content of the mudstone suggests

that anoxic bottom-conditions prevailed during the marine transgression.

The succeeding **Lilstock Formation** is represented in this district by about 6 m of pale green, soft, soapy-textured mudstone and subordinate, thin, upward-fining, rippled, siltstone laminae; the mudstone is rich in illite, chlorite and smectite clay minerals (Raymond, 1955). This unit has a restricted benthic fauna comprising fish fragments and abundant small branchiopod crustaceans (*Euestheria minuta*) and is assigned to the Cotham Member (Warrington et al., 1980).

Farther south, a limestone facies, the Langport Member, is developed above the Cotham Member in this formation, but it is not recognised in this district. The Cotham Member includes a brief lagoonal phase after which the marine incursion resumed, resulting in the deposition of intercalated grey mudstone, siltstone and limestone which comprise the lower part of the succeeding Redcar Mudstone Formation (Lias Group) (Ivimey-Cook and Powell, 1991). The base of the Jurassic system is defined (Cope et al., 1980) at the first appearance of *Psiloceras* so that the lowermost part of the Redcar Mudstone Formation in the district is of Triassic age (Table 4).

In this district, the Westbury Formation is exposed only in a few localities, and the Lilstock Formation (Cotham Member) is known only from boreholes; consequently it has not been possible to map the subdivisions of the Penarth Group, which is shown 'undivided' on geological maps.

Details

Thornton-le-Street to South Kilvington

The Westbury Formation is recognised in the north of the district, on the hilltop [390 872] west of Sunny Hill Farm, Thornton-le-Street, from soil brash comprising black fissile mudstone, grey siltstone and brown, bioturbated, fine-grained sandstone with bivalves. Further south, black mudstone containing an abundant fauna of thin-shelled bivalves is exposed in a stream section [4078 8505] south of Big Wood. West of Able Grange, the Penarth Group caps a prominent fault-bounded hill [3994 8417] upon which there is a soil brash of brown, fine-grained, flaggy sandstone derived from the Westbury Formation.

South Kilvington to Thirkleby and the Felixkirk Borehole

North of South Kilvington, large slabs of grey, rippled, fine-grained sandstone with the bivalve *Rhaetavicula contorta*, typical of the Westbury Formation, were extracted from a disused ballast pit [429 844] and incorporated in the embankment for the A19 Trunk Road. Slightly further east, Fox-Strangways et al. (1886) recorded a shallow pit [4316 8424], now infilled, which formerly exposed this formation as black shales with *Rhaetavicula contorta*.

Between South Kilvington and Thirkleby, the Penarth Group forms a small escarpment, but is entirely drift covered. However, excavations [4644 7868] near Stockhill Green, Thirkleby, exposed, beneath till, hard, dark grey to black, fissile mudstone with a few specimens of *Eotrapezium concentricum* and *Rhaetavicula contorta*, and yellow-brown to grey, cross-laminated, fine-grained sandstone of the Westbury Formation. The mudstone has yielded palynomorphs of Rhaetian (latest Triassic) age (Benfield and Warrington, 1988) (Figure 6; locality 9).

The BGS Felixkirk borehole [4835 8576] (Appendix 2; Powell *in* Institute of Geological Sciences, 1983; Ivimey-Cook and Powell, 1991) penetrated 4.57 m of dark grey to black organic-rich mudstone with thin beds and laminae of grey, fine-grained pyritic sandstone, which represent all but the lowest beds of the Westbury Formation. Convolute lamination and contorted slump balls occur in the upper 0.6 m. Bivalves (Appendix 2) are abundant, particularly in the mudstone beds, and include *Eotrapezium* spp., *Protocardia rhaetica* and *Rhaetavicula contorta*; the gastropod *Natica* sp. is also present. Bioturbation is common throughout and the trace fossils include *Diplocraterion* sp. Organic-rich laminae with finely comminuted bone fragments are present in the mudstone. The overlying Cotham Member of the Lilstock Formation comprises 5.71 m of pale grey-green mudstone with ripple cross-laminated siltstone laminae; the laminae have scoured bases and fine upwards. The small crustacean *Euestheria* sp. is the only macrofossil present; horizontal, pyrite-filled burrows are common. The mudstone is composed of illite, chlorite and smectite clay minerals; the last is prone to swelling and gives a 'soapy' feel to the rock. Palynomorphs from this sequence are listed in Figure 7.

Asenby – Coxwold area

The Penarth Group is not exposed within the Asenby – Coxwold Graben but its presence is proved by boreholes. A borehole [3979 7532] for water in the centre of Asenby proved 9.1 m of "Rhaetic Beds" on red marls with gypsum. A site investigation borehole [3989 7502] for the Asenby Bypass proved, beneath drift, 0.7 m of grey to black, silty mudstones of the Westbury Formation.

To the south of this fault structure, the outcrop of the Penarth Group is covered by thick drift deposits, and direct evidence for its presence is limited to a single confidential borehole. The Crayke Lodge Borehole [5458 6992], located east of Easingwold, within 1 km of the south-east corner of the district, penetrated the Westbury Formation, which yielded a Rhaetian palynoflora (Benfield and Warrington, 1988).

Figure 7 Palynomorphs from the Penarth Group succession, Felixkirk Borehole. Relative abundances expressed as percentages based upon a count of 200 specimens per sample.

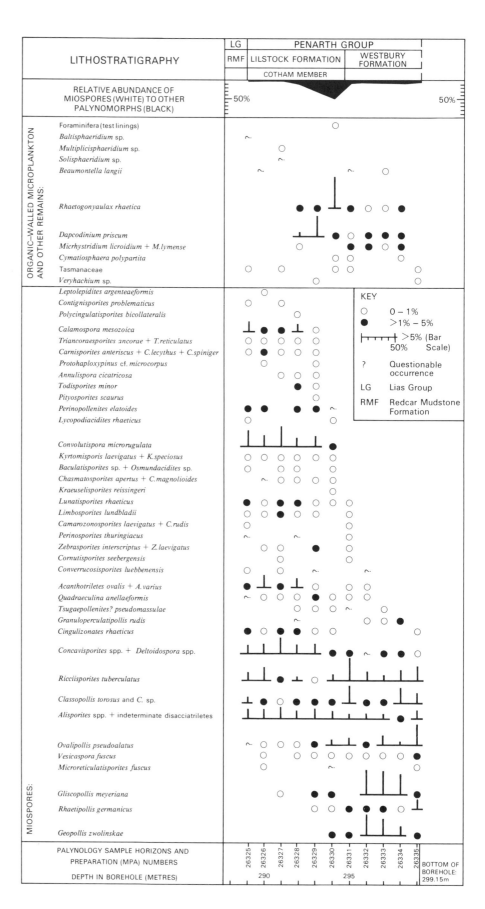

FIVE

Jurassic

Jurassic strata crop out over the eastern part of the district, although much of the sequence in the Vale of York, particularly the Lias Group, is obscured by drift deposits. Middle and Upper Jurassic strata form the high ground of the Hambleton Hills and also the area between Coxwold and Oulston (western margin of the Howardian Hills). The Jurassic rocks in the district were deposited near the south-western margin of the Cleveland Basin, which was centered on the eastern extremity of the present-day North York Moors, adjacent to the coast (Figures 22 and 23E).

Lower Jurassic rocks in this district predominantly comprise mudstone and siltstone, with subordinate sandstone, limestone and ironstone, which were deposited in a broad epeiric sea following the late Triassic marine transgression. Uplift and erosion at the end of early Jurassic times, probably the result of doming and rifting in the North Sea (Hallam and Sellwood, 1976), was followed by deposition of

the southward-prograding, regressive facies of the Ravenscar Group, comprising fluviodeltaic, fluvial and paralic sandstone, mudstone and thin coals, interrupted by brief, but regionally significant shallow-marine incursions from the south and south-east, which resulted in the deposition of carbonate and clastic lithofacies. A major marine transgression occurred in late mid Jurassic times, when the fine-grained sandstone and siltstone of the Osgodby Formation were deposited in a shallow shelf sea. Local uplift, faulting and erosion during this period and also during early late Jurassic times probably reflect major structural events that occurred in the North Sea. Following deposition of the Oxford Clay in relatively deeper water during the early part of late Jurassic times, the district was the site of warm, shallow-water, shelf sedimentation comprising predominantly oolitic limestone, spicule-rich sandstone and coral patch-reefs (Corallian Group). This phase was followed by a

Series	Stage	Yorkshire coast					Thirsk district
		Fox-Strangways & Barrow (1915)		Hemingway (1974)	Cope et al. (1980)	Powell (1984) & Knox (1984)		
Middle Jurassic	Aalenian	Dogger						
Lower Jurassic	Toarcian	Upper	Blea Wyke Series	Upper	Blea Wyke Sands	Blea Wyke Sands	Blea Wyke Sandstone Formation	Yellow Sandstone Member	not present
								Grey Sandstone Member	
					Striatulus Shales	Striatulus Shales	Whitby Mudstone Formation	Fox Cliff Siltstone Member	
					Peak Shales	Peak Shales		Peak Mudstone Member	
			Alum Shale Series		Cement Shales	Alum Shales Formation		Alum Shale Member	Whitby Mudstone Formation (undivided)
					Main Alum Shales				
			Jet Rock Series		Bituminous Shales	Jet Rock Formation		Jet Rock Member	
					Jet Shales				
			Grey Shale Series		Grey Shales	Grey Shales Formation		Grey Shale Member	
	Pliensbachian	Middle	Ironstone Series	Middle	Cleveland Ironstone Formation	Cleveland Ironstone Formation	Cleveland Ironstone Formation		Cleveland Ironstone Formation
			Sandy Series		Staithes Formation	Staithes Formation	Staithes Sandstone Formation		Staithes Sandstone Formation
		Lower	Bb	Lower	Ironstone Shales	Ironstone Shales	Redcar Mudstone Formation	'Ironstone/ Pyritous Shales'	Redcar Mudstone Formation
			Ba		Pyritous Shales	Pyritous Shales			
	Sinemurian		Ab		Siliceous Shales	Siliceous Shales		'Siliceous Shales'	
	Hettangian		Aa		Calcareous Shales	Calcareous Shales		'Calcareous Shales'	
Triassic	Rhaetian	Rhaetic			Penarth Group				

Table 5 Lithostratigraphical framework of the Lias Group in the Cleveland Basin, comparing the previous nomenclature with that adopted for the Thirsk district.

Table arranged by chronostratigraphy (Series / Stage) against four nomenclature schemes:

Chronostratigraphy (Series / Stage)	Yorkshire coast — Fox-Strangways et al. (1886), Fox Strangways (1892)	Yorkshire coast — After Wright (1968), Hemingway & Knox (1973) & Hemingway (1974)	Yorkshire coast — Parsons (Aalenian–Bathonian) & Wright (Callovian–Oxfordian) in Cope et al. (1980)	Hambleton Hills — Thirsk Sheet (52) after Hemingway & Knox (1973), Wright (1980), Powell & Rathbone (1983)
Upper Jurassic — Oxfordian	Lower Calcareous Grit	Corallian Group: Lower Calcareous Grit	Corallian Group: Lower Calcareous Grit; Oldstead Oolite	Corallian Group: Lower Calcareous Grit; Oldstead Oolite
Callovian	Oxford Clay; Kellaways Rock	Oxford Clay; Hackness Rock; Langdale Beds; Kellaways Rock	Upper Oxford Clay; Hackness Rock; Kellaways Rock; Osgodby Formation	Oxford Clay; Hackness Rock; Kellaways Rock; Osgodby Formation
Bathonian	Cornbrash; Upper Estuarine (Deltaic)† Series	Cornbrash; Ravenscar Group: Scalby Formation (Moor Grit)	Ravenscar Group: Scalby Formation	Ravenscar Group: Scalby Formation (Long Nab Member; Moor Grit)
Bajocian	Moor Grit; Scarborough or Grey Limestone Series; Middle Estuarine (Deltaic)† Series; Millepore Bed & Whitwell Oolite; Lower Estuarine (Deltaic)† Series	Scarborough Formation (Moor Grit; Crinoid Grit; Brandsby Roadstone; Gristhorpe Member); Cloughton Formation (Lebberston Member; Sycarham Member; Blowgill Member)	Scarborough Formation (Crinoid Grit; Brandsby Roadstone; Gristhorpe Member); Cayton Bay Formation (Cloughton Formation; Sycarham Member; Blowgill Beds)	Scarborough Formation (Crinoid Grit; Brandsby Roadstone); Cloughton Formation (Lebberston Member)
Aalenian	Eller Beck Bed or Hydraulic Lst.; Lower Estuarine (Deltaic)† Series; Dogger	Eller Beck Formation; Saltwick Formation; Dogger	Eller Beck Formation; Hayburn Formation; Dogger Formation	Eller Beck Formation (Ingleby Ironstone); Gormire Lst.; Saltwick Formation; Dogger Formation

(Lias Group)

* shows revised (upwards) position of Middle/Upper Jurassic boundary (Cope et al. 1980).
† the term 'Deltaic' was introduced by Hemingway (1949).
⊐⊏ denotes strata absent due to erosion or nondeposition.

Table 6 Lithostratigraphical framework of the Middle Jurassic strata in the Cleveland Basin, comparing the previous nomenclature with that adopted for the Thirsk district.

eustatic sea-level rise which, together with subsidence of the Cleveland Basin, resulted in the deposition of mudstone and bituminous mudstone, the latter reflecting stagnant, anaerobic bottom-conditions.

The lithostratigraphical nomenclature of the Jurassic strata in the Cleveland Basin has been subject to numerous revisions over the years; the terminology adopted for the Lower and Middle Jurassic strata in this district is compared with the previous nomenclature in Tables 5 and 6 respectively.

Biostratigraphical zonation of the Jurassic is based primarily on ammonites, although other fossils, notably foraminifera, ostracods and dinoflagellate cysts, are also used. The ammonites are generally considered to have evolved sufficiently rapidly for the life span of each species to have been approximately synchronous over wide regions. Hence 'biozones can be defined in common with chronozones at points in rock' (Cope et al., 1980, p.4), and can also be used chronostratigraphically to determine the limits of stages. Many of the Callovian and Upper Jurassic zones and subzones have formal definitions and type sections and, consequently, can be used as standard chronostratigraphical units; they are conventionally printed in 'Roman' type with capitals for the index. In the pre-Callovian stages, however, few formal definitions have been completed, and so the zones and subzones are here all treated as biostratigraphical units with the names of their nominal taxa in italics.

Biostratigraphical zonation of the Jurassic marine strata in the Cleveland Basin is based on ammonites (Cope et al., 1980; Ivimey-Cook and Powell, 1991), but where these fossils are scarce or lacking in this district, for instance in the Middle Jurassic sequence, age determination is based on lithostratigraphical correlation with equivalent ammonite-bearing sequences described from the Yorkshire coastal exposures (Hemingway, 1974; Cope et al., 1980).

Seismic stratigraphy, based on wireline-log characteristics, has also been used to correlate the Lower Jurassic sequence of this district with sequences further south (Powell, 1984; Whittaker et al., 1985).

LOWER JURASSIC

In the Cleveland Basin, marine conditions prevailed throughout early Jurassic times, but water depths and sediments varied. The basal sequence of relatively deep water, predominantly argillaceous sediments is succeeded by shallower-water sandstones, ironstones and mudstones which are, in turn, overlain by further deeper-water mudstones. These three broad lithostratigraphical units were termed the Lower, Middle and Upper Lias respectively, the Middle Lias originally being divided, where possible, into a "Sandy Series" and an "Ironstone Series" (Fox-Strangways et al., 1886; Fox-Strangways, 1908). Recently, the whole sequence has been redefined as the Lias Group (Powell, 1984) and subdivided into mappable formations (Hemingway, 1974; Powell, 1984). The succession in the district is shown in Table 5.

Elsewhere in the Cleveland Basin, particularly on the coast, the Lower Jurassic has also been biostratigraphically subdivided, principally on the basis of its ammonite faunas

(Cope et al., 1980). Although exposures of the Lias Group in the district are limited, due to an extensive cover of drift deposits, several localities, particularly in the Whitby Mudstones, have yielded ammonites, which have enabled biostratigraphical correlations with the type coastal sections to be established (Table 5). In addition, ammonite faunas collected from the BGS cored borehole at Felixkirk (Powell, in Institute of Geological Sciences, 1983; Powell, 1984) have confirmed the presence of all the Lower Jurassic stages and the majority of the constituent zones (Figure 8; Ivimey-Cook and Powell, 1991). The first appearance of the ammonite *Psiloceras*, which defines the base of the Jurassic (Cope et al., 1980), is about 10 m above the base of the Lias Group; consequently, the lowest strata are of Triassic age. For convenience, they are considered here with the remainder of the Group. Further information on the biostratigraphy of parts of the sequence, particularly in boreholes, has come studies of the bivalves, calcareous microfauna and palynomorphs.

LIAS GROUP (MOSTLY LOWER JURASSIC)

The Lias Group is about 270 m thick (Powell, in Institute of Geological Sciences, 1983) and is subdivided into four formations (Powell, 1984) that can be traced throughout the district; namely, in upwards sequence, the Redcar Mudstone, Staithes Sandstone, Cleveland Ironstone and Whitby Mudstone formations (Table 5; Figure 8).

Redcar Mudstone Formation

The Redcar Mudstone Formation crops out, beneath drift deposits, over the central parts of the Vale of York, where exposures are limited to a few stream sections and small areas of soil brash. However, the borehole at Felixkirk (Figure 8; Appendix 2, Powell, 1984; Ivimey-Cook and Powell, 1991) and others in the south-east of the district (see details) have provided much new information on the sequence.

The formation is about 200 m thick and consists mainly of dark grey, fossiliferous, fissile mudstone and siltstone with, in upward sequence, subordinate thin beds of shelly limestone (wackestone and packstone texture), and fine-grained, carbonate-cemented sandstone; sideritic and calcite concretions are present throughout, but are most common in the top 70 m. Bioturbation is extensive at some horizons and includes pyrite-filled burrows. There is generally a rich, shelly fauna comprising gastropods, bivalves, ammonites and belemnites; soil brash from the basal part of the formation includes *Gryphaea*-rich limestone (wackestone).

Three informal units are distinguished in the Felixkirk Borehole (Figure 8); these broadly correspond to the subdivisions recognised in the typical coastal sections (Buckman, 1915) and comprise, in ascending order, the 'Calcareous Shales', 'Siliceous Shales' and 'Pyritous Shales plus Ironstone Shales' (undivided). The distinction between the Pyritous Shales and the Ironstone Shales cannot be recognised in the Felixkirk cores where, in the topmost 70 m, both siderite concretions and pyritous burrows are common throughout. Furthermore, wireline logs over this interval show a smooth upward-coarsening trend (Figure 8). These

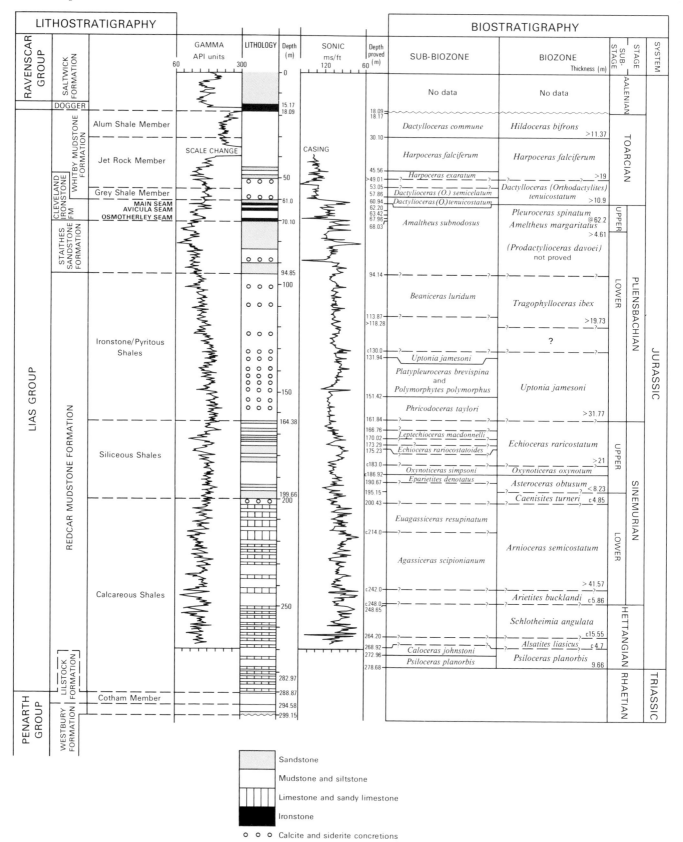

Figure 8 Generalised lithological log of the Felixkirk Borehole, together with geophysical logs and biozonation (after Ivimey-Cook and Powell, 1991).

informal subdivisions cannot be mapped at surface in the district; thus the formation is shown 'undivided' on the map.

The basal contact of the 'Calcareous Shales' with the underlying Cotham Member (Lilstock Formation; Penarth Group) in the Felixkirk Borehole is sharp and irregular. They are about 90 m thick and consist of grey mudstone, silty in part, with thin, harder beds of pale grey, shelly, calcareous sandstone and sandy limestone, which are extensively bioturbated; bivalves, particularly *Gryphaea* sp., are common. The overlying 35 m of grey mudstone with abundant beds of pale grey, bioturbated siltstones and very fine-to fine-grained sandstones, are assigned to the 'Siliceous Shales'. Small-scale, cyclic, sedimentary rhythms are present in this member, which have been interpreted as upward-coarsening cycles resulting from periodic shallowing of the sea (Sellwood, 1970). Study of the Felixkirk Borehole cores (Appendix 2), however, shows that most of the units can be interpreted as upward-fining cycles showing a gradual passage from a basal, extensively bioturbated sandstone, locally with a scoured, erosive base and bivalve shell-lags, to bioturbated sandstone, siltstone and mudstone with sparse bivalves, preserved in life position. The trace fossils include the narrow burrows of *Chondrites* sp., which are particularly common in the lower part of the coarser basal bed, where it produces a diffuse lower boundary as a result of the inter-mixing of sand-grade sediment with the underlying silt and mud. *Diplocraterion* sp. is also present, showing extrusive burrowfills. These coarse-grained sandy beds are interpreted as the deposits of major storms, which transported sand-grade sediment offshore, where the substrate was colonised by benthic fauna (van Buchem and McCave, 1989). The laminated siltstone and mudstone between each coarse unit represents the normal 'background' sediments deposited between each storm-induced pulse.

The uppermost 70 m of the formation, corresponding to the 'Ironstone Shales' and 'Pyritous Shales' of the coastal sections, comprise mudstone and siltstone with abundant beds of sideritic–calcitic concretions and pyritous burrows; an overall upward-coarsening (shallowing) trend of increasing sand content, illustrated by the wireline logs (Figure 8), is a precursor of the shallow-water conditions manifested in the overlying Staithes Sandstone. The base of the latter is taken at the base of the first thick, fine- to medium-grained sandstone and is clearly shown in the wireline logs (Figure 8).

The standard north-east European sequence of ammonite zones (Cope et al., 1980), representing the Hettangian, Sinemurian and part of the Pliensbachian stages, has been recognised in the Redcar Mudstone Formation in well-exposed coastal sections (Buckman, 1915; Bairstow, 1969). Most of these zones have also been identified in the Felixkirk cores (Figure 8; Ivimey-Cook and Powell, 1991).

DETAILS

Brawith Hall to north-east Thirsk

In the north of the district, small ditch and stream sections [4071 8758; 4180 8582; 5070 8696] near Brawith Hall expose up to 1.4 m of grey-brown, fissile mudstone with beds, 0.2 to 0.4 m thick, of blue-grey, shelly limestone. Khaki-grey clay and mudstone, with

carbonate nodules and small bivalves, is exposed in the bank of Cod Beck [4093 8664] and was dug out from pits [4043 8583] near Thornton-le-Street. The proximity of the Penarth Group outcrop indicates that these localities must all be stratigraphically low in the formation.

Soil brash comprising fragments of *Gryphaea*-rich bioclastic limestone with brown, fissile mudstone and siltstone was seen on the fault-bounded, south-west extension of the main outcrop around Abel Grange [4026 8396]. Comparison with lithologies in the Felixkirk Borehole suggests that these *Gryphaea*-rich limestone beds occur between 17 and 65 m above the base of the formation and are equivalent to the 'Calcareous Shales' of the coastal type section (Powell, 1984).

To the north-east of Thirsk, similar lithologies are exposed in Whitelass Beck, south-east of Hag House [4525 8400], and near Grizzle Field House [4494 8318 to 4510 8308], where the following strata are exposed:

	Thickness m
Mudstone, brown, silty, and micaceous siltstone, with bivalves including *Gryphaea* sp.	0.65
Limestone, blue-grey, argillaceous, with abundant *Gryphaea* sp.	0.25
Siltstone, blue-grey, micaceous, and lenses of blue-grey limestone with abundant *Gryphaea* sp.	1.20

At Plump Bank [446 823], about 1 km further south, the Primary Survey recorded shales with thin limestones containing "*Ostrea liassica*" (now *Liostrea hisingeri*) in temporary sections.

Beds above the 'Calcareous Shales' are exposed in the bank of Blackmill Beck [4416 8678], near Rush House. Here, 1.6 m of dark grey, shelly, fissile mudstone with brown-weathering siderite nodules, up to 0.10 m in length, are present below till. These beds are equivalent to the 'Pyritous and Ironstone Shales' of the coastal type section.

Bagby to Dalton

The Primary Survey (Fox-Strangways et al., 1886) recorded 'paper shales' with "*Ostrea liassica*" (now *Liostrea hisingeri*) in wells at Bagby, whose precise locations are unspecified, in the cellars of Thirkleby Hall [4703 7921] and in a stream section [4661 7894], no longer exposed, in Thirkleby Park. During the resurvey, large blocks of shelly, bioclastic limestone were seen, ploughed out on the hillside [4785 7904] overlooking Thirkleby Beck and excavated from a ditch [4817 7921 to 4827 7938] at Spring Wood.

South-west of Thirkleby, evidence for the presence of the Redcar Mudstone in the drift-covered, faulted ground just to the north of the Asenby–Coxwold Graben comes from a borehole [4674 7769] at Thirkleby Bridge Farm, which proved dark grey silty mudstone with bivalves, and which yielded a calcareous microfauna indicating an Early Sinemurian age (Figure 6; locality 10). Another borehole 4738 7739], north-west of Thirkleby Barugh, penetrated dark grey sandy shale.

Faults control the position of the Redcar Mudstone outcrop north and east of Dalton. In the area north of Dalton a borehole [4326 7677] penetrated, beneath drift, grey silty mudstones with bivalves, typical of the Hettangian and Sinemurian stages; another borehole [4471 7646], near Bruce House, proved grey, silty mudstones containing a calcarous microfauna indicative of a late Sinemurian to early Pliensbachian age (Figure 6; locality 11).

Asenby-Coxwold Graben

Within the Asenby–Coxwold Graben, the Redcar Mudstone is exposed near the westernmost limit of its outcrop at Asenby, where the following section [3994 7556] occurs in the south bank of the River Swale:

Bed No.		Thickness m
9	Limestone, grey, rubbly	0.3
8	Mudstone, grey-brown, friable, silty; bivalve fragments	0.7
7	Limestone, dark grey-brown, moderately hard, silty; small bivalves	0.2
6	Shale, dark grey, friable to moderately hard; abundant shell and crinoid debris; ammonite fragments, small bivalves; commonly bioturbated, with small circular burrows	0.7
5	Limestone, grey to yellow-brown, moderately hard, very silty, goethitic; large bivalves; irregular base	0.2
4	Mudstone, grey, silty; ammonite and bivalve fragments; concentrations of goethite ooliths; pyritic bands	0.7
3	Not exposed	0.8
2	Limestone, grey, hard, silty; sporadic small bivalves	0.2
1	Limestone, grey-brown, silty, pyritic; *Gryphaea* sp., abundant very small pyritised gastropods and sporadic ammonite nuclei	0.3

Ammonites collected from Bed 4 indicate either the top of the *liasicus* Zone or the *angulata* Zone of the Hettangian, while those from Bed 6 are certainly from the *angulata* Zone. Comparison with the Felixkirk Borehole cores suggests that this section lies about 25 m above the base of the Redcar Mudstone. About 300 m to the south-west, boreholes drilled for the Asenby–Topcliffe Bypass proved grey, fissile mudstone, which probably represents beds slightly higher in the sequence.

Further east, within the graben, 0.3 m of grey, silty mudstone exposed on the south bank of the River Swale [4084 7483] yielded ammonites indicative of a mid-Sinemurian age. Boreholes at Leckby Grange [4139 7472] and at Eldmire Cottage [4322 7471], to the east, proved grey silty mudstone with bivalves, and a calcareous microfauna indicative of a Hettangian to earliest Sinemurian age (Figure 6; localities 12 and 13).

A borehole [4408 7510] north of Eldmire Moor penetrated grey mudstones with bivalves, and a calcareous microfauna suggesting an earliest Pliensbachian age (Figure 6; locality 14); this represents the most easterly evidence of the formation within the graben.

At Angram Grange [5152 7691] palynomorphs indicative of an early Jurassic, possibly early Pliensbachian age were recovered from the Redcar Mudstone Formation immediately to the south of the southern boundary of the graben (Figure 6; locality 15).

Birdforth Hall to Raskelf

South-east of the Asenby–Coxwold Graben in Birdforth Beck [4863 7545], poorly exposed, dark grey, fissile mudstone with bivalves yielded a calcareous microfauna indicative of a mid-Sinemurian age (Figure 6; locality 16). Some 3 km further east, the Primary Survey recorded an exposure of the formation in the railway cutting near the former Husthwaite Station, but this is no longer visible.

Over the remainder of its outcrop within the district, the Redcar Mudstone Formation is entirely covered by drift, and evidence of its presence stems solely from boreholes. In a borehole at Brier Hill Farm [4780 7404], an old account records 29 m of blue shale and "hard stone", presumably limestone and probably within the "Calcareous Shales". A recent borehole near Cold Harbour [4980 7277] proved, below drift, 1 m of grey, fossiliferous mudstone with limestone beds, the calcareous microfauna from which indicates a Hettangian or earliest Sinemurian age (Figure 6; locality 17). A comparable age-range was obtained from similar studies of grey mudstone and siltstone penetrated beneath the drift in two boreholes [4968 7157; 4902 7102] within the faulted ground around Raskelf (Figure 6; locality 18 and 19). Finally, further east, similar lithologies were reported from boreholes at Boscar Moor [5010 7189] and Springfield Farm [5141 7212].

Staithes Sandstone Formation

The Staithes Sandstone generally forms a well-defined topographical feature which can be traced across the district, even in drift-covered terrain. Exposures are, however, rare and usually comprise soil brash in areas of thin drift on the crest of its escarpment.

The thickness of the formation varies from 20 to 25 m, and it consists of fossiliferous, micaceous, calcareous, fine- to medium-grained sandstone, and sandy siltstone; the colour ranges from blue-grey (unweathered) to yellow-brown (weathered). Cross-bedding and ripple cross-lamination are common, where not destroyed by extensive bioturbation. The bases of some sandstone beds seen in the Felixkirk Borehole cores exhibit erosive scours infilled with cross-bedded sandstone containing sandstone intraclasts and bivalve fragments. Calcite–siderite concretions are present in the more argillaceous beds. An abundant benthic marine fauna, which includes sparse rhynchonellid brachiopods, *Gryphaea gigantea*, *Modiolus* sp., ostreid bivalves, *Oxytoma inequivalvis*, *Protocardia truncata* and *Pseudopecten* sp., locally produces conspicuous shell beds; occasionally, whole shells are found in life position. Trace fossils (seen in the Felixkirk Borehole cores) include *Diplocraterion* sp., *Planolites* sp. and *Rhizocorallium* sp. in the sandy lithologies, and *Chondrites* sp. in the more argillaceous beds; indeterminate vertical and horizontal circular burrows are common throughout.

The base of the Staithes Sandstone Formation is taken at the junction between the lowest sandstone and the underlying siltstone or silty mudstone; this is at 94.85 m depth in the Felixkirk Borehole where the formation is 24.75 m thick (Powell, *in* Institute of Geological Sciences, 1983; Ivimey-Cook and Powell, 1991). The top of the formation is marked by the base of the Cleveland Ironstone Formation at the junction between sandstone and an overlying mudstone or ironstone bed (the Osmotherley Seam in Felixkirk Borehole). Wireline logs from this borehole show a gradual upward-coarsening trend from the upper part of the Redcar Mudstone Formation to the Staithes Sandstone Formation (Figure 8). This transition probably reflects shallowing of the basin to within wave-base, resulting from a eustatic sea-level fall. The lithological and faunal characteristics suggest that the Staithes Sandstone was deposited in the intertidal to subtidal zone of a shallow sea, which was colonised by a diverse benthic fauna and subjected periodically to the effects of storms.

The Felixkirk Borehole cores yielded few age-diagnostic ammonites from this formation (Ivimey-Cook and Powell, 1991); the presence of *Beaniceras* sp. at 94.14 m could imply that the lower part of the Staithes Sandstone is of *luridum* Subzone (*ibex* Zone) age (Figure 8). However, this genus is also recorded from the higher *maculatum* Subzone (*davoei* Zone) in the Winteringham Haven Borehole, Humberside (Gaunt et al., 1980, p.7), and so a slightly younger age may be possible. The uppermost part of the Staithes Sandstone Formation is probably of early *margaritatus* Zone age since ammonites and bivalves from the overlying Cleveland Ironstone Formation proved this zone. Revision of the stratigraphy in the coastal sections and north Cleveland (Howard, 1985) suggests that the base of the Staithes Sandstone Formation youngs southwards from the *capricornum* Subzone (middle *davoei* Zone) in north Cleveland, to the *figulinum* Subzone (late *davoei* Zone) in the Brown Moor Borehole, Humberside. Limited biostratigraphical evidence from the Felixkirk Borehole cores suggests that the age of the lowermost Staithes Sandstone in the district is of a similar age or slightly older than in the north Cleveland area.

DETAILS

Upsall to High Osgodby Grange and the Felixkirk Borehole

In the north of the district, soil brash comprising green-grey siltstone and yellow-brown, cross-laminated, fine-grained, calcareous sandstone occurs in fields [4477 8749 to 4498 8692] west of Upsall. Bivalves, including *Pseudopecten equivalvis*, are common, and the trace fossil *Chondrites* sp. is ubiquitous. In fragments from the lower part of the scarp, burrow-mottling has destroyed any original sedimentary structures. Water from springs issuing from the base of the sandstone, through thin till cover, is rich in dissolved calcium carbonate and has formed extensive 'aprons' of calcareous tufa. Sandstone with the bivalve "*Cardium truncatum*" (now *Protocardia truncata*) was recorded by Fox-Strangways et al., (1886) in the road below Upsall Castle [4526 8656], but it is no longer exposed.

In the Felixkirk Borehole [4835 8576], the formation is represented by 24.75 m of grey, extensively bioturbated, fossiliferous, micaceous, fine- to medium-grained sandstone with thin beds of grey siltstone and sporadic siderite nodules; cross-bedding and ripple cross-lamination are common where not destroyed by bioturbation (Powell *in* Institute of Geological Sciences, 1983). Further to the south-east, fragments of grey-yellow micaceous siltstone occur on the crest of the escarpment formed by the Staithes Sandstone at Hole Wood [4677 8425], south of Felixkirk, and near High Osgodby Grange, [4893 8043].

Asenby – Coxwold Graben

Within the Asenby–Coxwold Graben, the Staithes Sandstone forms a marked topographic feature at Barf Hill [429 752], south of Dalton, which protrudes conspicuously from the low-lying, drift-covered plain; soil brash comprising brown, fine-grained sandstone with bivalves is common on the upper slopes. Further east, in a borehole [4465 7562] at Cold Harbour, the presence of grey-green, very fine-grained sandstone proved a separate synclinal block within the graben.

Hutton Sessay to Easingwold

At Hutton Sessay, Fox-Strangways et al., (1886) reported a roadside exposure [4754 7616], no longer visible, comprising sandstone and mudstone with bivalves, indicating the presence of the Staithes Sandstone immediately south of the southern boundary fault of the graben. To the south-east, in the fault-bounded outcrop at Thormanby, a road-cutting [4941 7474] described by Fox-Strangways et al. (1886), exposed 0.5 m of brown, micaceous, cross-stratified, very fine-grained sandstone. In the adjacent fault-block, soil brash consisting of brown, shelly, fine-grained sandstone occurs on Watson Hill [492 741].

South of Coxwold, the formation forms a topographical feature which runs along the hillside to Husthwaite, where fragments of yellow ferruginous sandstone were exposed in a temporary section [5189 7515].

In the far south-east of the district, the Staithes Sandstone forms a prominent, north-west-facing escarpment from Oak Trees [551 778] south-west to the northern outskirts of Easingwold. At several localities to the south-west of Rising Sun Farm [5366 7140], soil brash consisting mostly of orange-brown and khaki, ferruginous, parallel- or ripple cross-laminated silty sandstone, shelly in part, is accompanied by fragments of nodular sideritic ironstone and khaki siltstone and silty mudstone. The exposure [5406 7125] of sandstone south-east of Hanover House, noted by the Primary Survey, is no longer visible, but 0.4 m of khaki, silty sandstone overlain by 0.2 m of khaki siltstone was located in a ditch [5382 7092] about 400 m to the south-west; similar lithologies were noted north-east of Haverwitz Farm [5402 7055] and at a number of places around Mount Pleasant [5535 7083].

Cleveland Ironstone Formation

This formation crops out in the east of the district above the topographical feature made by the Staithes Sandstone Formation, but it is mostly drift-covered. Small exposures are present within the Asenby–Coxwold Graben, to the south of the graben at Carlton Husthwaite, and in the south-east of the district.

The Cleveland Ironstone Formation comprises about 9 to 13 m of grey silty mudstone and siltstone with subordinate very fine-grained sandstone and three beds of fossiliferous, sideritic, berthierinitic, oolitic ironstone (Figure 9). In north Cleveland, where the formation has its maximum development, a total of six ironstone seams of workable quality occur. However, a southwards-descending, intraformational unconformity below the highest (the Main Seam) cuts out successively older beds (Chowns, 1968; Hemingway, 1974) and, in the Thirsk district, the Main Seam rests on beds which include only the Avicula Seam and the basal Osmotherley Seam. None of these seams is of workable quality or thickness. Previously it was thought that, between Felixkirk and Sessay, the Avicula Seam was cut out and the formation reduced in thickness to less than one metre (Chowns, 1968; Hemingway, 1974; Howard, 1985). Reappraisal of the evidence from around Sessay and new data from the south-east of the district show, however, that the Avicula Seam extends across the whole district and that the formation actually increases in thickness to the south-east (Figure 9).

The base of the formation in the district is taken at the junction between the Staithes Sandstone and the basal Osmotherly Seam, although in the type coastal sections (Howarth, 1955, 1973; Howard, 1985) it is drawn at the base of up to 2.6 m of siltstone and mudstone underlying the seam. The top is defined by the base of the Whitby Mudstone Formation and in the district (Felixkirk Borehole, Figure 9; Powell, 1984) is marked by the passage from ferruginous sandy mudstone and siltstone to grey micaceous mudstone of the Grey Shale Member above.

Figure 9
Comparative
lithological logs
of the Cleveland
Ironstone
Formation in
the the Felixkirk
Borehole and in
the Gallows Hill
area.

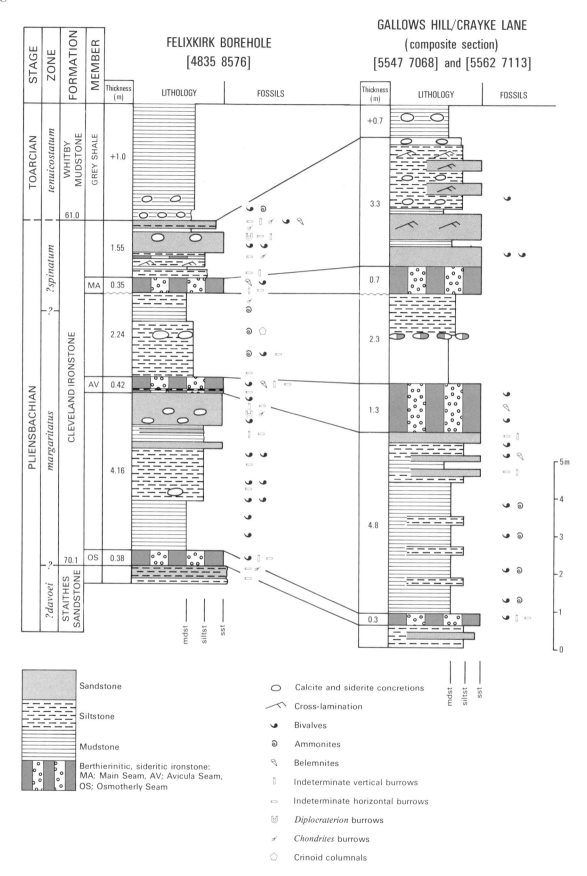

Sandstone

Siltstone

Mudstone

Berthierinitic, sideritic ironstone:
MA; Main Seam, AV; Avicula Seam,
OS; Osmotherly Seam

Calcite and siderite concretions

Cross-lamination

Bivalves

Ammonites

Belemnites

Indeterminate vertical burrows

Indeterminate horizontal burrows

Diplocraterion burrows

Chondrites burrows

Crinoid columnals

The age of the Cleveland Ironstone Formation in the Cleveland Basin, according to Howard (1985), ranges from early *subnodosus* Subzone to the *paltum* Subzone and, therefore, includes part of the *margaritatus* Zone, the *spinatum* Zone and the earliest part of the *tenuicostatum* Zone. Limited faunal evidence from exposures in the south-east of the district, and from the Felixkirk Borehole, indicates that the 'shales' overlying the basal Osmotherley Seam are of *subnodosus* Subzone age. The *spinatum* Zone was proved from interbedded siltstone and fine-grained sandstone beds overlying the Main Seam; these beds are lithologically transitional between the Cleveland Ironstone Formation and the overlying Whitby Mudstone Formation, but are included in the former unit (Figure 8; Ivimey-Cook and Powell, 1991).

The presence in coastal exposures of an abundant marine fauna dominated by suspension feeders (Hallam, 1975), together with extensive cross-lamination in the more arenaceous beds, indicates deposition within a shallow marine environment. The oolitic texture of the ironstones and their fauna of strongly ribbed bivalves suggest periods of strong wave and/or current activity. The amount of iron within this stratigraphically condensed sequence is clearly greater than during other periods in the early Jurassic; it must have been concentrated by early authigenic and diagenetic processes during periods of low terrigenous clastic input to the basin. The formation exhibits a distinct upward-coarsening cyclicity (Chowns, 1968; Howard, 1985), suggesting repeated shallowing episodes in the depositional basin. This is supported by the presence of the intraformational unconformity at the base of the Main Seam in the district.

The origin of berthierinitic, sideritic, oolitic ironstones has been discussed by many authors (Chowns, 1968; Curtis and Spears, 1968; Hallam, 1975) but the association of berthierine and siderite, which require anoxic, reducing conditions for their formation, with sediments that yield a benthic infauna and exhibit intense bioturbation, and which reflect aerobic mobile, turbulent substrates, remains an enigma.

DETAILS

Felixkirk and the Felixkirk Borehole

North of the Asenby–Coxwold Graben, the formation is almost totally masked by drift and its outcrop has been mapped from its position relative to the feature formed by the underlying Staithes Formation. A roadside exposure [4685 8475] at Felixkirk, recorded by Fox-Strangways et al. (1886), is no longer visible. More comprehensive information stems from two boreholes in the Felixkirk area. One, a trial borehole [4705 8488] for ironstone at Mount St-John (Phillips, 1858), proved 10.4 m of shales with beds of marlstone and nodular ironstone, which were allocated to the Cleveland Ironstone by Fox-Strangways et al. (1886).

More recently, the Felixkirk Borehole 4835 8576] (Powell *in* Institute of Geological Sciences, 1983; Powell, 1984; Howard, 1985; Ivimey-Cook and Powell, 1991) provided a cored section through the formation, which totalled 9.01 m in thickness (Figures 8 and 9). At the base of the formation in this borehole, the Osmotherley Seam comprises 0.38 m of pale grey, fossiliferous, sideritic ironstone with sparse berthierinitic ooliths; it rests directly on sandstones of the Staithes Sandstone Formation. It is overlain by 4.16 m of upward-coarsening grey silty mudstone, grey siltstone and very fine-grained sandstone of *subnodosus* Subzone age (Ivimey-Cook and Powell,

1991). The succeeding Avicula Seam, 0.42 m thick, consists of sideritic, berthierinitic ironstone with abundant thick-shelled bivalves. This ironstone is, in turn, overlain by grey, silty mudstone, 2.24 m thick, with a prominent band of sideritic ironstone nodules 1.14 m above the base. Fragmentary amaltheid ammonites occur both below and above the Avicula Seam, proving it to lie within the *margaritatus* Zone. The overlying Main Seam, 0.35 m thick, consists of fossiliferous, sideritic, oolitic ironstone; it rests with a sharp, disconformable junction on the underlying strata. The succeeding 1.55 m of grey siltstone and pale grey, very fine-grained sandstone with laminae and thin beds of mudstone yielded *Pleuroceras* sp., indicating a *spinatum* Zone age. This unit includes a distinctive bed, 0.35 m thick, consisting of grey-brown, bituminous, laminated siltstone, with small burrows, 0.32 m above the base; this may be a correlative of the Sulphur Band of the coastal succession (A S Howard, personal communication, 1986).

Asenby–Coxwold Graben

Within the Asenby–Coxwold Graben, the Cleveland Ironstone Formation crops out south of Dalton. The summit of Barf Hill [429 752] is capped by sparsely oolitic, sandy ironstone which is exposed as soil brash. Tate and Blake (1876, p.142) suggested that an unknown thickness of shales could be present between the underlying sandstones of the Staithes Formation and the lower ironstone bed. However, field evidence indicates that the ironstone rests directly on the sandstone, as it does in the Felixkirk Borehole. Its sparsely oolitic nature and its stratigraphical position indicate that the ironstone is the Osmotherley Seam.

Further east within the graben, the formation was formerly exposed in the railway cutting [4486 7573] at Sessay. Fox-Strangways et al. (1886, p.26) reported an exposure of 'gravelly' ironstone, which, from its stratigraphical position with respect to their record of the overlying Jet Rock to the south-west, probably represents the Main Seam. However, these exposures are no longer visible.

Carlton Husthwaite, Howe Hill, Gallows Hill and Mount Pleasant

The probable presence of the formation immediately south of the graben is indicated by a BGS borehole [4964 7658] at Manor House Farm, Carlton Husthwaite, which penetrated, beneath thick drift, 0.5 m of grey-brown, laminated, silty mudstone, which yielded palynomorphs indicating a Pliensbachian, possibly younger Pliensbachian, *margaritatus* Zone age and a marine depositional environment (Figure 6; locality 20). To the south-east, the formation subcrops beneath drift on the north-west-facing escarpment between Coxwold and Husthwaite, but it is not exposed.

In the south-east of the district, outliers of the Cleveland Ironstone Formation occur above the plateau-like feature formed by the underlying Staithes Formation. Soil brash comprising dark brown, oolitic ironstone occurs in areas of thin drift at several localities; mapping indicates that the Osmotherley Seam is present south-east of Rising Sun Farm [5376 7123] and east-south-east of Banks Farm [5442 7194]. The overlying Avicula Seam forms a small but distinctive feature around Howe Hill [543 715], and soil brash consisting of shelly oolitic ironstone occurs at several nearby localities [5440 7186; 5426 7143; 5430 7135; 5435 7139].

The Avicula Seam also forms a small feature east of Swallow Nest [5496 7236] and around the outlier [548 719] to the south, where fragments of oolitic ironstone occur in several fields. This outlier is capped by an outcrop [549 719] of the Main Seam which is exposed as a soil brash of sandy oolitic ironstone. Further south, oolitic ironstone fragments occur at a number of localities along the outcrop of the Avicula Seam east of Haverwitz Farm [5421 7053].

In the extreme south-east of the district, site investigation boreholes drilled for the construction of Gallows Hill Reservoir [5547 7068], temporary sections examined during its construction, and observations in a pipeline trench [5562 7113] just to the east of the district, have permitted the construction of the following composite section (Figure 9):

	Thickness m
WHITBY MUDSTONE FORMATION	
Mudstone, grey-brown, silty, micaceous	0.7
CLEVELAND IRONSTONE FORMATION	
Siltstone, yellow-brown, clayey, with bands of sideritic ironstone nodules at top	0.2
Siltstone, khaki, micaceous, cross-laminated, and sandstone, brown, cross-laminated, very fine-grained, with nodules of grey shelly limestone up to 0.1 m in diameter	1.6
Mudstone, black to dark grey; fine laminae of coarse siltstone [?Sulphur Band]	0.1
Sandstone, yellow, micaceous, very fine-grained, with bivalves and ammonite fragments, and siltstone, khaki, micaceous, clayey	0.7
Mudstone, grey-brown, silty	0.2
Sandstone, orange-brown, silty, ferruginous, very fine-grained; small bivalves; dark green in basal 0.1 m	0.5
Ironstone, dark brown, sideritic, sandy; sparse berthierinitic ooliths [Main Seam]	0.7
Mudstone, yellow-grey, slightly silty to silty; faint lamination	1.0
Ironstone, grey, sideritic, nodular	0.1
Mudstone, grey-brown, laminated, slightly silty in part	1.2
Ironstone, orange-brown, sideritic, with berthierinitic ooliths; large, strongly ribbed bivalves and sporadic belemnites [Avicula Seam]	1.3
Siltstone, grey, argillaceous, micaceous, laminated, bioturbated, with thin beds of grey, silty, bioturbated, very fine-grained sandstone and silty mudstone; bivalves and belemnites	1.3
Mudstone, dark grey, silty to very silty, micaceous, with beds of argillaceous siltstone; bivalves and ammonites	3.5
Ironstone, grey-brown, sideritic, bioturbated, with pale green berthierinitic ooliths and shell fragments [Osmotherley Seam]	0.3
STAITHES SANDSTONE FORMATION	
Siltstone, grey, and sandstone, pale grey, very fine-grained	0.5

The Avicula Seam forms a distinctive feature at Mount Pleasant [5535 7084], upon which soil brash of berthierinitic ironstone occurs sporadically. Samples from a pipeline trench [5544 7046] cutting the Avicula Seam yielded *Amaltheus subnodosus*, thus confirming that the Avicula Seam there is of the same biostratigraphical age as in the type section on the Yorkshire coast.

Whitby Mudstone Formation

This formation crops out in the east of the district below the Hambleton Hills escarpment, and also within the Asenby–Coxwold Graben and the western extension of the Howardian Hills. The outcrop is mostly drift covered except for scattered, small areas below the higher ground formed by the Middle Jurassic rocks.

The Whitby Mudstone Formation is about 40 m thick in the district (43 m in the Felixkirk Borehole) and predominantly consists of grey to dark grey, fossiliferous, fissile mudstone and silty mudstone, bituminous in part; thin beds of finely laminated siltstone and, more rarely, fine-grained sandstone are also present. Bands of carbonate (calcite–siderite) concretions are common at some horizons. Mudstone and silty mudstone comprise 90 per cent of the stratal thickness in the Felixkirk Borehole.

Fossils, variously preserved as calcite or pyrite, include inoceramid and pectinid bivalves, the latter often in thin shelly laminae, and also gastropods and belemnites. Ammonites are abundant at some levels, and have allowed a detailed biozonation to be established (Figure 8). Fish fragments are common in some of the bituminous horizons.

In the type section on the Yorkshire coast, the formation can be divided into five members (Cope et al., 1980; Powell, 1984; Knox, 1984), in ascending order: Grey Shale, Jet Rock, Alum Shale, Peak Mudstone and Fox Cliff Siltstone. Erosion in late Toarcian times resulted in only the lower three members being present in the district. Because of the absence of any marked lithological contrast, these units cannot be traced across the poorly exposed, mainly drift-covered ground; they can, however, be distinguished in the Felixkirk Borehole (Figure 8). Scattered exposures immediately below the Middle Jurassic escarpment indicate that the uppermost part of the Formation is represented in the district by the Alum Shale Member.

The ammonite and bivalve fauna collected from the Felixkirk Borehole shows that the formation ranges in age from the *tenuicostatum* Zone to the *bifrons* Zone, representing the lower part of the Toarcian Stage (Figure 8; Ivimey-Cook and Powell, 1991).

The lithology, the paucity of wave- or current-induced bedding structures and the presence of highly bituminous beds (Jet Rock Member), along with the relatively common nektic ammonite fauna, suggests that the formation was deposited under deeper water conditions than the underlying unit. Stagnant, anoxic conditions at the sediment–water interface during the deposition of the Jet Rock Member favoured the accumulation and preservation of bitumen (derived from marine phytoplankton) and drifted wood (jet mineral).

DETAILS

Borrowby Graben

The most north-westerly outcrop of the Whitby Mudstone Formation within the district occurs in the downfaulted area of the north–south-trending Borrowby Graben. Much of this ground is drift covered, but 0.7 m of grey mudstone with bivalves and grey siltstone representing the Alum Shale Member, overlain by berthierinitic ironstone of the Dogger Formation, are exposed in a stream section [4203 8986] north-west of Borrowby. To the south-west of here, dark grey silty mudstone at a slightly lower horizon is exposed beneath drift in a ditch [4255 8871]. About 3 km to the south-south-east, grey, fissile, micaceous mudstone with small siderite nodules is exposed in the bed of the Spittle Beck [4413 8584]; the high dip (40°) reflects close proximity to the eastern boundary fault of the graben. Palynological analysis indicates that, at Spital Beck [4405 8576] and Crake Bank Farm [4383 8566], these sediments are not older than late Pliensbachian (*margaritatus* Zone) and may be early Toarcian in age, indicating that they probably lie within the Whitby Mudstone. Further to the south-south-east, soil brash of orange-grey, fissile, organic-rich mudstones at Broom Hill [4435 8487], and an exposure [4542 8330] of grey mudstone with siderite nodules in the bed of Whitelass Beck, prove the continuity of the formation into the closure of the graben.

Cowesby to Hood Hill and the Felixkirk Borehole

To the east, the main outcrop of the Whitby Mudstone trends in a south-easterly direction below the escarpment formed by Middle and Upper Jurassic rocks, but is mainly drift covered. Grey mudstone high in the formation is exposed [473 898] south-east of Cowesby. The Alum Shale was formerly worked for brick and tile manufacture in shallow pits [4677 8865] north of Kirby Knowle, but these are now flooded. The topmost beds of the formation, comprising 1.2 m of pale grey mudstone immediately below the Dogger, are exposed in a section [4589 8875] further west along the Woolmoor Outlier.

Weathered grey mudstone of the Alum Shale is present as soil brash below the Dogger at numerous localities along the escarpments around Upsall and south of Kirby Knowle, and around the outliers at Knowle Hill [470 868] and Felixkirk [470 849]. The presence of springs at the base of the Dogger (or the Saltwick Formation, where the Dogger is absent) and the softness of the mudstone have led to deep weathering and the development of solifluction lobes at most of these localities. Less-weathered exposures occur near Pallet Hill [4742 8589], where micaceous fissile mudstones dip at 4° to the north-east in a ploughed embankment.

In the Felixkirk Borehole [4835 8576], Powell (1984) was able to distinguish the lower three members of the Whitby Mudstone Formation, which yielded fossils representative of the *tenuicostatum*, *falciferum* and *bifrons* zones (Figure 8; Ivimey-Cook and Powell, 1991). At the base, the Grey Shale Member comprises 4.99 m of fossiliferous mudstone and siltstone with carbonate concretions. This is overlain by the Jet Rock Member, comprising 24.71 m of fissile, bituminous, silty mudstone with subordinate thin beds of siltstone. Upward-fining, organic-rich, silty laminae, 5 to 50 mm thick, contain inoceramid-rich shell layers, pyritised shell fragments and fish debris. They occur as rhythmic pulses throughout the Jet Rock Member and may indicate seasonal/climatic variations (Hallam, 1967). The uppermost unit, the Alum Shale Member, is 13.21 m thick and consists of grey, nonbituminous, fossiliferous mudstone and silty mudstone with bands of carbonate concretions. Further south, in small pits [5006 8184] near Hood Hill, the Alum Shale is exposed below the till as brown-yellow weathering, fissile mudstone. The Dogger ironstone and limestone, formerly worked at Cleaves (some 400 m to the north), are absent in this area and the sandstone of the Saltwick Formation appears to rest directly on the Alum Shale; the pit may have been a trial for the Dogger ironstone. To the south-west, old clay pits [4932 8104] near Osgodby Hall expose dark grey mudstone beneath till.

South of Hood Hill, the upper part of the Whitby Mudstone Formation is exposed in a section [5035 8023] near Rose Cottage, in which grey fissile mudstone is overlain by about 1.5 m of dark grey mudstone with siderite nodules; the nodules are up to 0.25 m long, concentrically zoned, and contain abundant bivalves. The nodule-bearing bed is overlain by yellow, medium-grained sandstone of the Saltwick Formation. Hemingway (1974, fig. 48) considered the 'shales with ironstone-nodules' to be a facies of the Dogger Formation, overlying the Alum Shale. During the present survey, no ammonites were collected from these beds and it was not possible to prove a post-Toarcian (that is, post-Lias Group) age for them. Because of the lithological similarity of this mudstone to that of the Alum Shale below, it is not possible to map a line between the two units across poorly exposed country. The top of the Lias Group in this area is taken, therefore, at the junction between the grey mudstone (with or without siderite nodules) and the overlying sandstone of the Saltwick Formation.

Around Kilburn, the formation is exposed as dark grey, fissile mudstone along Tigtag Lane [5090 8032] and was formerly seen in the road between Stocking House [5055 7978] and the village (Fox-Strangways et al., 1886). The Jet Rock Member was formerly worked west of Kilburn (Fox-Strangways et al., 1886) where purple-brown fissile mudstone with sparse fragments of jet are present in spoil-heaps [5089 7951].

Asenby – Coxwold Graben

Within the Asenby – Coxwold Graben, the formation was formerly visible in the railway cutting [4490 7569] at Sessay, where Tate and Blake (1876, p.142) reported "shales of the *annulatus*-series", that is mudstones belonging to the Grey Shale Member, "followed down-dip by the Jet Rock". The latter observation, but not the former, was confirmed by Fox-Strangways et al. (1886), but the exposures are no longer visible. Further east within the graben near Highfield House [4655 7591], Fox-Strangways et al. (1886) reported that mudstone within the formation had been penetrated by a well and was exposed in ditches. A BGS borehole [4658 7589] in this area proved, beneath drift, 3.7 m of grey-brown, silty, micaceous mudstone, organic-rich in part, with subsidiary siltstone. Micropalaeontological analysis of these beds revealed a foraminiferal assemblage comprising only long-ranging agglutinating species. Comparison with the sequence in the Felixkirk Borehole suggests that this horizon could be between 12 and 15 m above the base of the formation, within the Jet Rock Member.

Newburgh Priory to Gallows Hill

South of the graben, the outcrop of the formation extends south-westwards from Newburgh Priory [542 764] but is mainly drift covered. However, a small exposure [5344 7571] within a landslip at High Leys and a temporary section [5197 7485] south of Husthwaite provide evidence of grey mudstone.

Further to the south-west, in the faulted ground around Thormanby Hill, the best exposure of the formation within the district occurs in an abandoned railway cutting [4964 7399], which exposes the following section:

	Thickness m
DRIFT	
Clay, sandy, with pebbles	1.8
WHITBY MUDSTONE FORMATION	
Mudstone, grey-brown, fissile, weathered	1.0
Mudstone, grey, fissile, fossiliferous	2.0
Not exposed	1.0
Mudstone, dark grey, blocky	3.0

Ammonites collected from the fossiliferous mudstone indicate the presence of the *falciferum* Zone of the Toarcian; comparison with the Felixkirk Borehole suggests that these beds lie between 12 and 25 m above the base of the formation, within the Jet Rock Member. Palynomorph assemblages from this site (Figure 6; locality 21) are also indicative of an early Toarcian age and include the dino-flagellate cysts *Nannoceratopsis ambonis* and *N. gracilis*, in addition to varied spore and pollen associations, acritarchs and tasmanitid algae. The outcrop of the Whitby Mudstone extends east from Thormanby Hill to south of Oulston [567 743], but is entirely drift covered. A temporary section [5239 7378] south of Sand Hill proved 1.0 m of grey fissile mudstone, below drift.

In the south-east of the district, outliers of the formation occur at Mallinson Hill [535 706] and Howe Hill [543 715], on both of which soil brash of grey fissile mudstone occurs. Palynomorphs recovered from a site [5343 7049] at Claypenny Hospital are indicative of a Toarcian, possibly early Toarcian age (Figure 6; locality 22). In the extreme south-east, a temporary section at Gallows Hill Reservoir [5546 7072] exposed 0.3 m of grey-brown, silty, micaceous mudstone with ironstone nodules, resting on the underlying Cleveland Ironstone Formation.

MIDDLE JURASSIC

At the end of the Early Jurassic (Toarcian), the Cleveland Basin was subjected to gentle folding followed by submarine erosion (Hemingway, 1974). Middle Jurassic sediments, between 120 and 140 m thick in the district, rest unconformably on the eroded surface of the Whitby Mudstone Formation (Alum Shale Member). The oldest unit is the Dogger Formation, a lithologically heterogeneous, marine unit comprising conglomerate, sandstone, shale, limestone and ironstone, which, elsewhere in Yorkshire, can be shown to be of Aalenian age (Parsons, 1980) (Table 6).

The succeeding Ravenscar Group, which makes up the larger part of the Middle Jurassic sequence, broadly represents a period of regression, when deltaic, fluvial and paralic sediments were deposited, broken only by three short periods of marine transgression (Table 7). Biostratigraphical data from these beds is confined to the occurrence of early Bajocian ammonites (*humphriesianum* Zone) in exposures of the Scarborough Formation on the Yorkshire coast (Parsons, 1980). Correlation with the typical coastal exposures is, however, tentative, and the Scarborough Formation in this district may be representative of the early *sauzei* Zone (Table 8; Parsons, 1980).

The upper boundary of the Ravenscar Group, defined by the base of the Cornbrash (or, where absent, by the base of the Osgodby Formation) was formerly taken as the junction between the Middle and Upper Jurassic Series in the Cleveland Basin (Fox-Strangways et al., 1886; Hemingway and Knox, 1973; Hemingway, 1974). However, a revision of the Jurassic stratigraphical column (Cope et al., 1980) has raised the Series boundary to include the Callovian Stage, represented in the district by the transgressive Osgodby Formation, within the Middle Jurassic. Consequently, the base of the Upper Jurassic strata in this district (Table 6) is now taken at the base of the Oxford Clay (Oxfordian Stage; Mariae Chronozone).

In the district, Middle Jurassic rocks form the bulk of the Hambleton Hills, and much of the sequence rises above the highest levels reached by glacial deposition. However, apart from scattered quarries and landslip scars, exposure is severely limited by landslips, head deposits and dense coniferous forests.

Dogger Formation

The Dogger Formation crops out at the base of the Middle Jurassic escarpment between Cowesby [475 898] and Cleaves [4965 8275], where it forms a small topographical feature. Southwards from the latter locality to the northern margin of the Asenby – Coxwold Graben its presence cannot be demonstrated; this may be due either to its removal by erosion prior to deposition of the overlying Saltwick Forma-

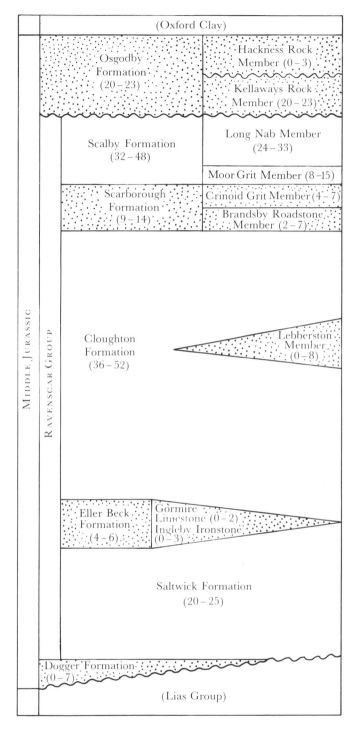

Table 7 Lithostratigraphical subdivisions of the Middle Jurassic strata in the district; stipple indicates predominantly marine strata. Thickness (in metres) of units shown in brackets.

tion, or to lateral passage into a predominantly shale facies (see p.38), which cannot be distinguished from the underlying Whitby Mudstone Formation in poorly exposed terrain (Figure 10). South of the Asenby – Coxwold Graben, the formation again forms a prominent topographical feature at Beacon Banks [5258 7507].

The lithologically heterogeneous Dogger Formation ranges in thickness from 0 to 7 m. Lithofacies vary throughout the district (Figures 10 and 11); it typically consists of shelly, sideritic ironstone with berthierine ooliths (Figure 10) but other lithologies include: bioclastic, oolitic, commonly sideritic, cross-bedded limestone (wackestone–packstone), calcareous mudstone with siderite concretions, calcareous fine-grained sandstone, and phosphatised pebbles. The presence of basal phosphatised pebbles in the formation, limited palaeontological evidence within the district (see details), and also information from elsewhere in the Cleveland Basin (Hemingway, 1974; Kent, 1980a; Cope et al., 1980), suggests that the formation represents a condensed sequence spanning the *opalinum* Zone and early *murchisonae* Zone (Table 8).

The lithological characteristics, bedforms and facies distribution suggest a marine depositional environment ranging from shallow-water, high-energy conditions on submarine highs, where carbonates and oolitic ironstones accumulated (Cleaves area; Figure 10), to quieter-water lagoons or barred depressions, where laminated mudstone was deposited and where early diagenetic ironstone concretions developed. The presence of phosphatic pebbles at the base of the formation at Cleaves, and the presence, outside the district, of abraded ammonites of Toarcian age (Black, 1934), testifies to the erosional phase and depositional hiatus between the top of the Lias Group (Alum Shale Member) and the Dogger Formation (Table 5).

DETAILS

Borrowby, Woolmoor and Kirby Knowle

In the north of the district, the predominant lithofacies of the Dogger Formation is a sideritic, berthierinitic, oolitic ironstone. On the western flank of the Borrowby Graben, a stream section [4208 8986] north-west of Borrowby exposes 1.4 m of ironstone overlying grey, fossiliferous siltstone of the Whitby Mudstone Formation. On the main escarpment, the ironstone extends south from Cowesby to near Kirby Knowle, where it was formerly worked in at least four adits (see chapter eight) between Black Plantation [4686 8867] and Storth Wood [4780 8640]. The adits are now closed, but nearby spoil tips provide evidence of the lithology of the ironstone. A small section [4788 8629] near Storth Wood exposes the following succession (Figure 11):

	Thickness m
SALTWICK FORMATION	
Sandstone, yellow, fine-grained, with coaly fragments and mudstone partings	4.0
DOGGER FORMATION	
Siltstone, greenish brown, with bivalve fragments; wood impressions and coaly laminae at base	0.33
Mudstone, pale grey, silty, with small bivalves	0.47
Ironstone, greenish brown, weathered, bioclastic; siderite matrix with berthierine ooliths	1.78
Siltstone, grey, calcareous, with crinoid columnals and abundant bivalves; limestone, in part	0.20
WHITBY MUDSTONE FORMATION	
Mudstone, grey, fissile	0.20

Dr H C Ivimey-Cook identified a number of bivalves collected from mine spoil by Dr R F Youell, including an arcid indet.,

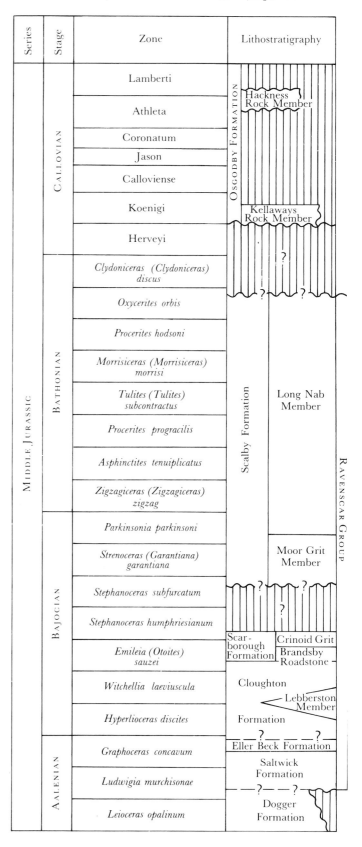

Table 8 Stratigraphical framework of the Middle Jurassic rocks in the district. Vertical ruled lines indicate an unconformity or depositional hiatus (after Cope et al., 1980)

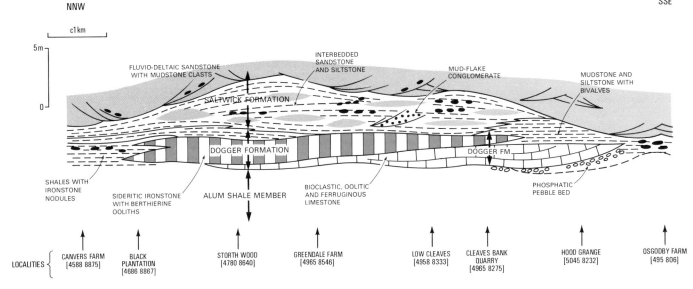

Figure 10 Diagrammatic cross-section showing the lithofacies of the Dogger Formation in the Hambleton Hills.

Chlamys?, *Cucullaea* sp., *Eopecten?*, *Gervillella* sp., *Gryphaea?*, *Lopha* sp., lucinid indet., *Modiolus* sp., ostreids indet., *Pholadomya lirata*, *Plagiostoma* sp., *Pleuromya* sp., *Pronoella* sp., *Propeamussium* cf. *pumilum*, *Protocardia?*, *Quenstedtia?*, and a trigoniid indet. The collection also included the gastropod *Procerithium* sp. and ammonite fragments including *Ludwigia?* sp. juv.

Also present are wood fragments, serpulids, rhynchonelloid, terebratuloid and echinoid fragments. The faunal assemblage is indicative of the *murchisonae* Zone.

The marked lateral facies change typical of the Dogger is illustrated by a section [4588 8875] near Woolmoor. Here, the formation solely comprises 1.20 m of grey mudstone and siltstone with bands of shelly siderite nodules and yet is less then 1 km west of the adit at Black Plantation [4686 8867] where oolitic ironstones were of sufficient thickness to be worked.

Boltby, Felixkirk and Cleaves

To the south and east of Storth Wood, the oolitic ironstone facies extends around the escarpment, past Boltby and south to Greendale Farm [4965 8546]. It also occurs at the foot of the Houseborough outlier where, in the Felixkirk Borehole [4835 8576], the Dogger comprised 2.92 m of yellow-orange, sideritic, limonitic, ironstone containing berthierine ooliths, shell fragments and bivalves, with a thin bed of grey shelly siltstone at the base (Powell, 1984).

To the south-west, the formation becomes more calcitic. In the Felixkirk outlier, a temporary section [4702 8493] north-east of the village exposed 2.0 m of grey-brown, sideritic limestone with pebbles of sideritic ironstone.

Between Greendale Farm and Skipton Hill [4967 8374], the ironstone is not exposed, and it appears that sandstones of the overlying Saltwick Formation rest directly on the Whitby Mudstone Formation, the Dogger possibly having been removed by penecontemporaneous erosion. Further south, at Cleaves Wood [4958 8333], Kennycow Quarry [5007 8252] and Cleaves Bank Quarry [4965 8275], limestones are again present (Figure 10), and a composite section for the last, based partly on data recorded by Fox-Strangways et al. (1886, p.33) when the quarry was better exposed, is as follows:

	Thickness m
SALTWICK FORMATION	
Sandstone, orange-yellow, micaceous, medium-grained, with wood impressions, mudstone clasts and siderite nodules	5.0
DOGGER	
Mudstone, grey, with shelly, argillaceous limestone concretions	c.4.0
Ironstone, yellow-brown, sideritic	0.5
Limestone, grey-buff, oolitic, with crinoid ossicles and shell fragments; sideritic matrix, in part	c.2.0
Phosphatic pebble bed, laterally impersistent	0.5

Further east, around Hood Grange [5045 8232], shelly sideritic ironstone occurs beneath the oolitic limestone bed, which forms a mappable feature and which is well exposed as field brash.

Hood Hill to Kilburn and the Asenby–Coxwold Graben

To the south, around Hood Hill and south-east towards Kilburn, the Dogger can no longer be traced, due either to erosion at the base of the Saltwick Formation, or to a lateral facies change into mudstones which cannot be distinguished from those of the Whitby Mudstone Formation (see p.35). Within the drift-covered ground of the Asenby–Coxwold Graben, there is no evidence for the presence of the Dogger and it is assumed that one or other of the same explanations applies.

Newburgh Priory to Beacon Banks

South of the graben, the outcrop of the Dogger extends south-west of Newburgh Priory and is mainly drift covered, but soil brash comprising grey, bioclastic, sideritic limestone with berthierine ooliths occurs at High Leys [5353 7572]. To the south-west, the formation forms the prominent topographical feature of Beacon Banks [5258 7507], where grey, bioclastic, sideritic, berthierinitic, oolitic ironstone is exposed. In the downfaulted ground to the south-west, the Dogger can be traced beneath drift as far as Providence Hill, where a small pit [5071 7448] exposes 1.5 m of a similar ironstone. The formation cannot be traced further east within the district.

RAVENSCAR GROUP

The Ravenscar Group ranges in thickness from 115 to 140 m, and predominantly comprises nonmarine siliciclastic rocks consisting of sandstone, siltstone and mudstone with subsidiary seatearths and thin coals; these lithologies were deposited in deltaic, fluvial and paralic environments during a regressive phase of sedimentation associated with uplift in the North Sea Basin (Sellwood and Hallam, 1974). The non-marine episode was interrupted by three transgressive marine units consisting of limestone, mudstone, ironstone and calcareous sandstone (Tables 6 and 7); these comprise, in ascending order, the Eller Beck Formation, Lebberston Member and Scarborough Formation, though not all can be traced throughout the district. A fourth marine unit, the Blowgill Member, was thought to be present (Hemingway and Knox, 1973; Hemingway, 1974; Kent, 1980a) but it has now been shown (Powell and Rathbone, 1983) that this unit represents a facies of the Eller Beck Formation, rather than a separate, later marine incursion.

The nomenclature of the Group has undergone frequent revisions (Table 6), but the terminology used herein follows broadly that of Hemingway and Knox (1973) with the exception noted above.

The chronostratigraphical framework (Table 8) of the Group is poorly known due to the paucity of age-diagnostic fossils (particularly ammonites). The coastal type sections have yielded sparse ammonites representative of the Lower Bajocian (*sauzei* Zone to *humphriesianum* Zone) from the Scarborough Formation (Parsons, 1980), but the upper part of the Bajocian Stage, and the whole of the succeeding Bathonian Stage, are represented only by the fluviodeltaic Scalby Formation (c.50 m thick); it is likely that this stratigraphical interval between the top of the Scarborough Formation and the base of the Osgodby Formation represents a period, or several periods of depositional hiatus (Leeder and Nami, 1979; Woollam and Riding, 1983; Fisher and Hancock, 1985). Study of palynofloras from the lowermost and uppermost Long Nab Member (Scalby Formation) from the Yorkshire coast and Newtondale, respectively, suggest, however that the Scalby Formation spans the uppermost Bajocian stage and the Bathonian stage (Riding and Wright, 1989).

Saltwick Formation

The Saltwick Formation forms the lower part of both the steep west-facing scarp of the Hambleton Hills and the western extension of the Howardian Hills, around Carlton Husthwaite. The outcrop is commonly obscured by landslip, solifluction deposits or coniferous forest, but feature-forming sandstones can be traced locally, and the formation is exposed in numerous quarries.

The Saltwick Formation (Hemingway and Knox, 1973) is synonymous with the Lower Estuarine Series (Fox-Strangways et al., 1886), the Lower Deltaic Series (Hemingway, 1949) and the Hayburn Formation (Parsons, 1980).

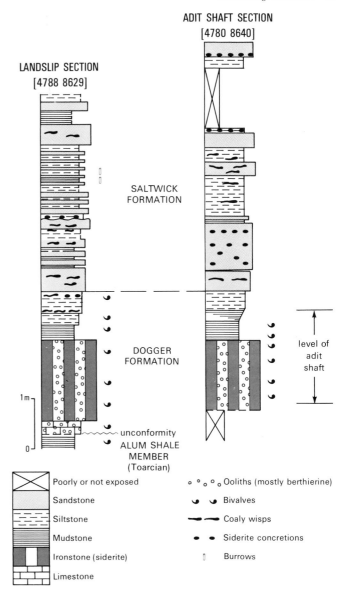

Figure 11 Lithological sections of the Dogger Formation and the overlying Saltwick Formation in Storth Wood [4780 8640], Kirby Knowle.

It is about 20 to 25 m thick in the district, and consists of sandstone, siltstone and mudstone deposited in fluviodeltaic and paralic environments.

The predominant lithology is fine- to medium-grained, micaceous sandstone, commonly containing plant fragments. Cross-lamination, large-scale cross-stratification of both trough and tabular types, erosion surfaces, obvious channel forms floored by mudstone-clast conglomerates, and upward-fining sequences from sandstone into siltstone and mudstone, together indicate deposition in fluvial channels. Mudstone clasts probably represent floodplain sediment eroded by the rivers during channel-switching. Coaly laminae are common at some horizons and suggest erosion of peat swamps situated in the interfluves. Thick, workable coal seams are, however, absent, in contrast with the Cloughton and Scalby formations in the district. This suggests deposition from rivers with a high velocity, high discharge regime during Saltwick times.

The absence of the topographical feature formed by the Dogger Formation between Hood Hill and Kilburn may indicate that the base of Saltwick Formation eroded down to the level of the Lias Group in this area. Elsewhere, the lower boundary of the formation is gradational with the clastic sediments of the underlying Dogger Formation (Figure 11); the junction is taken at the base of the lowermost sandstone, siltstone or mudstone of nonmarine aspect. For mapping purposes, however, this coincides with the base of the feature-forming sandstone or siltstone overlying the distinctive Dogger ironstone or limestone lithofacies or, where those are absent, the top of the Lias Group. The top of the Saltwick Formation is defined by the base of the marine Eller Beck Formation throughout most of the district. The latter formation, however, is absent north of Skipton Hill, except for a small outcrop in the southern part of the Woolmoor outlier, and the adjacent escarpment. Where the Eller Beck Formation is absent, the boundary between the Saltwick Formation and the similar fluviodeltaic strata of the overlying Cloughton Formation is shown on the map as a conjectural line.

The age of the Saltwick Formation is constrained by the fossiliferous Dogger Formation below and the Eller Beck Formation above, which have yielded early to middle Aalenian and late Aalenian faunas respectively (Table 8; Cope et al., 1980).

DETAILS

Upsall, Boltby and Cleaves

The Saltwick Formation has been extensively quarried for building stone, and the villages of Upsall [453 871], Boltby [492 867] and Thirlby [490 840] are largely constructed from it. Hence only those quarries and sections exhibiting an appreciable thickness of strata, or particular features, are mentioned below.

The formation crops out within the Borrowby Graben near the villages of Borrowby [428 894] and Knayton [432 877], but due to the absence of the Eller Beck Formation in this area, it cannot be distinguished from the overlying Cloughton Formation. Yellow-brown, medium-grained sandstone with siderite nodules is exposed in Swain Lane [4313 8771], near Knayton.

In the north of the main escarpment, beds low in the formation are exposed [4523 8750] near Upsall where the section is as follows:

	Thickness m
Sandstone, yellow-orange, fine-grained, cross-laminated	1.65
Siltstone, micaceous, with carbonaceous laminae	0.04
Siltstone, yellow-brown, micaceous, and thin beds of yellow sandstone with siderite nodules	0.31
Sandstone, yellow-orange, fine-grained, cross-laminated	0.80

To the south, at Hales Wood [4810 8589], near Boltby, the lower part of the Saltwick Formation, transitional with the underlying Dogger Formation, is exposed. The bases of the sandstone beds have vertical burrows but also include plant fragments, suggesting a paralic depositional environment, transitional between the marine ironstone unit below and the fluviodeltaic beds above. The section is as follows:

SALTWICK FORMATION	*Thickness* m
Sandstone, orange-brown, fine-grained, with plant fragments and thin (0.02–0.05 m) beds of siderite in basal 0.6 m	2.0
Sandstone, yellow, fine-grained, micaceous, with plant fragments; bioturbated in part; vertical burrows in basal 0.4 m	0.6
Siltstone, pale grey, finely laminated, micaceous, with plant fragments	0.2
DOGGER FORMATION	
Sandstone, orange, fine- to medium-grained, with ovoid siderite clasts; thin sandstone partings with vertical burrows in basal 0.6 m	1.4
Ironstone, grey-brown, sideritic, berthierinitic, oolitic, shelly	1.2

To the south-east, typical fluviodeltaic sediments can be seen in roadside quarries [4989 8520; 4990 8515] near Greendale. The former exposes orange-yellow, cross-bedded sandstone in which foresets with erosive bases dip at 20°; abundant mudstone (siderite) clasts are present towards the bases of the foresets. Nearby, a small quarry [5010 8435] near Southwood Hall exposes 2.8 m of yellow-orange, medium-grained sandstone; bed thickness decreases from the base to the top of the quarry face, suggesting an upward-declining flow regime.

Further south, Cleaves Bank Quarries [4962 8287; 4998 8258] expose beds higher in the formation, comprising orange, medium-grained sandstone with large-scale, trough cross-bedding. East of here, at Kennycow Quarry [5007 8252], yellow, medium-grained, cross-bedded sandstone (3.6 m) is exposed above the Dogger. The channel-fill geometry of the sandstone beds can be seen between the A170 road and the track leading to Rigg House [5062 8300]. Here, the erosional nature of the sandstone-filled channel and the thinner flanking beds is well displayed.

Osgodby, Kilburn and Beacon Banks

To the south, an old quarry [4951 8038] near Osgodby Wood exposes the following upward-fining sequence:

	Thickness m
Siltstone, yellow-buff, micaceous, passing up into cross-laminated silty mudstone	0.20
Sandstone, yellow-buff, micaceous, fine-grained, with small mudstone clasts; cross-bedded, with 3–4 mm coaly laminae; erosive base	0.23
Sandstone, yellow, micaceous, medium-grained, cross-bedded, with plant fragments	c.1.0

The nearby roadside quarry at Osgodby Bank [4967 8063] exposes 3.6 m of grey-yellow, fine- to medium-grained sandstone with large-scale, tabular cross-bedding.

North-east of Kilburn, an old quarry [5150 7986] exposes the following upward-fining sequence:

	Thickness m
Clay, grey, silty, with wood fragments	0.4
Siltstone, grey	2.4
Sandstone, orange, fine-grained, with wood fragments and siderite bands	1.7

Within the Asenby–Coxwold Graben, and to the south, in the vicinity of Newburgh Priory, the Saltwick Formation is totally drift covered. The formation is, however, exposed as soil brash comprising yellow, medium-grained sandstone above the Dogger Formation, near High Leys [5353 7573] and south-west of Beacon Banks [529 751].

Further to the south-west, an old quarry [5116 7463] at Bill Bank Plantation exposes 3.1 m of yellow, cross-stratified and cross-laminated, medium-grained sandstone.

Eller Beck Formation

This lithologically heterogeneous formation consists of berthierinitic, oolitic, sideritic ironstone, silty mudstone, argillaceous limestone, siltstone with sandstone lenses, and sandstone. It ranges in thickness from 4 to 6 m in this district and forms a small topographical feature. The Eller Beck Formation (Barrow, 1877; Hemingway and Knox, 1973) marks the first marine transgression within the Ravenscar Group; the incursion advanced from the east or south-east across the low-lying, delta swamp of the Saltwick Formation. The formation in this district shows a lithofacies transition from an ironstone-shale-sandstone sequence, both in the north and in the adjacent Northallerton (42) Sheet, to a limestone-shale-sandstone sequence, in the south (Powell and Rathbone, 1983).

In coastal sections, and throughout most of the Cleveland Hills, a distinctive sandstone bed (c.6 m thick) forms a prominent mappable marker horizon at the top of the Formation (Knox, 1973); this sandstone is not well developed in the district and hence the upper boundary is not well defined. The Eller Beck Formation can be traced across poorly exposed country, however, by the presence in soils of fragments of ironstone or limestone of distinctive types. Nevertheless, it was not possible to map the formation along much of the western escarpment, particularly the areas north of Skipton Hill [498 842], the north-west of the Woolmoor outlier and within the Borrowby–Knayton Graben. This may be due to the paucity of exposure, to rapid lateral facies changes (at the north-western limit of the transgression), or to penecontemporaneous erosion of the formation by prograding fluviodeltaic channels of the overlying Cloughton Formation.

Hemingway and Knox (1973) proposed two separate marine transgressions (represented by the Eller Beck Formation and the stratigraphically higher Blowgill Member) at this level in the Middle Jurassic. However, during the present survey, mapping evidence from around Skipton Hill [498 842] suggested that this was not so and a trench section [4980 8428] excavated on the west side of the hill proved the following section (Figure 12).

	Thickness m
CLOUGHTON FORMATION	
Sandstone, yellow-brown, cross-bedded, medium-grained, with plant fragments	1.60
Not exposed	0.50
ELLER BECK FORMATION	
Sandstone, greenish brown, fine- to medium-grained, cross-laminated, with symetrical	

ripples; siltstone with siderite nodules in basal 0.3 m	0.60
Mudstone, grey, calcareous, with large concretions and irregular beds of pale grey, argillaceous limestone (micrite); bivalves and gastropods [*Gormire Limestone*]	0.42
Mudstone, dark grey, with sparse bivalves and two beds of grey siderite (0.18–0.20 m)	1.95
Siltstone, grey, with abundant bivalves	0.01–0.14

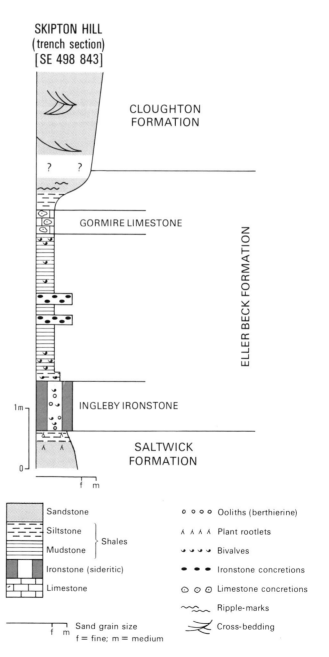

Figure 12 legend:

Sandstone	Ooliths (berthierine)
Siltstone ⎫	Plant rootlets
Mudstone ⎬ Shales	Bivalves
Ironstone (sideritic)	Ironstone concretions
Limestone	Limestone concretions
	Ripple-marks
Sand grain size f = fine; m = medium	Cross-bedding

Figure 12 Lithological section of the Eller Beck Formation at Skipton Hill (after Powell and Rathbone, 1983, fig. 2).

Ironstone, grey, yellow-weathering; siderite
matrix and berthierine ooliths; bivalves [*Ingleby
Ironstone*]   0.75

SALTWICK FORMATION
Siltstone, grey, with plant rootlets   0.20
Sandstone, yellow, medium-grained, with plant
rootlets   to 0.50

This section, together with additional mapping evidence from north of the district, demonstrates that there was only one transgression and that a change of facies occurred in the vicinity of Skipton Hill (Powell and Rathbone, 1983). To the north of the district, the ironstone bed, named the Ingleby Ironstone (Knox, 1973), is thicker and the limestone is thin or absent. South of Skipton Hill, the ironstone bed passes laterally into shales with siderite nodules and the limestone, now named the Gormire Limestone, but formerly known as the Hydraulic Limestone (Fox-Strangways et al., 1886), becomes more prominent. An exposure about 5 km to the north-west of Skipton Hill, at Coneygarth Hill [4653 8780], represents the most westerly outcrop of the formation in the Cleveland Basin. Here, the siderite ironstone and argillaceous limestone beds are both absent and, although the beds are poorly exposed, the following section can be demonstrated:

	Thickness m
Ironstone, red-brown, oolitic, berthierinitic, passing down to sandstone	c.2.0
Mudstone, grey, silty, with bivalves	1.0
Sandstone, fine-grained, with bivalves; base not seen	c.1.0

This atypical oolite facies has also been recognised at Winter Gill, north Cleveland (Knox, 1970). Both sequences represent local developments, possibly associated with the migration of iron-rich ooliths from laterally restricted sand banks. The oolitic ironstone can be traced for only about 500 m westwards from the main exposure at Coneygarth Hill.

The fauna of the Ingleby Ironstone includes abundant bivalves (*Astarte minima, Gervillia* sp., *Liostrea* sp. and *Pholadomya* sp.), sparse gastropods, and both vertical and U-shaped burrows (*Diplocraterion* sp.). Some of the infaunal bivalves are preserved in life position within the ironstone (Powell, 1982). Thin-shelled, small bivalves are also present in the micritic Gormire Limestone; they include "*Lima* sp., *Pecten* sp., *Pinna* sp., *Gervillia* sp., *Ostrea* sp. and *Meleagrinella* sp." (Arkell, 1933). The ostracod fauna (Bate, 1967) suggests a tentative correlation with the base of the Lincolnshire Limestone (Arkell, 1933) of late Aalenian to early Bajocian age (Cope et al., 1980).

The lithofacies and fauna indicate that the Eller Beck Formation was deposited in a shallow-marine environment. The absence of the formation in the north-west of the district probably indicates proximity to the shoreline in this area. The sharp lower boundary of the formation, where bivalve-rich, oolitic ironstone rests on sandstone with plant rootlets, points to a rapid incursion of the sea across the delta-top swamp. The distribution of ironstone in the north Cleveland Basin (Knox, 1969; Hemingway, 1974) compared to the increasing importance of micritic limestone to the south suggests that the sea advanced northwards across the Market Weighton Structure (Kent, 1980a; Powell and Rathbone, 1983). Oolitic, berthierinitic and sideritic muds were deposited in prodelta environments in the north where iron colloids, brought down by rivers draining from the north, were concentrated in shallow, but non-turbulent lagoons. Berthierine ooliths may have formed on local, shallow-water highs or in nearshore, tidal shoals, and subsequently been redeposited throughout the northern part of the basin by tidal or storm-induced currents. This iron-rich province passed gradationally, south of the Skipton Hill area, to a purer lime-mud province, which was a northern extension of the carbonate platform in Lincolnshire (Ashton, 1977).

DETAILS

Skipton Hill to High Kilburn

To the south of Skipton (see p.41), the outcrop of the Gormire Limestone can be traced along the main escarpment by the presence of pale grey argillaceous limestone fragments in the soil. At Gormire Lake [5019 8307], approximately 1 m of pale grey, argillaceous, shelly limestone is exposed on the western shore. The outcrop between Gormire Lake and Hood Hill is obscure, but large blocks of the limestone were found ploughed up in a forestry track on the south side of Hood Hill [5001 8078]. On the south side of the hill, the outcrop may be traced by the prominent feature formed by a sandstone overlying the limestone; Fox-Strangways et al. (1886) noted that the limestone was formerly worked in Penfoot Wood, but no exposures could be found here during the recent survey. The sandstone bed caps a small plateau at Acre House [5120 8054] and mudstone with both limestone fragments and siderite concretions are exposed below.

The Eller Beck Formation is next exposed, further south, near Ragged Ray [5136 8036]. Here, ferruginous mudstone with bivalves (0.3 m) overlies red-brown argillaceous limestone with small bivalves (0.35 m), which in turn rests on brown flaggy, bioclastic limestone with ironstone nodules (0.6 m). This atypical ferruginous limestone sequence can be traced south to Headstay Bank [5130 8008] where it overlies a prominent channel-fill sandstone of the Saltwick Formation. The Gormire Limestone is represented by typical facies south-east of High Kilburn, where fragments of grey, argillaceous limestone were seen at two localities [5235 7969; 5231 7933]; it can also be traced southwards to the northern margin of the Asenby–Coxwold Graben.

Husthwaite to Thornton Hill

Within the Asenby–Coxwold Graben, the Gormire Limestone is completely drift-covered; thus the mapped outcrop is conjectural and based on information to the north and south of the structure. In the ground south of Husthwaite, pale grey argillaceous limestone fragments have been observed at a number of localities [5134 7446; 5138 7434; 5178 7461; 5191 7461] around Highthorne.

Further east, on Thornton Hill, an old quarry [5302 7450] exposes the following section in the Gormire Limestone:

	Thickness m
Limestone, pale grey, argillaceous, in beds and nodules, with bivalves and gastropods	0.3
Mudstone, grey, fissile, with nodules of grey limestone	0.7
Mudstone, grey, micaceous, with shelly siderite nodules	0.3

The Gormire Limestone cannot be traced further east within the district, nor in the drift-covered ground between Husthwaite and Newburgh Priory.

Cloughton Formation

The Cloughton Formation (Hemingway and Knox, 1973) is synonymous with the upper part of the Lower Estuarine Series (Fox-Strangways et al., 1886) and the Middle Deltaic Series (Hemingway, 1949). The formation is between 36 and 52 m thick and predominantly comprises sandstone, mudstone and thin, laterally impersistent, coaly siltstone beds, of fluviodeltaic facies. Over much of the Yorkshire Basin, the formation is divided by a wedge of shallow-marine, calcareous sandstone and oolitic limestone, the Lebberston Member (Hemingway and Knox, 1973), which marks a marine incursion from the south and east. The north-west limit of the transgression lies within the north-east of the district and, consequently, the Lebberston Member is present only as small isolated outcrops which represent the 'feather-edge' of the unit.

The heterogeneous nature of the fluviodeltaic sediments that comprise the Cloughton Formation, and the steepness of the escarpment, result in few laterally persistent mappable horizons. Where these are present, usually as channel-fill sandstone units, they cannot be traced for any great distance. Some of the individual sandstone units can be mapped where the escarpment broadens out, for instance near Boltby [492 866], but over large areas the Cloughton Formation is mapped undivided.

Sandstones of the Cloughton Formation have been extensively quarried for building stone and there are many small quarries dotted along the outcrop. Yellow-orange, medium-grained sandstone, with lag deposits comprising mudstone clasts and wood fragments, is ubiquitous. The commonest sedimentary structure is trough cross-stratification, but planar cross-stratification, scoured channel bases and, more rarely, lateral-accretion units are also present. The predominant facies is clearly one of fluvial delta-top channels; associated facies such as interdistributary siltstone and mudstone or crevasse-splay sandstone are, however, not well exposed. Thin, locally developed lenses of coal and coaly siltstone, underlain by ganisteroid sandstone with rootlet traces, indicate colonisation of the delta-top by plants; none of these coals are of sufficient thickness to have been worked in the district.

The age of the Cloughton Formation is determined from its stratigraphical position between the underlying Eller Beck Formation (late Aalenian to Lower Bajocian age) and the overlying Scarborough Formation (late Lower Bajocian age) (Table 8). The marine Lebberston Member has not yielded ammonites, but its ostracod fauna suggests that these beds are coeval with the *discites* Zone of the Lincolnshire Limestone (Bate, 1967). The Cloughton Formation, there-fore, probably spans the *discites, laeviuscula* and *sauzei* zones (Table 8; Cope et al., 1980, fig. 4a).

DETAILS

Borrowby, Woolmoor and Brockholes

Within the Borrowby Graben [42 89], in the north of the district, the Eller Beck Formation cannot be traced and thus the Ravenscar Group is mapped undivided. However, yellow, thin-bedded, fine-grained sandstone high in the succession, and thus probably within the Cloughton Formation, is exposed at the roadside in Borrowby [4279 8972] and in a temporary section [4325 8791] at Knayton.

Excellent exposures of the sandstone of the Cloughton Formation occur around the Woolmoor outlier. A prominent sandstone near the base of the formation forms 'The Belt' [4571 8765], a scarp feature north of Newbuildings. A number of small quarries along the outcrop of the sandstone expose the ubiquitous yellow-weathering, medium-grained sandstone exhibiting large-scale, trough cross-bedding, with scoured, channelled bases and lag-deposits composed of large mudstone clasts. Up to 7.6 m of the same sandstone is also exposed in a quarry [4558 8752] on the downthrown side of the Woolmoor fault. Here, large-scale, trough cross-sets have foreset dips up to 25° with deeply channelled bases; large, rounded mudstone clasts form basal lag-deposits up to 0.6 m thick at the base of the channels.

On the main escarpment, the outcrop is obscured by extensive Head deposits, landslips and coniferous forest. However, at Brockholes [4742 8775] the backscar of a landslip exposes the upper part of the formation, below the Scarborough Formation (Figure 13):

	Thickness m
SCARBOROUGH FORMATION	
Limestone, grey, argillaceous	0.48
CLOUGHTON FORMATION	
Mudstone, pale grey, micaceous, and siltstone, buff, with ripple cross-lamination and carbonaceous fragments	3.0
Sandstone, yellow, fine- to medium-grained, micaceous, thin-bedded in top 1.8 m; low-angle, trough cross-bedding throughout	4.70
Mudstone, grey, micaceous	0.30
Sandstone, orange, medium-grained, thick-bedded, with large-scale, trough cross-bedding; carbonaceous fragments on bedding planes	5.30

The two sandstone units, together, form one of the more laterally persistent beds in the district and the feature they form can be traced along the escarpment to a small quarry [4699 8860]. A number of feature-forming sandstones are exposed on the bluffs north-east and south-west of Ravensthorpe [4807 8668]. A small quarry [4833 8697] exposes a cross-bedded sandstone displaying lateral-accretion units indicating point-bar deposition in a meandering river (Allen, 1963).

Boltby to Oldstead and High Kilburn

Sandstone at about the same stratigraphic level is exposed in a disused quarry [4925 8682] above Boltby. The quarry exposes about 8.7 m of orange, medium-grained sandstone; the basal 4.6 m show 1.3 m-thick sets of trough cross-strata; these are truncated by a 0.4 m unit of planar-bedded sandstone with small mudstone clasts and abundant wood fragments; a trough cross-bedded unit, 1.2 m thick, followed by a planar-bedded unit, with ripple-drift lamination and coaly fragments, 2.5 m thick, form the top of the quarry face. To the south, a 15 m-thick sandstone crops out immediately

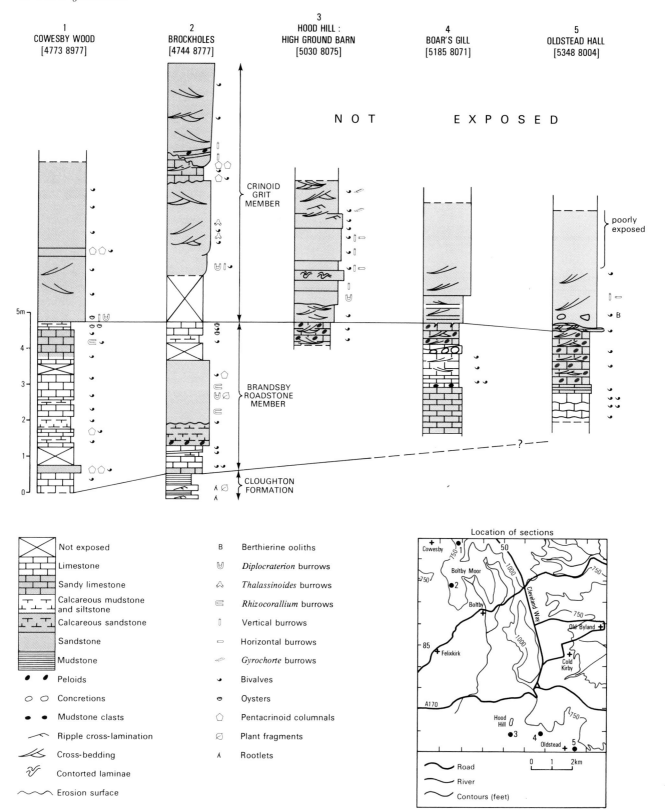

Figure 13 Comparative lithological sections of the Scarborough Formation in the Hambleton Hills.

below the Scarborough Formation, west of Little Moor; it can be traced southwards to Catstone Bank [5012 8530] where small exposures of yellow, medium-grained, cross-bedded sandstone are present. South of this locality, the outcrop is mostly obscured by large landslips near Southwood Hall [505 847] and Sutton Bank [511 827].

Sandstones of the Cloughton Formation form much of Gormire Rigg, a prominent ridge which surrounds Gormire Lake on three sides. Some of the sandstone beds have erosive, channelled bases; exposures of the ubiquitous orange-yellow, medium-grained sandstone are limited to small quarries along Gormire Rigg [5012 8327] and south of High Rigg [5038 8286]. On High Rigg, beds above the Lebberston Member comprise mudstones and feature-forming sandstones which are exposed as soil brash. Between Sutton Bank and Hood Hill, the formation is largely obscured by head deposits and landslip. Further south, the lateral thinning of channel-fill sandstones is well displayed near Penfoot Wood [5063 8076]. Here, a yellow, medium-grained sandstone with coaly fragments, some 15 m thick, thins out over a distance of about 150 m.

The features seen here and at Brockholes are indicative of sedimentation in erosively based fluvial channels; bedforms suggest periodic deposition as subaqueous dunes, passing upward, with declining flow, to planar-bedded and rippled units. Carbonaceous fragments were probably eroded by the rivers from emergent peat swamps in interchannel areas during periods of channel migration.

Exposures of coaly siltstone near the top of the formation indicate that the delta-top swamp (or marsh) was periodically colonised by plants. The following section was measured in a stream bed [5323 8041] near Oldstead:

	Thickness m
Sandstone, white, yellow-weathering, cross-laminated	0.40
Mudstone, blue-grey, with sandstone clasts (0.03 to 0.05 m)	0.10
Coaly siltstone, black, soft	0.03
Sandstone, pink-grey, fine- to medium-grained, ganisteroid, with black vertical rootlets 0.5 m in length	0.70

East of High Kilburn, an old quarry [5242 7970] exposes 2.0 m of orange, cross-stratified, medium-grained sandstone overlain by 8.5 m of sandstone and limestone of the Lebberston Member.

Newburgh Priory and Husthwaite

The outcrop of the Cloughton Formation is completely drift covered within the Asenby – Coxwold Graben. To the south of the structure, around Newburgh Priory, drift cover is also extensive but soil brash of orange-brown, medium-grained sandstone occurs sporadically. A much-degraded spoil tip [5538 7572], south of Hunt House, probably marks the site of the former Newburgh Park Colliery (Fox-Strangways et al., 1886; Hemingway and Owen, 1975), which worked a 0.4 m-thick coal within the formation at a depth of some 15 m below ground level.

In the faulted ground south and south-east of Husthwaite, the outcrop of the formation is mainly covered by drift. Further east, quarries at Oulston [5492 7404; 5494 7305] expose up to 2.7 m of yellow-grained sandstone resting on the Lebberston Member.

LEBBERSTON MEMBER

The Lebberston Member (Hemingway and Knox, 1973), formerly the Millepore Bed or Whitwell Oolite (Fox-Strangways et al., 1886), comprises a 'wedge' of calcareous sandstone and sandy, oolitic limestone, up to 8 m thick, deposited during a marine transgression which advanced northwards from the East Midlands Shelf into the Cleveland Basin (Kent, 1980b).

The Lebberston Member is a correlative of the Cave Oolite (Hemingway, 1974; Gaunt et al., 1992), which crops out south of the Market Weighton Structure, and is probably equivalent to the upper part of the Lincolnshire Limestone (Cope et al., 1980, fig. 4a). The Millepore Bed and the Whitwell Oolite are synonymous; the former name was mostly adopted for the coastal exposures and the Hambleton Hills (Fox-Strangways et al., 1886), whilst the latter term was used in the Howardian Hills. Parsons (1980) elevated this transgressive marine unit to formation status and reintroduced the geographical epithet Cayton Bay (Richardson, 1912), but the established nomenclature of Hemingway and Knox (1973) is adopted here.

In the Howardian Hills, the member consists of a basal, poorly fossiliferous, calcareous sandstone, which passes gradationally upwards to an oolitic grainstone with abundant fragments of bivalves, crinoids, corals and gastropods. The carbonates thin northwards, and in the district the Lebberston Member is represented by a thick, laterally persistent sandstone bed with a highly variable, cross-bedded shelly and oolitic base. The north-western limit of the transgression lay within the district, and on the main escarpment the member has not been recognised north of Gormire Lake, although there is evidence of its presence in the Woolmoor outlier (see details).

The fauna includes the echinoid *Pygaster semisulcatus*, the bivalves '*Ceratomya bajociana*', '*Gervillia*' sp., '*Lima*' sp., '*Pecten*' sp. and '*Trigonia*' sp., and the bryozoan *Haploecia straminae* (formerly *Millepora*) (Hemingway, 1974); crinoid columnals are also common. The ostracod fauna (Bate, 1964, 1967) is of Lower Bajocian age and the Lebberston Member probably spans the *discites* and *laeviuscula* zones (Hemingway, 1974).

The lithological and faunal characteristics, and the palaeogeography of the Lebberston Member in the district suggest that it was deposited in a marine, shallow-water environment, probably within the shoreface zone.

DETAILS

Woolmoor, High Rigg, Hood Hill and Oldstead

At Woolmoor, the Primary Survey maps show the prominent sandstone, exposed around 'The Belt' [4571 8765], as the Lebberston Member (Millepore Bed). However, the bedforms and stratigraphical position indicate that these exposures represent fluviodeltaic, channel-sandstone typical of much of the Cloughton Formation. Nevertheless, in two small quarries [4556 8819; 4540 8810], planar-bedded, calcareous, medium-grained sandstone occurs in the top 2 m of the exposure, and sparse bivalves were found in soil brash further along the outcrop. Thus there is some evidence for a brief marine incursion in this area, which perhaps took the form of a short-lived, marine-influenced embayment.

To the south-east, the crinoid-rich sandstone at Wind Egg [4740 8703], shown on Primary Survey maps as the Lebberston Member (Millepore Bed), has now been identified as either a downfaulted or a slipped block of the Scarborough Formation.

Some four kilometres further to the south-east, the member can be traced around the outlier of High Rigg, where it is exposed in a small, mostly overgrown, quarry [5044 8305] as follows:

	Thickness m
CLOUGHTON FORMATION	
Mudstone, yellow, silty, micaceous	0.45
LEBBERSTON MEMBER	
Siltstone, grey, with quartz granules and bivalves	0.25
Limestone, red-grey, argillaceous, with quartz granules; thin haematite partings; bivalves	0.20
Limestone, buff-grey, argillaceous, cross-laminated, with sandy laminae	0.75
CLOUGHTON FORMATION	
Sandstone, orange-yellow, fine- to medium-grained	0.55

On the south side of Hood Hill, at High Ground Barns [5024 8058], the Lebberston Member forms a small feature with sandy, oolitic, bioclastic limestone fragments in the soil. On the west side of the Oldstead outlier, it is exposed adjacent to a forestry track [5234 8020] in Cowling Wood. Here, 0.3 m of grey, thin-bedded, bio-clastic limestone rests on 0.7 m of yellow-grey, cross-laminated sandstone. The member can be traced from High Kilburn [5180 7978] to the north of Scencliff Grange [5272 7930] by the presence of soil brash, comprising grey oolitic limestone fragments.

Newburgh Priory to Oulston

Due to drift cover, the member cannot be distinguished within the Asenby–Coxwold Graben, but it is mappable south of this struc-ture near Newburgh Priory, where argillaceous limestone with crinoid ossicles and shell fragments is exposed [5444 7559] south-east of Newburgh Grange.

Despite faulting, the Lebberston Member is readily identified in the ground south and south-east of Husthwaite by the presence of grey, bioclastic, oolitic, partly sandy, limestone fragments in the soil, or, more rarely, at infilled, disused quarries [5174 7450; 5408 7387]. At the south end of Oulston Quarry [5494 7305], the follow-ing section in the Member was exposed below sandstones of the Cloughton Formation:

	Thickness m
Sandstone, pale grey, cross-bedded, with mudstone clasts and bivalves	0.8
Siltstone, green-brown, cross-laminated, and silty mudstone with plant fragments	1.3
Sandstone, yellow-grey, cross-laminated, fine-grained	0.5
Sandstone, grey, cross-bedded, calcareous, medium-grained, with mudstone clasts and shell fragments	1.9

Scarborough Formation

The Scarborough Formation, formerly known as the Grey Limestone Series (Fox-Strangways et al., 1886) (Table 6), comprises fossiliferous limestone, shale, siltstone and calcareous sandstone. The formation represents a major marine transgression during the deposition of the Ravenscar Group. It is the only marine unit within the group that can be traced throughout the Cleveland (Yorkshire) Basin and, furthermore, is the only unit to have yielded ammonites. These were collected from exposures on the Yorkshire coast, and they indicate the *humphriesianum* Zone (Parsons, 1977); they suggest a connection with the Tethys Ocean which lay to the south. Tentative correlation with inland exposures (Helmsley Moor) indicates that, in the district, the formation may also include beds of *sauzei* Zone age (Parsons, 1980,

fig.5). The Scarborough Formation ranges from 9 to 14 m in thickness (compared to c.20 m in coastal exposures) and forms a major topographical feature (or features), which can be traced throughout the district, even in poorly exposed terrain.

Over much of its outcrop the Scarborough Formation is subdivided into two members, the Brandsby Roadstone and the overlying Crinoid Grit (Figure 13; Hemingway, 1974). A third unit, above the Crinoid Grit, consisting of 'shales with fossils', was included in the formation by Fox-Strangways et al. (1886, p.39). They gave no thickness for this bed but noted that it formed a bank of wet ground beneath the Moor Grit Member (Scalby Formation). This shale bed has been mapped as a 'slack' below the Moor Grit over much of the district during the present survey, but it is nowhere exposed and is included as an unnamed mudstone within the overlying Scalby Formation. Furthermore, in many places this 'shale' slack is not present, probably due to penecontemporaneous erosion at the base of the Moor Grit.

BRANDSBY ROADSTONE MEMBER

The Brandsby Roadstone Member (Phillips, 1829) ranges in thickness from 2 to 7 m and consists of grey, argillaceous, siliceous, peloidal limestone (micrite and wackestone tex-tures), with subordinate beds of grey calcareous siltstone and yellow-grey calcareous sandstone (Plate 3). The limestones show planar-lamination and trough cross-lamination with shallow, erosive scours; bi-directional foresets are common. Bivalves are common in both the planar-bedded limestones and the calcareous siliciclastics; they include *Astarte minima*, *Gervillella scarburgensis*, *Lopha marshii*, *Meleagrinella* sp., *Modiolus* sp., *Protocardia* sp., *Pseudomonotis lycetti*, and *Trigonia signata* (Hemingway, 1974). The sandstones contain sparse crinoid columnals and the trace fossils *Diplocraterion* sp. and *Asterostoma* sp.

CRINOID GRIT MEMBER

The Crinoid Grit Member (Richardson, 1912) forms a prominent topographical feature above the Brandsby Roadstone throughout the district (Plate 3). It ranges in thickness from 4 to 7 m, and comprises orange-yellow, fine-, medium- and coarse-grained, geothitic, calcareous sand-stone with sporadic quartz granules. At outcrop, it is com-monly decalcified and highly porous, and is characterised by moulds of pentacrinoid columnals and scattered bivalves. The coarser beds are commonly cross-stratified with both bi-directional foresets and low-angle cross-bedding. Ichnofossils include simple vertical burrows (cf. *Arenicolites* sp.) as well as *Diplocraterion* sp. and *Gryochorte* sp. traces (Powell, 1992).

The Scarborough Formation (Figure 13) in this district represents an upward-coarsening sequence. The lowermost, transgressive carbonate facies (Brandsby Roadstone) was probably deposited in a non-turbulent, shallow-water lagoonal embayment, which was subjected to oscillating cur-rent activity with periodic influxes of quartz sand derived, during storm events, from offshore banks or beach zones. The sharp junction of the carbonate facies with the overlying sandstone (Crinoid Grit) suggests a sudden change in condi-tions and/or a depositional hiatus; bi-directional and low-angle cross-bedding, and the ichnofauna, are indicative of

Plate 3 Scarborough Formation; Brandsby Roadstone overlain by Crinoid Grit. High Ground Barns (L3054).

beach or shore-face environments (Elliot, 1978), and it seems likely that the Crinoid Grit represents a beach or an offshore-bank sand facies that prograded rapidly across the carbonate lagoon.

DETAILS

Cowesby Moor, Brockholes

In the following account, both members are treated together (Figure 13). In the far north of the main escarpment, trackside quarries [4773 8980] and a dry stream gully [4773 8977] in Cowesby Wood give the following composite section:

	Thickness m
Crinoid Grit	
Sandstone, orange-yellow, medium-grained, cross-bedded, with bivalve casts; hard, calcareous-cemented band (0.20 m) at base	2.40
Sandstone, orange, medium- to coarse-grained, with low-angle cross-bedding; *Liostrea* sp. in basal 0.10 m	1.80
Siltstone, calcareous, grey, with abundant bivalves including *Liostrea* sp.	0.21
Brandsby Roadstone	
Limestone, grey, argillaceous, with bivalves (biomicrite); sparse quartz grains	0.80
Siltstone, grey, calcareous	0.18
Limestone, grey; mostly argillaceous biomicrite with beds of calcareous mudstone and siltstone (0.10 to 0.20 m)	3.90

The formation is well exposed, about 2 km further south, at Brockholes [4744 8777], near Kirby Knowle. The section (Figure 13) was described by Fox-Strangways et al. (1886, p.41), but is given in more detail below:

	Thickness m
Crinoid Grit	
Sandstone, yellow, thick-bedded, cross-bedded, coarse-grained; bivalves and vertical burrows common	2.8
Sandstone, yellow, calcareous, with crinoid-rich, cross-bedded lenses; bivalves present	0.8
Sandstone, yellow, cross-bedded, medium-grained, with thin mudstone partings; burrows common; basal 0.6 m bioturbated, with *Pleuromya* sp. and *Trigonia* sp.	2.6
Not exposed	1.1
Brandsby Roadstone	
Limestone, grey, argillaceous, with abundant *Liostrea* sp. and *Meleagrinella* sp.	0.5
Siltstone, grey, calcareous, with *Modiolus* sp.	0.2
Not exposed	0.7
Sandstone, yellow, calcareous, medium-grained, with bivalve voids and sparse crinoid columnals; various burrows including *Diplocraterion* and *Asterostoma*	2.5
Limestone, red-grey, argillaceous, with *Gervillella* sp. and *Protocardia* sp.	0.2
Siltstone, grey, finely laminated, with bivalves	0.1
Limestone, grey, argillaceous, with bivalves including *Gervillella* sp. and *Cardium* sp.	0.6
CLOUGHTON FORMATION	
Mudstone, pale grey, and siltstone, buff, with ripple cross-lamination and carbonaceous fragments	c.3.0

The crinoid-rich, cross-bedded unit of the Crinoid Grit is well exposed at Wind Egg [4740 8703], where the exposure is part of a slipped block which Fox-Strangways et al. (1886, p.38) erroneously described as an exposure of the Lebberston Member. About 4 m of yellow, cross-bedded, medium-grained sandstone with bivalve voids is exposed; one bed, 0.95 m thick, has abundant pentacrinoid columnals and mudstone clasts parallel to the foreset laminae.

Boltby to Sutton Bank and Hood Hill

Both members are only sporadically exposed around the head of Gurtof Beck, north-north-west of Boltby, but their features can be traced around Boltby Moor to Boltby Reservoir. Blue-grey, argillaceous limestone was found in the stream bed [4934 8863] to the west of the reservoir, and also to the north-west, where the following section [4920 8875] in the Crinoid Grit is exposed:

	Thickness m
Sandstone, orange-yellow, thin-bedded, medium-grained, with bivalves including *Meleagrinella* sp.	0.70
Sandstone, grey-yellow, thin-bedded, fine-grained, micaceous	0.45
Sandstone, grey, fine-grained, extensively bioturbated; burrows include *Diplocraterion* sp.	0.80

Southwards along the escarpment, landslip largely obscures the formation until Little Moor where, at Catstone Bank [5012 8538], the following section in the Crinoid Grit is exposed:

	Thickness m
Sandstone, yellow-orange, medium-grained, with decalcified voids of *Meleagrinella* sp.	1.0
Limestone, yellow-grey, sandy, with crinoid ossicles and shell fragments	1.0
Sandstone, orange-yellow, medium-grained, massive-bedded	1.4

The Scarborough Formation is again obscured by landslip in South Wood, but southwards to Garbutt Wood, it forms a prominent mappable feature. The formation caps the outlier at High Rigg [504 830] but is masked by extensive landslip and head deposits on the main escarpment at Sutton Bank and Roulston Scar.

The formation can be traced around the Hood Hill outlier, where a stream bed [5012 8122] exposes buff-brown, fine-grained sandstone with abundant decalcified *Lopha marshii* shells forming a lumachelle. Further south an old quarry [5030 8075] near High Ground Barn, exposes the following section (Figure 13):

	Thickness m
Crinoid Grit	
Sandstone, yellow-orange, medium- to coarse-grained; bi-directional cross-bedding with sinuous current-ripples; sparse *Meleagrinella* sp; *Gyrochorte* burrows; erosive base	0.86
Sandstone, yellow-grey, medium- to coarse-grained, cross-laminated; abundant bivalve voids in top 0.12 m	0.25
Sandstone, yellow, medium-grained, extensively bioturbated, with sparse bivalves; parallel lamination in top 0.2 m; fine-grained and with vertical burrows in basal 0.27 m	1.20
Sandstone, yellow-brown, fine-grained, thin-bedded, with sparse bivalves including *Meleagrinella* sp.; extensively bioturbated; low-angle cross-bedding in basal 0.5 m; gradational base	1.06
Brandsby Roadstone	
Limestone, grey, siliceous, peloidal, cross-stratified, with shallow scours; planar-bedded in part	0.68

Boars Gill and Oldstead

On the main escarpment, the following section in the Brandsby Roadstone is exposed at Boars Gill [5185 8071] (Figure 13):

	Thickness m
Brandsby Roadstone	
Limestone, grey, peloidal, cross-laminated, siliceous in part; laterally impersistent nodular limestone band (0.2 m) at base	0.70
Limestone, buff-grey, siliceous, peloidal, planar-bedded; small bivalves present	0.70
Limestone, red-brown, sideritic, argillaceous, siliceous; mudstone clasts and wood fragments; bivalves present	0.24
Limestone, buff-grey, siliceous, planar-bedded	1.20

The Scarborough Formation can be traced south-eastwards around the escarpment; at Sand Lane, Oldstead, disused quarries [5314 8069 to 5315 8001] reveal the following composite section (Figure 14) below the base of the overlying Moor Grit:

	Thickness m
Not exposed (? mudstone slack)	1.4
Crinoid Grit	
Sandstone, yellow-orange, medium-grained, cross-bedded, thick-bedded, soft, decalcified; bivalve voids	c.3.0
Sandstone, yellow, coarse-grained, with angular quartz granules and comminuted shell fragments; cross-laminated	0.1–0.3
Brandsby Roadstone	
Limestone, blue-grey, cross-laminated, thin-bedded, peloidal, siliceous; bivalves common; poorly exposed	1.4

Further to the south-east, a more complete section in the Brandsby Roadstone occurs in a disused quarry [5348 8004] near Oldstead Hall, where the following section (Figure 13) was measured:

	Thickness m
Crinoid Grit	
Sandstone, orange-yellow, medium- to coarse-grained, with bivalve voids and horizontal burrows; calcareous nodules with bivalves present near base	1.70
Sandstone, yellow, calcareous, coarse-grained, with sparse quartz granules and shell fragments; finely laminated and convoluted in part	0.10
Brandsby Roadstone	
Limestone, grey, siliceous, peloidal, cross-laminated, with shallow scours; sparse bivalves	1.52
Limestone, grey, siliceous, peloidal, planar-laminated, with thin sandy partings	0.25
Limestone, grey, argillaceous, irregularly bedded, with abundant bivalves including *Gervillella* sp. and *Meleagrinella* sp.	0.70

Both members can be mapped around the outliers north of High Kilburn [517 796] and east of Scawling Wood [527 804]. South-east of Oldstead, the outcrop of the formation broadens out and a disused quarry [5317 7692] north of Oldstead Grange exposes the following section in the Brandsby Roadstone:

	Thickness m
Limestone, grey, siliceous, peloidal, with bivalves	to 0.4
Limestone, grey, siliceous, with abundant bivalves	1.3
Siltstone, pale grey, micaceous, calcareous	0.2

Asenby – Coxwold Graben and Oulston

Within the Asenby–Coxwold Graben, the westernmost exposures of the formation were formerly seen in the quarries [4782 7716 to 4801 7685] at Thirkleby Barf. Here, Fox-Strangways et al. (1886) noted hard, fossiliferous limestone overlain by soft, massive, sandstones "with casts of fossils" but gave no thicknesses. Their description suggests that both the Brandsby Roadstone and the Crinoid Grit members are present, but due to the extent of drift-cover within the graben, the formation has been mapped 'undivided'. Slightly further east, at Quarry Banks, 0.3 m of grey, siliceous limestone is still visible at the top of the degraded quarry [4882 7680] adjacent to the Carlton Husthwaite road; however, the more extensive Birdforth Quarry [4877 7690], which formerly exposed fossiliferous sandstones, is now completely infilled.

The Scarborough Formation can be traced eastwards along the graben by following the lines of the old quarries, which mainly exploited the limestone beds. At Wildon Hill, a partially infilled quarry [5112 7725] exposes 1.5 m of yellow, coarse-grained, cross-stratified sandstone; loose blocks of grey, flaggy, bioclastic limestone indicate the presence of the Brandsby Roadstone. Further east, brash at disused quarries [5267 7699 to 5308 7687], west of Coxwold, includes fragments of grey, argillaceous limestone with bivalve voids typical of this member. The most easterly sections within the graben occur in the beck [5342 7687] south of Coxwold, where discontinuous exposures reveal yellow-grey, siliceous limestone (0.2 m thick), resting on grey, bioturbated mudstone (0.4 m thick), overlying white, fine-grained sandstone (0.4 m thick).

South of the Asenby–Coxwold Graben, the Scarborough Formation crops out only in a restricted area on the eastern margin of the district, north-east of Oulston. Here, north-west of Whincover Farm [5549 7459], soil brash of yellow, fine- to medium-grained sandstone with bivalves occurs in fields. A bed of grey siltstone with bivalves, included within the Scarborough Formation, crops out locally above this sandstone and is exposed in a small pit [5538 7497] north of the Oulston–Yearsley road.

Scalby Formation

The Scalby Formation (Hemingway and Knox, 1973) is the uppermost subdivision of the Ravenscar Group, and is synonymous with the Upper Esturine Series (Fox-Strangways et al., 1886) and the Upper Deltaic Series (Hemingway, 1949) (Table 6). It crops out in the upper part of the Hambleton Hills escarpment and forms a broad tract of ground on Boltby Moor [48 88]; a narrow, poorly exposed outcrop is also present within the Asenby–Coxwold Graben.

The formation is 32 to 48 m thick in the district, and is made up of mudstone, siltstone and sandstone, together with seatearths and thin coals. The Moor Grit Member, 8 to 15 m thick, at the base of the formation, is a prominent, mappable sandstone which can be traced throughout much of the district.

The Long Nab Member (Nami and Leeder, 1978), above the Moor Grit, comprises a higher proportion of fine-grained clastics (mudstone and siltstone) compared to the nonmarine Saltwick and Cloughton formations, which predominantly consist of sandstone in this district. Sandstone units within the member, exposed on Boltby Moor, are also less persistent laterally than in the stratigraphically lower, fluviodeltaic formations. These characteristics suggest that the Long Nab Member was deposited in an alluvial plain environment characterised by marshy swamps, lagoons and meandering rivers. This interpretation is supported by studies of similar facies of the Scalby Formation, exposed on the Yorkshire coast (Nami and Leeder, 1978; Leeder and Nami, 1979). Sedimentological and palynological studies of the Yorkshire coastal exposures, however, have indicated paralic conditions in environments ranging from delta-top distributary channel to fully marine interdistributary bay during deposition of the Long Nab Member (Fisher and Hancock, 1985).

The age of the Scalby Formation has been the subject of much debate (Leeder and Nami, 1979; Woollam and Riding, 1983; Fisher and Hancock, 1985; Riding and Wright, 1989). Its stratigraphical position, between beds of definite Bajocian age (Scarborough Formation) below and beds of Callovian age above, may indicate that the Scalby Formation spans the whole of the Bathonian Stage (eight ammonite zones) (Table 8). Leeder and Nami (1979) have pointed out that, based on known rates of fluvial sedimentation, the thickness of the Scalby Formation could have been deposited in a fraction of this time. They suggest that a major depositional hiatus must occur somewhere in this sequence, and they favour the break between the Scarborough Formation and the Moor Grit. However, in contrast with Yorkshire coastal exposures, the Moor Grit in this district does not have a strongly erosional base indicative of a major break in sedimentation (Powell, 1983b). Furthermore, recent study of palynofloras (Riding and Wright, 1989) suggests that the Long Nab Member spans most of the Bathonian Stage, and, taken together with the underlying Moor Grit Member, the Scalby Formation represents a period of relatively continuous sedimentation from late Bajocian to late Bathonian times. These authors envisage minor breaks in sedimentation at the junction of the Scarborough and Scalby formations, and at the boundary between the Scalby Formation and the overlying Callovian strata (Cornbrash Formation or Osgodby Formation).

Moor Grit Member

The Moor Grit forms a marked, step-like feature directly above the outcrop of the Scarborough Formation. Its lateral persistence, stratigraphical position and characteristic lithology all serve to distinguish it from the more lenticular, channel sandstones present within the overlying Long Nab Member.

The Moor Grit is a grey to white, fine-grained, orthoquartzitic sandstone, about 8 to 15 m thick. Some beds are cross-stratified, with large-scale, tabular-planar and, more rarely, trough-shaped cosets; others are parallel-bedded or appear 'massive'. Small-scale cross-lamination and convolute lamination are also present. Coaly plant fragments are common, and rootlet horizons topped by thin, coaly siltstone occur in the upper part of the member. Studies elsewhere in the Cleveland Basin (Nami and Leeder, 1978; Leeder and Nami, 1979) have indicated that the Moor Grit was deposited in the anabranches of a braided river. However, some of the features displayed within the district, such as the uniform fine-grain size, tabular cosets and the absence of strongly erosive channel bases, suggest that sheet-flood or crevasse-splay processes may also have been involved. Coaly siltstone and rootlet beds (seatearths) in the upper part of the member indicate periodic colonisation of the marshy interfluves by plants.

Details

Cowesby to Thirlby Bank

The Moor Grit can be traced along the escarpment from Cowesby Moor, on the northern margin of the district, southwards to Boltby Moor. Exposures are limited, but those above Wind Egg [4745 8704], in Gurtof Wood [4792 8821] and to the north [4942 8872] and south-east [4969 8837] of Boltby Reservoir all exhibit the characteristic features of the unit.

Between Low Paradise Farm [501 881] and Little Moor [502 858], the outcrop is largely obscured by landslip, but a section at the top of Catstone Bank [5018 8528] exposes about 6 m of white, thin-bedded, fine-grained, orthoquartzite with large-scale, trough cross-bedding. Further south, a quarry [5036 8386] north of Thirlby Bank exposes the following section:

	Thickness m
Sandstone, white-buff, fine-grained, with alternating cross-laminated and structureless beds; convolute lamination in part; grey mudstone partings with plant fragments; rootlets common	2.4
Sandstone, white, fine-grained, thin-bedded, with parallel lamination; cross-laminated near base	3.6
Sandstone, yellow-buff, fine- to medium-grained, cross-bedded in part; thin (0.01 to 0.03 m) hard, siliceous beds with plant rootlets	3.1

Sutton Bank to Hood Hill, Kilburn and Oldstead

Southwards, the outcrop is completely covered by landslip and Head deposits along the escarpment below Sutton Bank and Roulston Scar. However, the member can be traced around the drift-free Hood Hill outlier where about 6.6 m of grey, cross-stratified, fine-grained sandstone are exposed in a quarry [5027 8159] on the north-west side. On the outlier north of Kilburn, a temporary section [5165 8032] in the back-scar of a landslip south of Oldstead Road exposed the uppermost, coal-rich facies of the member as follows:

	Thickness m
Sandstone, white, finely laminated, fine-grained	2.00
Clay, grey	0.02
Sandstone, white, fine-grained	0.20
Coaly siltstone, dark grey	0.10
Sandstone, grey, fine-grained, with rootlets in top 0.15 m	0.55
Coaly siltstone, black, soft	0.15
Sandstone, yellow, fine-grained	0.16
Coaly siltstone, black	0.20
Sandstone, white, fine-grained, with rootlets in top 0.05 m; cross-laminated	c.1.50
Coaly siltstone, black, with thin partings (0.05 m) of fine-grained sandstone	0.40
Sandstone, yellow, fine-grained, with rootlets in top 0.15 m	0.85

Despite areas of landslip, the Moor Grit Member can be traced along the escarpment from Roulston Scar eastwards to the vicinity of Oldstead, where a small quarry [5314 8086] adjacent to Sand Lane exposes 5 m of pale grey to white, cross-stratified, fine-grained sandstone (Figure 14). The upper part of this sandstone (Plate 4; Figure 14) is exposed in a small quarry and adit [5319 8066] about 60 m to the south-east, as follows:

	Thickness m
Coaly siltstone, black, soft	0.05
Sandstone, white, fine-grained, with plant fragments and vertical rootlets	0.70
Coaly siltstone, black, soft	0.10
Sandstone, white, fine-grained, with vertical rootlets	0.15
Coaly siltstone, black, soft	0.02
Sandstone, white, fine-grained, with vertical rootlets in top 0.50 m; thin-bedded in top 1.2 m; cross-laminated with convolute laminae in the basal 1.3 m	2.50

The sequence and sedimentary structures in these two quarries suggest that the Moor Grit hereabouts was deposited under conditions of upper flow regime, probably as a sheet-flood or crevasse-splay deposit. The freshwater lagoon or marsh in which the sands were deposited was subsequently colonised by plants at repeated

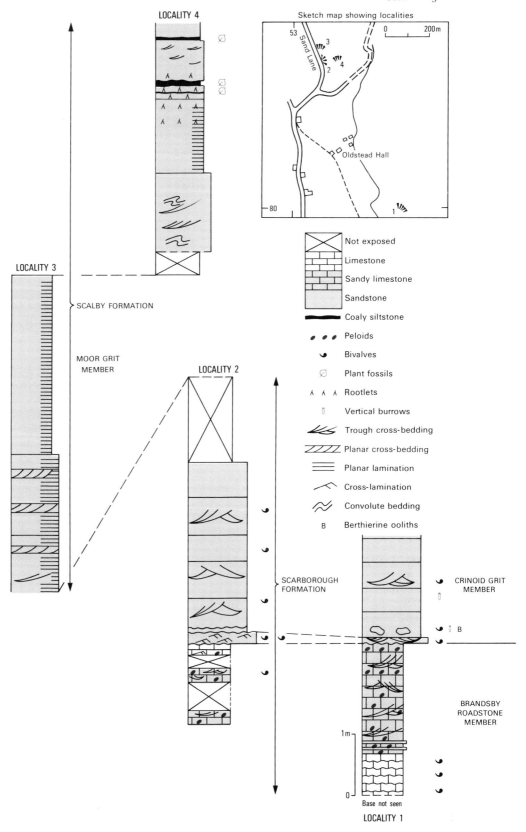

Figure 14 Composite sections in the Scarborough and Scalby formations near Oldstead Hall.

Plate 4 Scalby Formation; disused trial adit, near Oldstead Hall (L3185).

intervals to form thin coaly beds with underlying rootlet-bearing seatearths.

Byland Abbey and Oulston

To the south-east and east, the outcrop of the Moor Grit is covered by extensive landslip along the face of the escarpment. Below this level, however, it crops out widely in the ground to the north-west of Byland Abbey, where sporadic exposures and abundant soil brash of white, fine-grained sandstone occur. Within the Asenby–Coxwold Graben, the Moor Grit, although almost certainly present, cannot be distinguished due to the thickness of drift, the steepness of the dips and the absence of quarries. To the south of the graben, it crops out near Oulston, in a small area on the eastern margin of the district, north of Whincover Farm [555 745].

LONG NAB MEMBER

The upper part of the Scalby Formation, the Long Nab Member (Nami and Leeder, 1978), is 24 to 33 m thick and largely consists of mudstone and siltstone, with only sporadic, discontinuous, channel-fill sandstones. Consequently, these beds are not well exposed and are little quarried. Coals, with associated seatearths, occur towards the base and have been exploited from bell-pits and shafts. Where the beds lie below the Upper Jurassic escarpment, they are commonly covered by landslip and Head. Studies of well-exposed sections of this member on the Yorkshire coast (Black, 1929; Leeder and Nami, 1979) concluded that it was deposited in a spectrum of subenvironments, including meandering channels, marshes and flood basins on an alluvial plain. However, subsequent reports of *Ophiomorpha* burrows, together with bioturbation and mud-grade sediments in channel-fill deposits (Livera and Leeder, 1981), supported by the discovery of marine microplankton (Hancock and Fisher, 1981), have suggested at least some degree of marine influence. On the basis of detailed sedimentological and palynofacies investigations of the coastal suc-

cession, Fisher and Hancock (1985) have recently reinterpreted the upper part of the Scalby Formation as a saline-influenced delta-plain, interrupted by small distributary channels, some of which may have been tidal. However, it is not known whether this marine-influenced facies extended to the Thirsk district at the western margin of the Cleveland Basin.

DETAILS

Cowesby Moor and Boltby Moor

In the north of the district, the Long Nab Member crops out widely on Cowesby Moor, Boltby Moor and south-east of Boltby Reservoir, and it has been possible to map several laterally impersistent sandstones of probable channel-fill origin. The best section of the interfluvial facies is along a stream bed [4990 8773 to 4955 8774] north of Lunshaw House, where thin, fine-grained sandstones with asymmetrical ripples are interbedded with grey mudstones containing coaly fragments. Mudstone, which forms the bulk of the member, was formerly worked in an old clay pit [4944 8829] some 600 m further north.

Hawnby

In the north-east of the district, the Long Nab Member crops out in the Rye valley around Hawnby. A thin, impersistent sandstone can be traced on the western slopes, where a section [5355 8961] south-west of Hawnby Church proved 1.8 m of yellow, cross-bedded, medium-grained sandstone. The nature of the argillaceous strata is illustrated by an exposure [5411 8928] in the bank of the River Rye, west of Hawnby Bridge, which shows the following section:

	Thickness m
Mudstone and siltstone, grey	1.1
Sandstone, grey-green, fine-grained	0.3
Mudstone, grey, with sparse siderite nodules	0.4

Boars Gill and Kilburn

Southwards along the main Jurassic escarpment, the Long Nab Member is largely covered by landslips (see chapter seven), but soil brash comprising yellow-grey, fine-grained sandstone is exposed on channel-fill sandstone features at Little Moor [501 857] and Boars Gill [518 809]. At the latter locality, the presence of fragments of black mudstone and coal in spoil from an old bell-pit [5188 8084] indicates that coal of workable thickness occurs within the member. The stratigraphical level of this seam (or seams) is about 3 to 5 m above the top of the Moor Grit. Although the member caps the outliers north of Kilburn and north-west of Oldstead, only yellow sandstone brash is seen, while along the escarpment south-eastwards from here to the margin of the district, it is mostly covered by landslip and Head.

Asenby – Coxwold Graben

Within the Asenby–Coxwold Graben, the outcrop of the Long Nab Member is totally drift covered. However, in the west, opencast coal exploration boreholes around Burtree House [482 768] have confirmed the presence of the two coal seams worked in the late 18th century at the former Birdforth Colliery (Fox-Strangways et al., 1886; Owen, 1970; Hemingway and Owen, 1975). Calculations suggest that the lower seam lies about 16 m above the top of the Scarborough Formation and is, therefore, at the same stratigraphical level as the coal worked in the Boars Gill bell-pit (see above). The upper seam is about 3 m higher in the sequence; both vary in thickness, and the lower is reported to reach 1.2 m. The seams lie within strata reported to be predominantly sandstone.

Cornbrash Formation

The Cornbrash Formation (Wright, 1977) on the Yorkshire coast and in north Cleveland comprises the Cornbrash Limestone Member and the overlying Shales of the Cornbrash Member. The Cornbrash Limestone (equivalent to the Upper Cornbrash of southern England) marks the base of the Callovian Stage (Macrocephalus Zone) and consists of oyster-rich, sandy limestone (1 m thick) which represents the initial transgression across the delta-top marsh or alluvial plain of the Scalby Formation. The overlying Shales of the Cornbrash typically consist of dark grey calcareous mudstone and siltstone with phosphatic nodules. The Cornbrash Formation, however, has not been found in the district, where the basal sandstone (Kellaways Rock) of the Osgodby Formation appears to rest directly on the Scalby Formation (Table 8). The absence of the Cornbrash may be real or, in part, due to the paucity of exposures at the base of the Osgodby Formation. The only exposure in the district, in Northwoods Slack [4982 8920], noted by Fox-Strangways et al. (1886, p.43), is no longer visible. They recorded 'a little grey sandy limestone with *Ostrea*', but this may have been a fallen block of oyster-rich Kellaways Rock, which is exposed in a quarry above the stream. Senior (1975) logged sections through this part of the sequence in 1967 when the area was temporarily deforested. He also noted that Fox-Strangway's locality was no longer exposed, but he recorded several small exposures of grey silty clay with bivalve fragments (c.1 m) at the base of the sandstone. This bed was not regarded by Senior as positive identification of the Cornbrash Limestone and the unit was not mapped during the present survey.

Osgodby Formation

The term Osgodby Formation was introduced by Wright (1978) for the predominantly sandstone beds of Callovian age in the Cleveland Basin (Table 6). In the typical Yorkshire coastal sections it is subdivided into the following members, in ascending order: Kellaways Rock, Langdale Beds and Hackness Rock (Wright, 1968, 1978). Only the Kellaways Rock and the Hackness Rock are present in the district, where the Osgodby Formation ranges in thickness from 20 to 23 m. Furthermore, due to the paucity of exposure, the Hackness Rock has been identified at only one locality (see details) and the formation is shown 'undivided' on the map. In the area near Roulston Scar, the Hackness Rock and the overlying Oxford Clay have both been removed by erosion below the unconformable Lower Calcareous Grit (Figure 15).

The stratigraphy of the Callovian (and Oxfordian) rocks in the Cleveland Basin has been refined by Wright (1968, 1977, 1978, 1983), particularly for the eastern part of the Basin. The stratigraphy and nomenclature of the Lower Callovian strata has recently been revised (Page, 1989) but the nomenclature of Wright (1977) is used herein. Wright's studies and mapping in the district (Powell, 1982) have demonstrated many unconformities in a seemingly conformable sequence (Table 6).

KELLAWAYS ROCK MEMBER

The Kellaways Rock ranges from 20 to 23 m in thickness and consists of orange, yellow and grey, fine- to medium-grained, thick-bedded sandstone, locally with scattered berthierine ooliths; large bivalves and belemnites, often preserved as decalcified moulds and casts, are conspicuous in some beds, particularly in the upper part of the member (Figure 16). Some beds show trough cross-bedding and the rock is usually soft and decalcified at outcrop. Vertical burrows and burrow-mottling are common in some beds. The bivalve fauna includes the oysters *Gryphaea dilobotes*, *Liostrea* sp. as well as *Chlamys fibrosa*, *Meleagrinella braamburiensis*, *Trigonia* sp. and *Unicardium* sp.; rhynchonellid brachiopods are also present. The Kellaways Rock has yielded ammonites indicating the Calloviense Zone (Wright, 1978). The lithology is consistent over most of the district and represents an upward-coarsening sequence with a more abundant shelly fauna in the uppermost 4 m. In the extreme south-east of the district, however, there is some evidence, in poorly exposed terrain, that the sandstone passes laterally into grey sandy siltstone.

The lithological and faunal characteristics suggest that the Kellaways Rock was deposited in a shallow-water, littoral environment, probably the subtidal shoreface zone of a beach, passing offshore to finer-grained siliciclastics in the south-east of the district.

The base of the Kellaways Rock is not exposed, but is presumed to rest unconformably on the Scalby Formation (see previous discussion of the Cornbrash Formation).

The upper boundary, north of Whitestone Cliff is defined by the base of the Hackness Rock, but due to successive, overstepping unconformities, the member is overlain by the Oxford Clay and, in turn, by the Lower Calcareous Grit between Whitestone Cliff and Raven's Gill (Figures 15 and 16).

HACKNESS ROCK MEMBER

The Hackness Rock, where present, is about 3 m thick, and consists of buff-grey siltstone with alternating soft and hard calcite-cemented bands; fossils include bivalves, belemnites and sparse ammonites, the last belonging to the Athleta Zone (Wright, 1978). The member has been identified above the Kellaways Rock at one exposure [5072 8506] in South Wood (see details), north of Whitestone Cliff, and is probably locally present north of this locality (Figure 15). However, to the south-east, between Whitestone Cliff and Raven's Gill, it is cut out by low-angle, overstepping unconformities at the base of the Oxford Clay, and at the base of the Lower Calcareous Grit. Due to poor exposure, the Hackness Rock cannot be traced south-east of Raven's Gill; it may again be present between the feature-forming Kellaways Rock and the base of the Oxford Clay, but the Osgodby Formation is shown 'undivided' on the map.

DETAILS

In the following account, the members of the Osgodby Formation are treated together.

Boltby Moor

The Osgodby Formation forms a broad tongue-shaped outcrop in the north of the district on Windy Ridge [482 895], and can be traced around the escarpment to Cracoe Slack [4925 8966] and Northwoods Slack [4984 8927]. The section in Cracoe Slack has degraded since 1967 when it was logged by Senior (1975), but orange-weathering, medium-grained sandstone with decalcified voids of bivalves and belemnites was observed in the stream bed and adjacent track [4919 8964]. The formation, represented here solely by the Kellaways Rock, is better exposed in Northwood Slack and adjacent trackside quarries, where the following composite section was recorded:

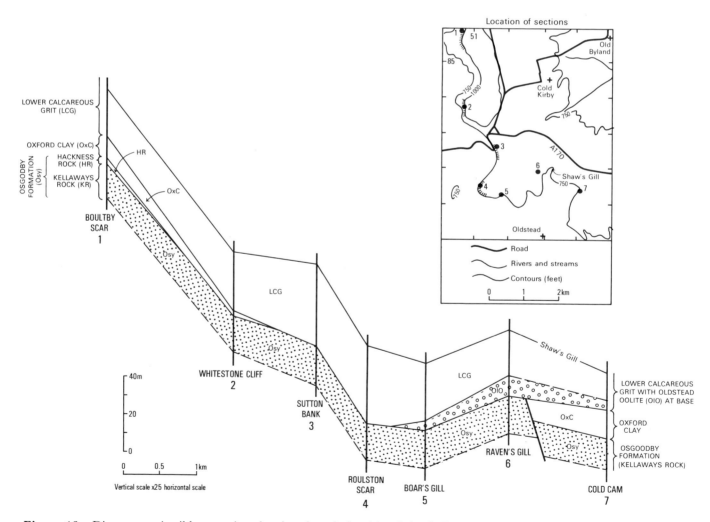

Figure 15 Diagrammatic ribbon section showing the relationship of the Callovian and Lower Oxfordian rocks in the Hambleton Hills, and the postulated post-Oxford Clay/pre-Lower Calcareous Grit fault between Raven's Gill and Shaw's Gill.

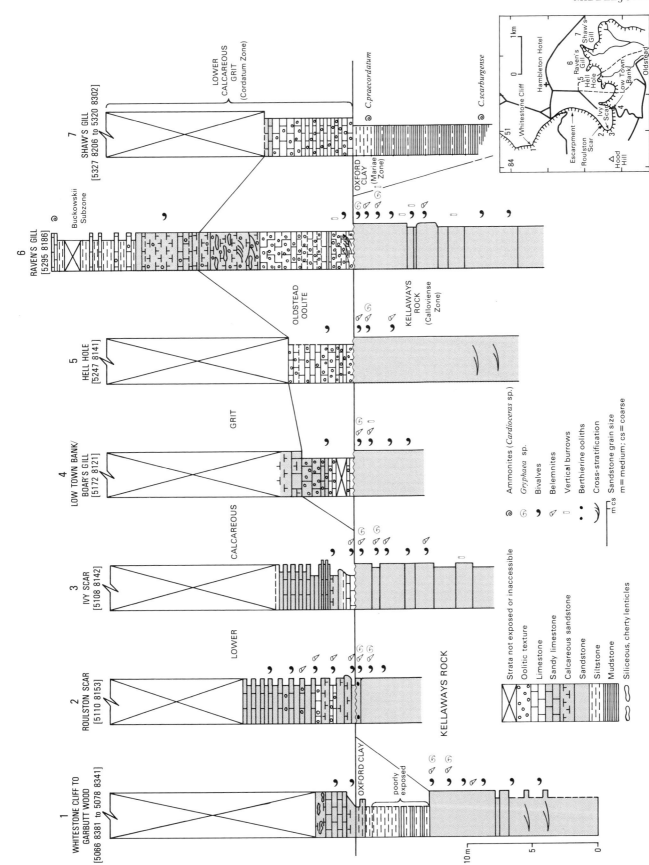

Figure 16   Comparative lithological sections showing the correlation of the Osgodby Formation (Kellaways Rock and Hackness Rock), Oxford Clay and Lower Calcareous Grit (Callovian/Oxfordian) in the Roulston Scar area (Hambleton Hills).

	Thickness m
OXFORD CLAY	
Mudstone, grey-green; poorly exposed	0.05
OSGODBY FORMATION	
Kellaways Rock Member	
Sandstone, yellow-grey, medium-grained, with bivalve and belemnite voids; voids and joint spaces in top 0.10 m infilled with mudstone from bed above	0.90
Sandstone, as above, but with abundant belemnites and bivalve voids including large *Gryphaea dilobotes*, *Liostrea* sp., *Chlamys fibrosa* and *Meleagrinella braamburiensis*	1.40
Sandstone, green-brown to orange-grey, medium-grained, massive-bedded, with sparse bivalve and belemnite voids	2.44
Sandstone, yellow-grey, thick-bedded, medium-grained, with thin (0.2 m) burrowed beds; sparse bivalves; base not seen (estimated 15 m to base of the formation)	3.0

Senior (1975) observed large calcareous concretions, no longer exposed, near the base of the formation at this locality; these yielded bivalves and a proplanulitid ammonite suggesting a Callovian age.

Low Pasture to Whitestone Cliff

The formation can be traced southwards along the escarpment and is exposed at Low Pasture [5002 8861], High Barns [5032 8672] and in the back-scar of a landslip below Boltby Scar [5061 8594]. The upper bivalve-rich sandstone of the Kellaways Rock is exposed in a quarry [5039 8560] above Little Moor; here, the beds are extensively bioturbated and contain a higher proportion of berthierine ooliths; sandy limestone concretions are present in the lower, fine-grained sandstone. To the south, in South Wood, the outcrop is largely obscured by landslip, but the upper part of the formation is exposed adjacent to a forestry track [5072 8506] as follows:

	Thickness m
OXFORD CLAY	
Clay, green-grey, soft, weathered	0.3
OSGODBY FORMATION	
Hackness Rock Member	
Siltstone, buff-grey, with alternating hard (calcareous) and soft bands; fragments of belemnites, bivalves and fragments of kosmoceratid ammonites (K. (*Lobokosmokeras*) *duncani*, K. (K.) *bigoti; Peltoceras* sp.) indicating the Athleta Zone	3.25
Kellaways Rock Member	
Sandstone, orange, fine- to medium-grained; sparse berthierine ooliths present in basal 0.38 m; abundant, large, calcitic and decalcified bivalves and belemnites; bivalves include *Gryphaea dilobotes, Chlamys fibrosa, Unicardium* sp. and *Oxytoma* sp; rhynchonellid brachiopods and wood fragments also present; *Sigaloceras* sp. indicates the Calloviense Zone	1.53

This locality represents the only exposure of the Hackness Rock in the district.

The Osgodby Formation forms a prominent topographical feature above Thirlby Bank and can be traced southwards to Garbutt Wood near Whitestone Cliff (Figures 15 and 16) where a dry stream gully 5078 8341] exposes the following section:

	Thickness m
OXFORD CLAY	
Siltstone, green-grey to brown, micaceous; plant fragments and small mudstone clasts	0.35
Not exposed (probably mudstone)	4.1
OSGODBY FORMATION	
Kellaways Rock Member	
Sandstone, red-brown, medium-grained, medium- to thick- bedded, with limonite laminae and abundant decalcified bivalves and belemnites	5.5
Sandstone, yellow-grey, fine- to medium-grained, thick-bedded; sparse bivalves; cross-bedded in part	14.1
Siltstone, grey-buff, clayey, micaceous	0.2

Roulston Scar to Raven's Gill

Between Whitestone Cliff and Roulston Scar [5110 8153], the Oxford Clay and the Hackness Rock are cut out by the overstepping unconformity at the base of the Lower Calcareous Grit which, in this area, rests directly on the Kellaways Rock (Figures 15 and 16); the sequence at Ivy Scar [5108 8142] is as follows:

	Thickness m
LOWER CALCAREOUS GRIT	
Sandstone, grey-buff, finely laminated, with thin siltstone partings; abraded fragments of *Gryphaea dilobotes* and other bivalves	0.50
Limestone, grey-buff, with shell fragments and silty laminae; abundant bivalves and belemnites in basal 0.10 m (probably derived from the Kellaways Rock)	0.47
Kellaways Rock Member	
Sandstone, orange-brown, medium-grained, with sparse berthierine ooliths in basal 1.7 m; abundant decalcified voids of bivalves, including *Gryphaea dilobotes*, and belemnites; more fossiliferous upwards	5.34
Sandstone, yellow fine- to medium-grained, thick-bedded; sparse bivalves; vertical burrows	4.05

At Roulston Scar (Figure 16), a few hundred metres to the north, the sequence is similar, but here, a bed (0.13 m thick) of soft sand with abundant bivalves and belemnites probably represents the product of winnowing, following erosion of the Hackness Rock and the Oxford Clay, prior to deposition of the Lower Calcareous Grit. The Osgodby Formation forms a prominent topographical feature below the Lower Calcareous Grit on Hood Hill [504 813], but the sequence is not well exposed. The unconformity can be traced eastwards along the main escarpment to Low Town Bank [5172 8126] and Hell Hole [5247 8141] (Figure 16). At the latter locality and at Raven's Gill [5295 8186], the Kellaways Rock is overlain by the Oldstead Oolite Member at the base of the Lower Calcareous Grit; the sequence at Raven's Gill (Plate 5) is given below:

	Thickness m
LOWER CALCAREOUS GRIT	
Oldstead Oolite Member	
Limestone, grey, oolitic, with grainstone texture; cross-laminated; erosive base	1.7
OSGODBY FORMATION	
Kellaways Rock Member	
Sand, yellow-orange, with small grey-green clay pellets	0.3
Sandstone, orange, medium-grained, with abundant	

Plate 5 Oldstead Oolite (Lower Calcareous Grit) unconformably overlying the Kellaways Rock (Osgodby Formation). Raven's Gill (L3183).

decalcified voids of bivalves, including *Gryphaea dilobotes, Trigonia* sp. and *Meleagrinella* sp., and belemnites; vertical burrows; geothite laminae   4.3

Sand, grey, clayey   0.3

Sandstone, yellow-orange, medium-grained, with sparse belemnite and bivalve voids; burrows   1.2

Sandstone, yellow-grey, fine-grained, with sparse bivalve voids; burrow-mottled; hard goethite-rich cemented bed (0.5 m) 0.7 m from top   7.4

The clay pellets in the unconsolidated sand at the top of the Kellaways Rock at this locality may have been derived from the Oxford Clay during the erosive phase that removed both the Oxford Clay and the Hackness Rock and reworked the top of the Kellaways Rock (Powell, 1982). This unconformity is equivalent to five ammonite zones and represents a considerable time span (Cope et al., 1980, fig. 8).

East of Raven's Gill, the Oldstead Oolite can be traced through at the same topographical level to Shaw's Gill [5308 8198] where it overlies the Oxford Clay. The abrupt termination of the Kellaways Rock feature, below the Oldstead Oolite, is attributed to a post-Oxford Clay–pre-Lower Calcareous Grit fault (Powell, 1982), which preserves the Oxford Clay above the Kellaways Rock on its downthrow side (Figure 15).

Shaw's Gill to Wass

The Osgodby Formation is mostly obscured by landslip and head deposits between Shaw's Gill and Snever Wood [5365 8038], but yellow sandstone typical of the Kellaways Rock is exposed in a forestry track at the latter locality. The stratigraphical relationships in the south-east margin of the outcrop are obscure due to lack of exposure. Exposures in a stream section in Duckendale [554 803], near Wass, suggest that the typical bivalve-rich sandstone at the top

Table 9 Stratigraphical framework of the Upper Jurassic rocks in the district. Vertical lines indicate a depositional hiatus (after Cope et al., 1980)

Series	Stage	Zone	Subzone	Lithostratigraphy
Upper Jurassic	Kimmeridgian (part)	Eudoxus		Kimmeridge Clay Formation and Ampthill Clay Fm. (undifferentiated)
		Mutabilis		
		Cymodoce		
		Baylei		
	Oxfordian	Rosenkrantzi		
		Regulare		
		Serratum	Serratum	
			Koldeweyense	Upper Calcareous Grit Fm. (undivided)
		Glosense	Glosense	
			Ilovaiskii	
		Tenuiserratum	Blakei	Coral Rag
			Tenuiserratum	Malton Oolite
		Densiplicatum	Maltonense	Middle Calcareous Grit
			Vertebrale	
		Cordatum	Cordatum	Hambleton Oolite / Birdsall Calcareous Grit
			Costicardia	
			Bukowskii	Lower Calcareous Grit / Oldstead Oolite
		Mariae	Praecordatum	Oxford Clay Formation
			Scarburgense	

Corallian Group; Coralline Oolite Formation

*Brink Hill beds

Not exposed, proven in boreholes in adjacent sheet (53)

Asenby–Coxwold Graben

Not exposed

Hambleton Hills

of the Kellaways Rock passes laterally into dark grey, micaceous siltstone, which is overlain by grey-green silty mudstone typical of the Oxford Clay. The dark grey siltstone has been mapped as the Osgodby Formation in this area; it may represent a lateral change of facies in the Kellaways Rock Member, or possibly the presence one or both of the stratigraphically higher units, the Hackness Rock Member and the Langdale Member.

Fox-Strangways et al. (1886) postulated that the Osgodby Formation (Kellaways Rock) is not present in both the Wass area and the northern part of the Howardian Hills (Pickering (53) Sheet), so that the Oxford Clay unconformably overlies the Scalby Formation. However, about 12 km to the south-west of Wass, in the vicinity of Hovingham, the 'normal' sequence of the Oxford Clay overlying the Kellaways Rock (referred to as the Kellaways Sand in this area) is shown on Sheet 53 (see also Wright, 1978, fig. 4). This hypothesis requires very rapid thickening of the Oxford Clay from about 25 m to about 50 m between Snever Wood [5365 8083] and Duckendale [554 803], at the expense of the Osgodby Formation. This could be explained by invoking penecontemporaneous erosion of the Osgodby Formation in this area prior to deposition of the Oxford Clay (cf. the erosional unconformity at the base of the Lower Calcareous Grit in the Roulston Scar area). A detailed study of the poorly exposed lithofacies and their faunas in both the south-west of the district and the northern Howardian Hills is required in order to resolve this problem.

The Osgodby Formation does not crop out within the largely drift-covered Asenby–Coxwold Graben and its subdrift crop, is shown conjecturally on the map. The formation may, however, be absent if the relationship postulated by Fox-Strangways et al. (1886), described above, is extrapolated westward from the northern Howardian Hills to the Asenby–Coxwold area.

Cadell and Rye Valley

The Kellaways Rock Member crops out in Cadell and in the Rye Valley, in the north-east margin of the district; orange, medium-grained, oyster-rich sandstone at the top of the member is exposed adjacent to the ford at Cadell Mill [5426 8676], and at Dale Town [5356 8869], Low Pasture Wood [5384 8924], North Bank Wood [5328 8955], Spring Wood [5226 8992] and Easterside Farm [5226 8992]. At the last locality, and around Hawnby Village, the Osgodby Formation forms a prominent topographical feature, but is subject to cambering.

UPPER JURASSIC

The base of the Upper Jurassic Series is defined at the lower boundary of the Oxfordian Stage (Cope et al., 1980), which in this district (Table 9) is at the base of the Oxford Clay. The youngest Jurassic strata in the district, the Kimmeridge Clay, belong to the Kimmeridgian Stage. These predominantly deep-water, clay formations are separated in the Cleveland Basin by the Corallian Group, comprising mixed shallow-water carbonates and calcareous sandstones, which accumulated on the inner- and mid-shelf zones of a broad epeiric sea. South of the Market Weighton Structure, coeval strata are represented by deeper water mudstones and siltstones.

The Upper Jurassic rocks in the district are wholly of marine origin and mark a continuation of the major marine transgression which began during the Callovian Stage. The overall eustatic sea-level rise in north-west Europe (Hallam, 1975) was interrupted by a regressive phase during the deposition of the Corallian Group, but culminated in restricted, basinal environments with anoxic bottom-conditions during the deposition of the bituminous Kimmeridge Clay.

The lower part of the Upper Jurassic sequence (Oxford Clay and Lower Calcareous Grit) in this district includes a marked local unconformity, which reflects a continuation of the tectonic activity that resulted in depositional hiatuses during the Callovian (Tables 6 and 9). This is manifested in the uplift and tilting of the Roulston Scar 'block', where the Lower Calcareous Grit rests with unconformable overstep on the Kellaways Rock (Osgodby Formation) (Figures 15 and 16).

The lithostratigraphy of the Upper Jurassic in the Cleveland Basin was established by Fox-Strangways et al. (1886) and Fox-Strangways (1892), and was later refined by Wright (1972, 1983), who formalised the nomenclature, which is adopted herein, and provided a detailed chrono-stratigraphical framework based on ammonite zones (Table 9).

Upper Jurassic rocks form the greater part of the Hambleton Hills; the Oxford Clay, where present, marks a topographical slack below the towering cliffs of the scarp face formed by the Lower Calcareous Grit and the Coralline Oolite formations. These formations also produce gentle dip slopes towards the east and south-east which, in turn, are deeply incised by the River Rye and its tributaries. Upper Jurassic rocks also crop out in largely drift-covered terrain at the eastern end of the Asenby–Coxwold Graben, where beds high in the sequence, such as the Upper Calcareous Grit and Kimmeridge Clay, are downthrown against Lower and Middle Jurassic strata in a series of rhomb-shaped fault blocks (see chapter seven).

Oxford Clay Formation

The Oxford Clay ranges in thickness from 0 to 25 m along its outcrop, and consists of grey-green mudstone and silty mudstone; where present, it forms a topographical slack between the Osgodby Formation below and the Lower Calcareous Grit above.

The formation is mostly obscured by landslip and head deposits, but there are sufficient critical exposures to establish its gradual thinning southwards from Boltby Moor, in the north of the district, to Whitestone Cliff, its absence below the unconformable Lower Calcareous Grit between Roulston Scar and Raven's Gill, and its presence south-east of Raven's Gill (Figures 15, 16 and 18). The Oxford Clay also crops out in deeply dissected valleys in the east of the district, and within the Asenby–Coxwold Graben.

There are no complete sections through the formation, but scattered exposures along the outcrop indicate an overall upward-coarsening sequence from mudstone to silty mudstone and siltstone. The stratigraphical relationship with the underlying Osgodby Formation is obscure due to both the paucity of exposure and the lithological similarity in the district between the Oxford Clay and the underlying Hackness Rock Member. The latter has been identified below the Oxford Clay at one locality (see p.56), but on Boltby Moor [498 892] and near Whitestone Cliff [5078 8341] the Oxford Clay rests directly on the Kellaways Rock, suggesting a local unconformity at the base of the Oxford

Clay. The upper boundary, defined by the base of the Lower Calcareous Grit, appears to be gradational in exposures in the north-east of the outcrop (Ryedale, Cadell), but immediately to the north and east of the Roulston Scar 'block' the junction is sharp, due to erosion at the base of the overlying unconformable unit.

The absence of the Oxford Clay between Sutton Bank and Raven's Gill along the main escarpment, and also at Hood Hill [504 813], is the result of uplift and subsequent submarine erosion of the Oxford Clay and, in places, the Hackness Rock prior to deposition of the Lower Calcareous Grit. This area appears to have been an uplifted block, tilted gently towards the north, since the Oxford Clay thins gradually southwards towards Roulston Scar [5110 8153], but is present abruptly between Raven's Gill and Shaw's Gill where a penecontemporaneous post-Oxford Clay – pre-Lower Calcareous Grit fault is invoked (Figures 15 and 18). The uplift and erosion must have been short-lived because the Oxford Clay and the overlying Lower Calcareous Grit have yielded ammonites of the Mariae Zone and Cordatum Zone (Bukowskii Subzone) respectively in the Shaw's Gill area (Powell, 1982).

The Oxford Clay in this district has yielded an abundant ammonite fauna from a number of horizons. From one of these, about 10 m above the base of the unit, well-preserved, goethitic, small specimens of *Quenstedtoceras mariae* (d'Orbigny) and *Cardioceras scarburgense* (Young and Bird), indicating the Mariae Zone, Scarburgense Subzone have been collected. Other sections near the top of the formation have yielded small casts of *Cardioceras praecordatum* Douvillé, proving the later Praecordatum Subzone. Additional fauna includes sparse small bivalves and goethitic burrows.

Characteristics such as the fine-grained lithology, absence of current structures, paucity of benthic fauna and the presence, locally, of nektic fauna, suggest an offshore, moderately deep-water environment of deposition.

DETAILS

Boltby Moor

Senior (1975) recorded a prolific ammonite fauna from a bed about 18 m above the base of the Oxford Clay in Northwood Slack [4925 8966], in the north of the district. These sections have deteriorated, but a similar fauna was collected during the present survey from grey-green mudstone exposed in trackside trenches [4890 8981 and 4936 8952]. The small, goethitic specimens include *Quenstedtoceras mariae* (d'Orbigny) and *Cardioceras praecordatum* Douvillé, indicating the Mariae Zone.

Low Paradise Farm to Whitestone Cliff

The outcrop can be traced south-eastwards to Low Paradise Farm, where green-grey clay is exposed in drainage trenches north-east of the farm; the estimated thickness here is 25 m. South of this locality the outcrop is largely obscured by landslip, but the base is exposed, above the Hackness Rock, in South Wood [5072 8506] where the formation, 15 m thick, has yielded ammonites of the Mariae Zone; these include *Cardioceras (Scarburgiceras)* cf. *scarburgense* and *Peltoceras (Parawedekendia)* sp. Also present are small bivalves, including *Meleagrinella* sp. and *Oxytoma* sp., the gastropod *Dicroloma* sp. and the belemnite *Hibolites* sp. Below Whitestone Cliff [5066 8381 to 5069 8348] the formation thins southwards, from 15 m to 8 m, beneath the unconformable Lower Calcareous Grit (Figure 15); the upper

boundary is not exposed here, but 5 m of grey-green, micaceous siltstone were seen above the Kellaways Rock. A dry gully [5078 8341] in Garbutt Wood, about 150 m south-west of Whitestone Cliff, exposes the following section (Figure 16):

	Thickness m
LOWER CALCAREOUS GRIT	
Limestone, buff, siliceous, with decalcified bivalves	3.2
Siltstone, red-brown, calcareous, passing up to fine-grained sandstone	0.50
OXFORD CLAY	
Siltstone, olive-grey to brown, micaceous; plant fragments and small mudstone clasts	0.35
Not exposed (probably mudstone in break of slope)	4.1
OSGODBY FORMATION	
Kellaways Rock Member	
Sandstone, red-brown, medium-grained, with abundant decalcified bivalve and belemnite voids	5.5

Sutton Bank to Shaw's Gill

The formation thins rapidly below the unconformable Lower Calcareous Grit to the south of Whitestone Cliff, and is not present at Sutton Bank [5153 8275]. The absence of the Oxford Clay between Sutton Bank and Raven's Gill has been discussed in previous sections. The abrupt reappearance of the Oxford Clay on the northwest side of Shaw's Gill [5308 8198] and along the outcrop to the south-east is attributed to its preservation on the downthrow side of a penecontemporaneous fault, which uplifted the Roulston Scar 'block' after deposition of the Oxford Clay (that is, in late Mariae Zone – early Cordatum Zone times). The Oxford Clay was removed from this 'high', and there is evidence (p.59) that the top of the Kellaways Rock was reworked by submarine erosion (Powell, 1982). The section in Shaw's Gill [5327 8206] (Figure 16) is as follows:

	Thickness m
LOWER CALCAREOUS GRIT	
Oldstead Oolite Member	
Limestone, buff-grey (oopackstone), with bivalve fragments; sharp base	5.8
OXFORD CLAY	
Siltstone, grey-green, micaceous, with bivalves and casts of *Cardioceras (Scarburgiceras)* cf. *praecordatum*	1.5
Silty mudstone, with goethitic *Cardioceras scarburgense*; poorly exposed downstream from bed above	12.0

Shaw's Gill to Snever Wood

Landslips obscure most of the Oxford Clay outcrop between Shaw's Gill and Mount Snever [544 801], but green-grey mudstone weathering to soft clay is exposed in a few forestry tracks; one locality [5349 8154] has yielded a goethitic ammonite assemblage, including *Cardioceras (Scarburgiceras) scarburgense, C.(S.) praecordatum, Goliathiceras* sp. and *Quenstedtoceras mariae*, indicative of the Mariae Zone. This assemblage is similar to that recorded from Shaw's Gill, South Wood and Boltby Forest. Also present are the bivalves *Gryphaea* sp., *Nuculoma* sp. and *Rollierella* sp., and the gastropod *Dicroloma* sp.

The probable upward passage of the Kellaways sandstone into a siltstone lithofacies to the south-east of Snever Wood, is obscured by extensive landslip and dense coniferous forest. Hence the boundary between the Oxford Clay and the underlying Osgodby Formation is very difficult to trace in the south-east of the main escarpment.

Hawnby, Flassen Dale and Nettle Dale

Exposures in the north-east of the district are limited to small sections in forestry tracks and streams. Grey-green, micaceous, silty mudstone (1.4 m thick) is exposed at a spring-head [5421 8991] near Hawnby. Micaceous siltstone, near the top of the formation, is exposed at Shatwith House [5350 8909], adjacent to Murton Bank [5417 8892], and in the track below Peak Scar [5288 8839]. The upper formational boundary, at the base of the Lower Calcareous Grit, is exposed in Flassen Dale [5292 8336; 5338 8352] as follows:

	Thickness m
LOWER CALCAREOUS GRIT	
Sandstone, buff, calcareous, with grey sandy limestone beds; base gradational	1.6
OXFORD CLAY	
Siltstone, grey-green, micaceous	0.7
Mudstone, grey-green, silty, with pyrite and goethite burrowfills, and small nodules	0.5

The gradational, upward-coarsing passage is also exposed in drainage trenches at the confluence of Flassen Dale and Nettle Dale [5519 8475] as follows:

	Thickness m
LOWER CALCAREOUS GRIT	
Sandstone, buff-grey, fine-grained, calcareous, with sparse ooliths	0.60
Sandstone, buff-grey, fine-grained, calcareous, with dark-grey laminae; burrow-mottled, with sparse horizontal burrows	0.61
OXFORD CLAY	
Siltstone, grey-green, calcareous, burrow-mottled, with small ammonite fragments; finer-grained, with mudstone laminae in basal 0.90 m	1.74

Asenby–Coxwold Graben

The Oxford Clay crops out in largely drift-covered terrain at the eastern end of this structure, near Wildon Grange [5164 7806], where grey-green micaceous siltstone with sparse ammonite fragments is exposed as soil brash. The junction with the overlying Lower Calcareous Grit is exposed in a disused railway cutting [5368 7706 to 5378 7712] at Coxwold, where the Oxford Clay is represented by up to 5 m of dark brown-grey, fissile mudstone passing gradationally up to buff-grey, sandy siltstone (0.7 m).

CORALLIAN GROUP

The Corallian Group ranges in thickness from 70 to 150 m in the district, and predominantly comprises oolitic and micritic limestone and calcareous, spiculitic, fine-grained sandstone, which were deposited in a warm, shallow sea during a low relative sea-level stand in the Cleveland Basin. These rocks from the bold west-facing escarpment and the moors of the Hambleton Hills, and also crop out as prominent features within the Asenby–Coxwold Graben, in marked contrast with the clay formations, above and below. The group is subdivided into three formations (Wright,

1972, 1983) and spans the Middle and Upper Oxfordian stages (Table 9; Wright, 1980).

Lower Calcareous Grit Formation

The Lower Calcareous Grit crops out along the upper part of the bold, west-facing escarpment of the Hambleton Hills, but many of the exposures are inaccessible because of the sheer cliff faces. It also crops out, downdip, in the deeply incised valleys in the north-east of the district, and in the Asenby–Coxwold Graben. The formation is 22 to 48 m thick and forms a prominent topographical feature above the Oxford Clay (Plate 10) or, locally, above the Osgodby Formation (Plate 5).

The Lower Calcareous Grit consists predominantly of yellow, buff, fine- to medium-grained, calcareous sandstone, with subsidiary beds and concretions of blue-grey, micritic limestone; both lithologies are variably oolitic and peloidal. Siliceous spicules of the sponge *Rhaxella perforata* form much of the clastic component (Hemingway, 1974), and diagenesis of these has produced secondary, thin beds of chert, particularly in the lower part of the formation. *Thalassinoides* burrows are very common at some horizons; the burrowfills have a high spicule content and are more resistant to weathering, giving an irregular, nodular appearance to weathered faces. The micritic limestone concretions reach up to 1.5 m diameter, and are locally concentrated in the upper part of the formation (the 'Ball Beds' of Arkell, 1945) (Plate 6).

In addition to the fauna noted above, the formation has yielded a benthic assemblage including bivalves and brachiopods ("*Avicula, Pecten, Trigonia, Modiola, Ostrea* and *Rhynchonelloidea*"; (Hemingway, 1974), but these are rarely well preserved. The carbonate concretions contain the richest fauna and have yielded many large ammonites which, although poorly preserved, indicate the Bukowskii Subzone of the Cordatum Zone (Table 9; Wright, 1980).

Between Low Town Bank [5156 8121] and Shaw's Gill [5327 8206], the **Oldstead Oolite Member** (Wright, 1980) is distinguished in the lower part of the formation. This member, up to 11 m thick, consists of grey to yellow-grey, bioclastic, oolitic wackestone-grainstone, and is cross-bedded in part. It exhibits an erosive base above the Kellaways Rock in the Raven's Gill area [5295 8186] (Plate 5; Figure 16). To the east, in Shaw's Gill, it overlies Oxford Clay with a sharp base (Figure 16).

The unconformable (overstep) boundary between the Lower Calcareous Grit and the Kellaways Rock at Roulston Scar, Ivy Scar and Raven's Gill is described above (pp.53–57), and the lower boundary with the Oxford Clay at Shaw's Gill, Whitestone Cliff, Flassen Dale and Nettle Dale is described on pp.60–61. The upper formational boundary is defined by the base of the Coralline Oolite Formation. Where the Hambleton Oolite Member is present, the junction is distinct and is taken at the base of the first thick bed of oolitic limestone (Figure 17; Plate 6). However, in the south-east of the district the Hambleton Oolite Member passes laterally into a coeval, predominantly siliciclastic facies, the Birdsall Calcareous Grit (Table 9; Figure 18). The base of this member is marked by a bed of richly oolitic sandstone (Wright, 1972), but, in places, the

Plate 6 Corallian Group, Cleave Dyke Quarry (L3041).

lithological contrast with the Lower Calcareous Grit is not strong, and the boundary is difficult to trace over poorly exposed moorland; in these areas, such as the southern part of Byland Moor [503 803], a conjectural boundary has been mapped between the Lower Calcareous Grit and the overlying Coralline Oolite Formation.

Away from the Roulston Scar 'block', the gradational upward-coarsening sequence at the base of the Lower Calcareous Grit, together with the shelly benthic fauna, abundant sponge spicules and *Thalassinoides* burrows, suggest sedimentation under shallower-water conditions than prevailed during deposition of the underlying Oxford Clay. The absence of small-scale sedimentary structures in the siliciclastic deposits may be due to intense bioturbation of the substrate soon after deposition; *Thalassinoides* burrows are well preserved on bedding planes, but intense activity within individual beds has produced a homogeneous fabric. Despite the absence of primary current structures, the lithological and faunal characteristics indicate deposition in shallow to moderate depths (c.5 to 30 m) in the offshore zone.

The Oldstead Oolite was deposited in shallow-water, turbulent conditions on the south-eastern flanks of the Roulston Scar 'block'. Cross-bedding, oolitic grainstone texture and basal erosional scours indicate shoaling conditions within

wave-base. The upward decrease in the proportion of ooliths (wackestone texture) at the top of the member suggests increasing water depths through time.

DETAILS

The following account includes the most accessible exposures, which demonstrate the lithological heterogeneity of the formation in the district when traced from north-west to south-east.

The Lower Calcareous Grit crops out in the north-west of the main escarpment where up to 3 m of yellow, calcareous sandstone are exposed adjacent to a forestry track [4945 8960] in Cracoe Forest. It can be traced southwards along the escarpment to Cleave Dyke Quarry [507 862], where calcareous sandstone with large carbonate concretions, exposed in the quarry floor, are overlain by the lower leaf of the Hambleton Oolite (Plate 6). The formation is also exposed at Boltby Scar [5056 8559] to the south, and at Peak Scar [5300 8832 to 5308 8828], but only the latter locality is accessible; the section at Peak Scar is as follows:

Thickness
m

CORALLINE OOLITE FORMATION

Hambleton Oolite Member
Limestone, grey-buff, sandy, bioclastic, oolitic   3.6

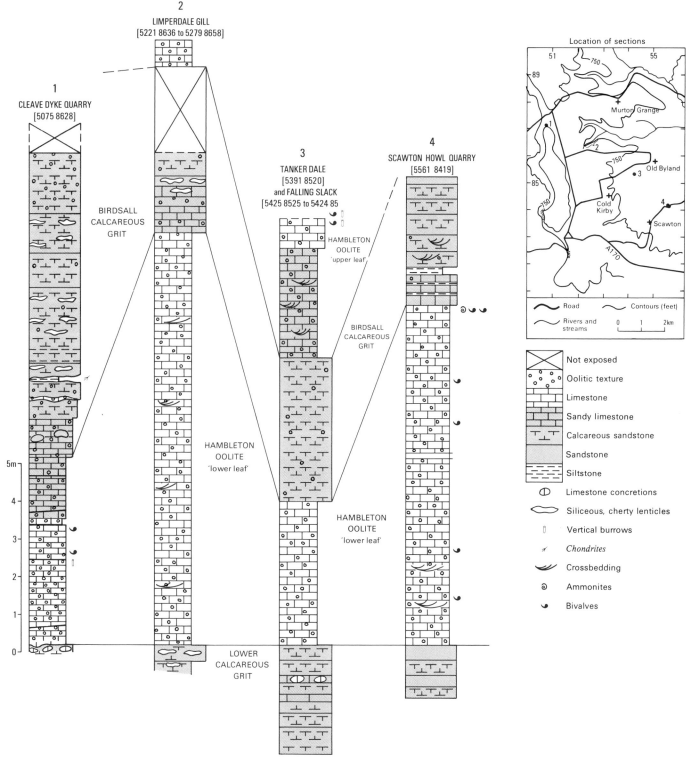

Figure 17 Comparative lithological sections showing the correlation of the Hambleton Oolite and the Birdsall Calcareous Grit in the Hambleton Hills.

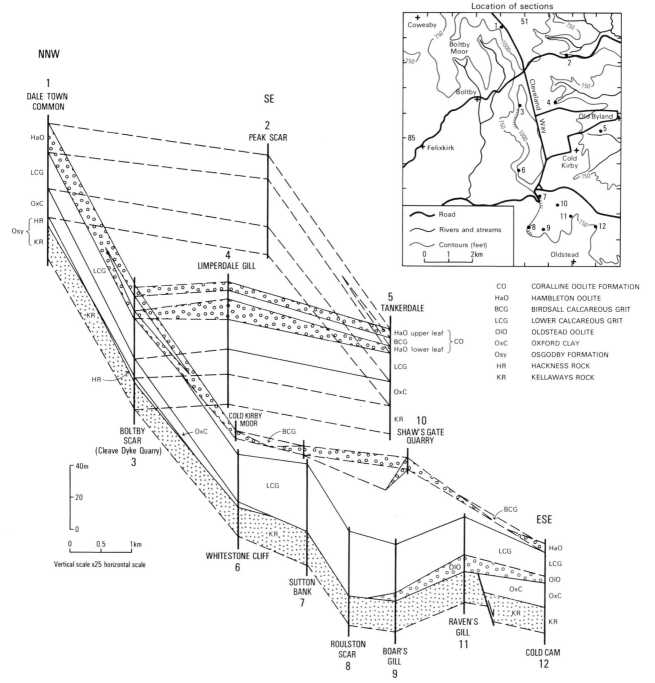

Figure 18   Diagramatic ribbon-section showing the stratigraphical relationships of the Callovian and Oxfordian strata in the Hambleton Hills.

LOWER CALCAREOUS GRIT

Limestone, grey-buff, sandy, with scattered ooliths; nodular, in part; siliceous beds; sparse *Thalassinoides* burrows   1.0

Limestone, grey-buff, slightly oolitic, interbedded with grey-buff, oolitic calcareous sandstone containing grey microcrystalline limestone concretions; siliceous *Thalassinoides* burrows; *Nucleolites* sp. present. ('Ball Beds')   10.5

Sandstone, pale grey, calcareous, intercalated with thin beds of grey limestone with sparse peloids and

ooliths; laterally impersistent beds of grey chert; abundant *Thalassinoides* burrows   9.0

(Base not exposed: estimated 10 m to top of Oxford Clay).

The amount of silica, derived from *Rhaxella* spicules, decreases up the section; diagenesis of the siliceous rock has resulted in the formation of thin-bedded chert. The boundary with the overlying Hambleton Oolite is gradational, the percentage of ooliths increasing upwards. Similar lithologies are present at the top of the formation at Limperdale Gill [5230 8660] and King Spring Gill [5203 8686].

Southwards along the main escarpment, the Lower Calcareous Grit is well exposed at Whitestone Cliff [5066 8381 to 5069 8348], Sutton Bank [5151 8280] and Roulston Scar [5110 8153] (Figure 16). Two very distinctive lithologies can be seen in the cliffs at these localities, but they are best observed in fallen blocks; these comprise the 'Ball Beds' and the 'nodular beds'. The former are grey to blue-grey, microcrystalline limestone concretions which contain sparse peloids and ooliths; they weather out from softer, decalcified, yellow, fine-grained sandstone. At Fairy Table [5238 8106] and Roulston Scar [5110 8153], concretions pass laterally into bedded limestone, suggesting early diagenetic migration of carbonate to concretion centres within an originally mixed carbonate–siliciclastic sediment. The nodular bedform is due to the differential weathering of cross-sections through harder, silica-rich *Thalassinoides* burrows; bedding-plane surfaces show the ramifying network of these crustacean burrows. The lower part of the section at Roulston Scar is given below:

	Thickness m
LOWER CALCAREOUS GRIT (upper part of the section is inaccessible)	
Sandstone, buff-yellow, fine- to medium-grained, calcareous; and limestone, buff-grey, sandy, with sparse ooliths; bed thickness c. 0.4 m in sandstone and 0.25 m in limestone; shell fragments and sparse belemnites	6.0
Limestone, buff, sandy, with shell fragments and belemnites	0.23
Sandstone, yellow-orange, medium-grained, calcareous, with belemnite and oyster fragments in basal 0.4 m; red-brown goethite laminae	0.74
Limestone, buff-yellow, with sparse ooliths; shelly band (0.05 m) with bivalve and belemnite fragments at top	0.40
Sandstone, yellow-orange, medium-grained, with bivalve and belemnite fragments common in basal 0.2 m; structureless	0.56
Sandstone, yellow, medium- to coarse-grained, with abundant abraded fragments of belemnites and bivalves, including oysters (reworked from Kellaways Rock); laminated in basal 0.20 m	0.43

(Kellaways Rock, below)

South and east of Low Town Bank [5172 8121] the Oldstead Oolite Member (Figures 16 and 18) is present at the base of the formation. At Hell Hole [5247 8141] and Boar's Gill [5172 8127] it is 4.8 m and 3.85 m thick respectively, and it thickens to 11 m at Raven's Gill [5286 8191 to 5295 8186] (Plate 5) where the following section [5286 8191] is exposed:

	Thickness m
Sandstone, yellow, calcareous, fine-grained, spicular, with irregular grey microcrystalline limestone concretions (sparsely peloidal) which yielded a number of ammonites including *Cardioceras* (*Scarburgiceras*) *harmonicum* Maire, *C.* (*Plasmatoceras*) spp. and *Cardioceras* sp. indet.(a large smooth body-chambered macroconch) indicating the Bukowskii Subzone	c.5.0
Limestone, sandy, yellow-buff to grey, with scattered ooliths (bed thickness 0.20 to 0.60 m), intercalated with fine-grained calcareous sandstone and siltstone; poorly exposed at base	c.9.6

Sandstone, grey-buff, calcareous, spicular, fine-grained, and beds of grey calcareous siltstone with dark grey, wispy cross-laminae; thin beds of grey, sandy, peloidal, sparsely oolitic limestone also present	8.85
Oldstead Oolite Member	
Limestone, yellow-grey, sandy, with sparse ooliths	1.5
Limestone, yellow, sandy, with abundant large ooliths and sparse, siliceous burrowfills; limestone concretions	1.4
Limestone, grey oolitic, bioclastic, cross-bedded in part; erosional scours	4.2
Limestone, grey, bioclastic, with discrete oolitic beds	2.2
Limestone, grey, oolitic, with grainstone texture; cross-laminated, with erosive base	1.7

(Kellaways Rock, below)

The Oldstead Oolite is also present in Shaw's Gill [5327 8206], where it overlies the Oxford Clay (Figure 16) with a sharp base (p.60). South-west of this locality, oolitic, sandy limestone and oolitic, calcareous sandstone beds at the base of the formation can be traced to Mount Snever [5377 8070] and Duckendale [5446 8001]. However, to the south-west of Mount Snever, the basal beds become increasingly sandy and the Oldstead Oolite cannot be distinguished.

Asenby-Coxwold Graben

The Lower Calcareous Grit is exposed near Coxwold Village, at the eastern end of the Asenby–Coxwold Graben. Buff-grey, fine-grained, spicule-rich, calcareous sandstone with chert beds is exposed in largely overgrown quarries at Holmtop [5387 7698] and Coxwold [5308 7732], and in a series of smaller quarries [5473 7658 to 5499 7672] north-east of Newburgh Priory. In the largely drift-covered terrain near Wildon Grange, small quarries [5163 7789; 5243 7769; 5195 7802] expose calcareous siltstone and fine-grained sandstone beds with brachiopod, bivalve, belemnite and ammonite fragments, interpreted to represent the lower part of the formation. The section exposed in a quarry [5195 7802] east of Wildon Grange is as follows:

	Thickness m
TILL	
Sandy clay and clay with pebbles	0.40
LOWER CALCAREOUS GRIT	
Siltstone, grey-green, with cross-laminated, fine-grained sandstone laminae	0.21
Sandstone, buff-grey, fine-grained, with carbonaceous wisps	0.18
Siltstone, grey-green, thin-bedded; small bivalves and finely ribbed ammonites; dark grey bituminous wisps	1.68
Sandstone, buff-grey, fine-grained	0.30
Limestone, dark grey, sandy	0.20
Siltstone, buff-grey, calcareous	0.18

Coralline Oolite Formation

The Coralline Oolite Formation (Wright, 1972) crops out in the north-east corner of the district where it forms broad easterly and south-easterly dip slopes, dissected by the deeply incised tributaries of the River Rye. The formation comprises the following five members, in upward sequence: Hambleton Oolite, Birdsall Calcareous Grit, Middle Calcareous Grit, Malton Oolite and Coral Rag (Table 9).

The lower three members crop out in the Hambleton Hills, but the upper two members are present only within the Asenby–Coxwold Graben, where they are almost entirely obscured by drift deposits. Only the Coral Rag Member has been definitely identified at outcrop in the graben (Fox-Strangways et al., 1886), and this single exposure is now obscured by quarry spoil (p.70). The estimated thickness of the formation ranges from 60 to 70 m, but the true thickness is not determinable in this district because of both the paucity of exposure and extensive faulting in the Asenby–Coxwold Graben.

The Coralline Oolite Formation consists of a varied sequence of grey, predominantly oolitic and peloidal limestone (oowackestone to oograinstone texture) intercalated with wedges of buff-yellow, sparsely oolitic, calcareous sandstone; subsidiary lithologies include micritic limestone, and reefal boundstone rich in corals and algae. Over most of the Cleveland Basin, from Scarborough in the east to the North-allerton in the west, the stratigraphical relationship of the members assumes a 'layer-cake' sequence (Wright, 1972; Hemingway 1974, fig. 53). However, as the formation is traced from the north-west of the district to the south-east, and beyond to the Howardian Hills, lateral changes in litho-facies are prevalent, particularly in the lower three members, the Hambleton Oolite, Birdsall Calcareous Grit and Middle Calcareous Grit (Figure 18). South-east of Murton Common [509 885], the Hambleton Oolite is separated into 'upper' and 'lower' leaves by the intervening Birdsall Calcareous Grit (Wright, 1972). This relationship can be traced to the area between Sutton Bank and Scawton [549 836], but south-east of here the oolite 'leaves' thin rapidly and are present as discontinuous lensoid bodies intercalated with sparsely oolitic calcareous sandstone. On parts of Byland Moor, south of Cold Cam [542 813], the oolitic limestones cannot be traced and there is a continuous sequence of calcareous sandstone from the top of the Lower Calcareous Grit, through the Birdsall Calcareous Grit, up to the base of the Middle Calcareous Grit, which is marked by a topographical feature; in these poorly exposed areas the base

of Coralline Oolite Formation is shown as a conjectural line on the map.

Over most of the district, however, the base of the Coralline Oolite Formation is clearly defined at the base of the Hambleton Oolite, as pale grey, oolitic limestone (oopackstone–oograinstone texture) overlying buff-yellow calcareous sandstone (Lower Calcareous Grit) (Plate 6). The top of the formation is defined by the base of the Upper Calcareous Grit (Wright, 1972) which rests on the Coral Rag Member in this district; this boundary is poorly exposed near Snape Hill Quarry [5110 7876], south-west of Kilburn.

The lithologies, fauna and facies distribution suggest that the Coralline Oolite Formation was deposited in a warm, shallow-sea which covered an extensive carbonate platform, across which oolite shoals prograded south-eastwards from the nearshore zone situated to the north of the district. Micritic carbonates developed in sheltered lagoons that were protected, in part, by coral–algal patch reefs during deposition of the Coral Rag Member (Reeves et al., 1978). Intercalation of oolitic carbonates and calcareous sandstones in the lower part of the formation, and lateral passage to increasingly siliciclastic-dominated lithofacies to the south-east, suggest a south-easterly transition from nearshore to offshore zones.

HAMBLETON OOLITE MEMBER AND BIRDSALL CALCAREOUS GRIT MEMBER

The **Hambleton Oolite** caps the escarpment of the Hambleton Hills and forms extensive dip slopes on the moors. It is 0 to 34 m thick and consists of pale grey to white, oolitic limestone (packstone to grainstone texture) with a variable proportion of quartz sand and fragmented shells; chert nodules are common in places. Thin beds of calcareous sandstone with scattered ooliths are present in the southern part of the outcrop. Cross-bedding and shallow scours are locally common in the oolitic limestone and the beds are frequently penetrated by circular, vertical burrows, up to 1 cm in diameter. Slump structures and injection phenomena (Plates 7 and 8; Hemingway and Twombley, 1963) are local-

Plate 7 Synsedimentary deformation in the Hambleton Oolite. Shaw's Gate Quarry. Bed numbers correspond to those in Figure 19 (L3066).

Plate 8 Hambleton Oolite in Shaw's Gate Quarry; opposite face to Plate 7. Bed numbers correspond to those in Figure 19 (L3074).

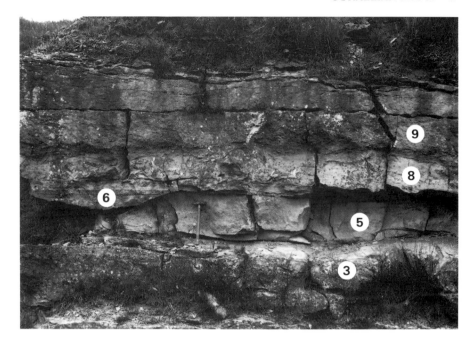

ly present at Shaws Gate Quarry [5233 8236] and Old Byland Grange Quarry [5454 8567] in the south of the outcrop (see details). The fauna includes the ammonites *Cardioceras, Goliathiceras, Aspidoceras* and *Perisphinctes*, as well as sporadic bivalves including "*Exogyra, Lima, Astarte, Ostrea, Modiola* and *Pholadomya*". Echinoids are common in some beds and include "*Cidaris, Nucleolites* and *Hemicidaris*" (Hemingway, 1974). Rare specimens of *Rhaxella perforata* and a brittle-star have been collected. Ammonites indicate an age (Table 9) ranging from the upper Bukowskii Subzone to the Vertebrale Subzone, spanning parts of the Cordatum and Densiplicatum zones (Wright, 1972).

The Hambleton Oolite is thickest in the north of the district, near Dale Town Common [50 89] and Murton [536 880], where it overlies the Lower Calcareous Grit (Figures 17 and 18). To the south and east of these localities, however, the stratigraphy is more complex (see Birdsall Calcareous Grit).

The **Birdsall Calcareous Grit Member** is a sandstone facies which was deposited coevally with the Hambleton Oolite. It is up to 12 m thick and consists of yellow-buff, calcareous, fine-grained sandstone with scattered ooliths and lenses of grey chert. Nodular texture is common and is due to abundant silica-rich *Thalassinoides* burrows. *Chondrites* burrows are locally present in thin-bedded siltstone. The Birdsall Calcareous Grit has yielded the subzonal ammonite *Cardioceras cordatum* (Wright, 1972) as well as bivalves, including *Chlamys fibrosa*.

In the northern part of the outcrop the Hambleton Oolite is split into upper and lower 'leaves' by the intervening Birdsall Calcareous Grit, which is well exposed between Cleave Dyke Quarry [507 863] (Plate 6) and Boltby Scar [506 857] (Frontispiece), near King Spring House [519 868], in Limperdale Gill [527 865] and Old Byland/Tanker Dale [5391 8520] (Figures 17 and 18), and also, to the south-east of the latter locality, at Flassen Dale and Nettle Dale. The

Birdsall Calcareous Grit wedges out along the main escarpment south of Boltby Scar, and also along the Caddell valley, so that the upper and lower 'leaves' of the Hambleton Oolite are not distinguishable (Figure 18; and details). On Scawton Moor, in the south-east of the outcrop, the Hambleton Oolite passes laterally into thin lensoid bodies comprising hard, pale grey oolitic grainstones, within a 'background' sediment consisting of calcareous, sparsely oolitic sandstone (Birdsall Calcareous Grit facies). South of Cold Cam, on Byland Moor [540 805], the Hambleton Oolite lithofacies wedges out (Figure 18) and there is a continuous upward succession of calcareous sandstones, comprising the Lower Calcareous Grit and Birdsall Calcareous Grit. Consequently, in this poorly exposed area, the boundary between Lower Calcareous Grit and Coralline Oolite formations is shown by a conjectural line on the map. The stratigraphy of the Byland Moor area is further complicated by the lateral thinning of the Lower Calcareous Grit to about 22 m, and an increase in the oolith content of this formation in the south-east of the outcrop.

The temporal relationship between the oolite and sandstone facies is difficult to resolve because of the lack of ammonite faunas. The overall facies pattern of these two members, as deduced from their outcrop pattern, indicates a depositional environment ranging from shallow-water oolite shoals in the north of the district, interdigitating with, and passing offshore to marine siliciclastics towards the southeast. The lithological characteristics of the oolite facies, taken together with the low-dipping, multidirectional crossbedding and shallow scours, suggest periodic migration of oolitic shoals on a shallow-water carbonate platform, influenced by waves and oscillating tidal currents. Long vertical burrows indicate temporary stability of the substrate. Similar facies have been described from the modern-day Great Bahama Bank (Purdy, 1963; Bathurst, 1975).

DETAILS

The Hambleton Oolite and Birdsall Calcareous Grit members are treated here together; the localities are described from the north-west to the south-east of the district.

The Hambleton Oolite outcrops on Dale Town Moor [50 89] and Murton Heights [536 880] where it forms a dip slope or bevelled dip slope capping the moors. There are no continuous sections in this area, but the oolitic limestone has been worked for walling stone or lime in many small, shallow disused quarries. The outcrop is partly obscured by loess deposits on Dale Town Common, but oolitic limestone is exposed in numerous swallow holes. An old quarry [5049 8875] near High Paradise exposes 2.8 m of grey, cross-bedded, shelly oolitic limestone with sparse pisoliths and shelly lenses, which yielded the echinoid *Nucleolites* sp. and small oysters. A specimen of the siliceous sponge *Rhaxella perforata* was found near-by in soil brash. The oolite has a grainstone texture with a sparite cement; this lithology is found in all the small quarries on the moor, and in soil brash, but as the outcrop is traced to the east, chert nodules become more common. These often take the form of a *Rhaxella* sponge colony or, locally, silica may replace both the sparite cement and the ooliths. Quarries near Sunny Bank [530 894] show anomalously high dips resulting from cambering near the edge of the escarpment. The cherty beds are exposed in a small disused quarry [5260 8945] as follows:

	Thickness m
Hambleton Oolite	
Limestone, buff, oolitic (grainstone), with sparse small chert concretions	0.6
Limestone, pale grey to buff, oolitic (grainstone), with elongate, irregular chert concretions passing laterally to bedded chert; relict ooliths in chert	0.2
Limestone, pale grey to buff, shelly, oolitic (grainstone); thin- to medium-bedded with undulating bedding planes; low-angle cross-bedding	2.2

The lower boundary with the underlying Lower Calcareous Grit is exposed nearby at the head of Gower Dale [5142 8935], where grey oolitic limestone (grainstone, with large ooliths) overlies buff, sandy limestone and calcareous sandstone with nodular siliceous bands (*Thalassinoides* burrow-fills). The gradational nature of this boundary at Peak Scar is described on p.62. Many of the quarries close to the edge of the escarpment show that the Hambleton Oolite is steeply cambered; these quarries [507 8798, 5206 8991, 5460 8855, 5597 8751] have often exploited natural scars within the camber gulls.

The lateral passage from oolite facies (Hambleton Oolite) to calcareous sandstone facies (Birdsall Calcareous Grit) occurs around Silver Hill Farm [514 882], where the transition is seen in the soil brash. The boundary here is poorly defined, but further south, near Sneck Yate Bank, there is a prominent break of slope [5095 8753] at the base of the upper oolite 'leaf'. The 'wedge' of calcareous sandstone separating the upper and lower 'leaves' is well exposed at King Spring Gill [5198 8688], Moor Ings [5183 8775], Limperdale Gill [5221 8636] and Cleave Dyke Quarry [5075 8628] (Figure 17); these are described as follows:

	Thickness m
King Spring Gill and Moor Ings	
Hambleton Oolite, upper 'leaf'	
Limestone, grey-buff, oolitic	2.0

Birdsall Calcareous Grit	
Sandstone, orange-yellow, fine-grained, calcareous, with siliceous *Thalassinoides* burrowfills	c.8.0
Hambleton Oolite, lower 'leaf'	
Limestone, grey, oolitic, with sparse pisoliths; small-scale cross-bedding	c.11.5
LOWER CALCAREOUS GRIT	
Sandstone, yellow, calcareous, fine-grained, with siliceous cherty bands and grey sandy limestone, in beds or concretions	15.0

Limperdale Gill	
Hambleton Oolite, upper 'leaf'	
Limestone, buff-grey, sandy, oolitic, shelly	1.8
Birdsall Calcareous Grit	
Sandstone, yellow-buff, calcareous, fine-grained, with grey limestone beds; poorly exposed in top 2.3 m	c.5.0
Hambleton Oolite, lower 'leaf'	
Limestone, grey, oolitic, with sparse pisoliths; small-scale cross-bedding	11.5
LOWER CALCAREOUS GRIT	
Sandstone, yellow, calcareous, fine-grained, with siliceous *Thalassinoides* burrowfills and beds or concretions of grey sandy limestone	15.0

Cleave Dyke Quarry	
Birdsall Calcareous Grit	
Sandstone, buff-yellow, calcareous, fine-grained, with shelly, slightly oolitic limestone beds	1.7
Sandstone, buff-yellow, calcareous, fine-grained, with irregular siliceous *Thalassinoides* burrowfills; shelly in part	1.1
Sandstone, buff, calcareous, fine-grained, decalcified in part, with sparse ooliths and irregular siliceous *Thalassinoides* burrowfills; calcareous siltstone partings (0.02 m)	3.1
Siltstone, grey-buff, calcareous, with abundant *Chrondrites* burrows in basal 0.2 m	0.38
Siltstone, grey-brown, with sparse ooliths and abundant *Chondrites* burrows	0.15
Sandstone, buff, calcareous, fine-grained, with sparse ooliths and a concretionary band (0.06 m) of grey oolitic limestone	0.95
Limestone, grey, sandy, partly decalcified, with sandy concretions	1.1
Hambleton Oolite, lower leaf	
Limestone, grey-buff, oolitic, sandy, partly decalcified	1.70
Limestone, grey, argillaceous, oolitic, with sparse pisoliths	0.25
Limestone, grey-buff, patchily oolitic, sandy in part; shell fragments and vertical burrows; erosional base, with cross-laminated scour-fill	3.20
LOWER CALCAREOUS GRIT	
Sandstone, buff, calcareous, fine-grained, with shell fragments; grey limestone concretions	0.4

The 'lower leaf' can be traced along Boltby Scar, but the two oolite units come together at the expense of the Birdsall Calcareous Grit, south of this locality, to form a single member overlying the Lower Calcareous Grit (Figure 18). The thinning out of the Birdsall Calcareous Grit can also be traced along Limperdale Gill and Cadell where the 'lower leaf' and the Birdsall Calcareous Grit are exposed at [5279 8658], as follows:

Birdsall Calcareous Grit

	Thickness m
Sandstone, yellow-buff, calcareous, fine-grained, with shells and sparse ooliths; decalcified in part	0.67
Sandstone, buff, fine-grained, calcareous in part; interbedded with grey-buff, slightly oolitic, sandy limestone; *Rhaxella perforata* colonies and siliceous *Thalassinoides* burrowfills present	1.55

Hambleton Oolite, 'lower leaf'

Limestone, grey-buff, thin-bedded, oolitic, with shell fragments and sparse pisoliths	c.11.5

The Birdsall Calcareous Grit wedges out along the escarpment about 1 km to the east of the above exposure, and the undivided Hambleton Oolite Member (about 15 m thick) is exposed adjacent to the track leading to Cadell [5475 8654]. The lateral thinning of the calcareous sandstone facies can also be seen in the track above Yowlass Wood [5223 8746 to 5239 8736] where the sandstone is only 4 m thick and has a higher percentage of ooliths; this bed dies out about 400 m to the east.

The tripartite division of oolitic limestone – calcareous sandstone – oolitic limestone is also present in Low Gill [5495 8573], Tanker Dale [5373 8520], Flassen Dale [530 834], Nettle Dale [552 848] and the deeply dissected valleys near Scawton [548 835].

The following sections in Tanker Dale [5368 8524] and Falling Slack [5424 8530 to 5426 8523] illustrate the lateral and vertical lithological variation of these beds:

Tanker Dale

Hambleton Oolite, 'upper leaf'

Bed No.		Thickness m
3	Limestone, grey, oolitic, shelly, with abundant vertical burrows, oysters and *Nucleolites,* sp.	1.1
2	Sandstone, brown, cross-laminated, medium-grained, with vertical burrows	0.10 – 0.30
1	Sandstone, grey-buff, cross-laminated, with abundant small ooliths and vertical burrows	1.8

About 30 m along the track, bed 1 passes laterally into a grey, cross-bedded, sandy oolite, bed 2 is not present and bed 3 remains unchanged. The Birdsall Calcareous Grit is present below bed 1 in exposures about 40 m to the south-east.

Falling Slack

Hambleton Oolite 'upper leaf'

	Thickness m
Limestone, grey-buff, sandy, with bivalves and abundant vertical burrows	1.0
Limestone, grey, sandy, with small ooliths; cross-bedded; shallow scours	3.1

Birdsall Calcareous Grit

Sandstone, buff, calcareous, fine-grained	c.4.0

Hambleton Oolite 'lower leaf'

Limestone, pinkish-grey, oolitic, with sparse pisoliths	c.4.0

LOWER CALCAREOUS GRIT

Sandstone, yellow, calcareous, fine-grained, with grey sandy limestone beds and concretions	3.0

The pinkish grey colour and large diameter ooliths are typical of the lower oolite in this area, and they serve to distinguish it from the upper oolite; similar sections can be seen in Low Gill, near Old Byland.

The 'lower leaf' increases in thickness from 2 m in Flassen Gill to 3 m near Scawton [5494 8380], and reaches 9.4 m in Scawton Howl Quarry [5561 8419]; the section at the last locality is given below:

Birdsall Calcareous Grit

	Thickness m
Sandstone, buff, fine-grained, calcareous with grey wisps; cross-laminated in part; sparse ooliths	2.5
Siltstone, grey with buff laminae, micaceous	c.0.2
Limestone, grey-buff, sandy, with dark grey silty wisps; small ooliths (decrease in abundance upwards)	0.8

Hambleton Oolite 'lower leaf'

Limestone, grey to pink-grey, oolitic, shelly in top 0.4 m; sparse pisoliths and small pectinid bivalves	4.2
Limestone, buff, variably oolitic, sandy (fine-grained) in part; grey wispy laminae; thick-bedded; sparry matrix in part; sparse bivalves and wood fragments	5.2

LOWER CALCAREOUS GRIT

Sandstone, yellow-buff, fine-grained, medium-bedded (exposed by roadside)	1.6

South of Cold Cam [5424 8136], the upper and lower 'leaves' pass into sandstone facies with sparse ooliths; the oolitic limestone reappears around Duckendale Gill [552 806] and Crief Gill [558 803], but it is thinner here and can be traced only a short distance around the heads of these valleys. The attenuated sequence measured in a forestry track in Ducken Dale [5518 8058 to 5524 8048] is as follows:

Birdsall Calcareous Grit

	Thickness m
Sandstone, yellow, fine-grained, and grey, sandy limestone	4.0

Hambleton Oolite 'lower leaf'

Limestone, buff, oolitic, sandy	3.0

LOWER CALCAREOUS GRIT

Sandstone, yellow, calcareous, fine-grained, with chert concretions	6.7

OXFORD CLAY

Siltstone, olive-grey, calcareous	2.0

The upper oolite was seen in a track above the valley [5518 8068]. It is also exposed in small quarries [5452 8192; 5430 8166; 5490 8200; 5521 8181] adjacent to the A170. The lithology here is pale grey, thin-bedded, cross-bedded (in part), shelly, oolitic limestone (grainstone); burrows are common at some horizons. The upper boundary with the Middle Calcareous Grit is marked by a moderate topographical feature which crosses the A170 near High Lodge [545 818]. Near Scawton and on Scawton Moor [54 83], the upper 'leaf' of the Hambleton Oolite maps out as thin lenses of oolite limestone which pass laterally, over a short distance, into sandstone facies (Birdsall Calcareous Grit). This interdigitation of facies is consistent with an interpretation of the depositional environment as migrating oolite shoals passing south-eastwards into offshore-marine siliciclastic sands; multidirectional cross-bedding azimuths, measured in quarries in this area, suggest that the oolite shoals were influenced by oscillating tidal currents.

An interesting feature of the Hambleton Oolite in the district is the evidence of synsedimentary deformation, manifested as repeated occurrences of slumping and convolute bedding (Plates 7 and 8). This has been described from Shaw's Gate Quarry [5233 8236] and Old Byland Quarry [5454 8567] by Hemingway and Twombley (1963). The sequence (Figure 19) at Shaw's Gate Quarry is described briefly below:

	Thickness m
Hambleton Oolite	
Limestone, grey, oolitic, with small oysters and *Nucleolites* sp.	0.70
Limestone, yellow, sandy, sparsly oolitic	0.32
Limestone, buff, sandy, with sparse ooliths (grainstone) and contorted sandy laminae; erosive base with laminated, siliceous limestone and cross-bedded, calcareous, fine-grained sandstone infilling channels and troughs of slump folds	0.65 – 0.82
Limestone, pale grey, oolitic (grainstone), laminated; shows slump folding, penecontemporaneous faulting and injection into overlying beds	0 – 0.40
Siltstone, buff, calcareous, laminated	0 – 0.50
Limestone, buff, sandy, with sparse ooliths and shell fragments; burrowed in top 0.2 m; grey, sandy oolitic limestone present as slump balls in top 0.5 m	0.55 – 0.70
Limestone, buff, very sandy, with shell fragments and sparse ooliths	0.70
Limestone, buff, sandy, oolitic, with shell fragments; large blocks of contorted siliceous limestone and chert at all angles to bedding	1.20

The slump structures and contorted bedding at discrete intervals have been attributed to repeated seismic shocks displacing pore-waters held in the semilithified sediments (Hemingway and Twombley, 1963). Some of the convoluted sandy beds, particularly the basal bed, have features such as erosive bases and planar, trun-cated, upper bedding surfaces, indicating deposition as submarine debris flows.

MIDDLE CALCAREOUS GRIT MEMBER

This member crops out in the south-east of the Hambleton Hills, on Byland Moor [54 81]. Up to 8 m of the Middle Calcareous Grit are exposed in this area although the maxi-mum thickness is reported to be 12 m (Wright, 1972). Ex-posures are restricted to soil brash of yellow, fine-grained sandstone with sparse ooliths and pisoliths. The rock is decalcified at surface, and only relict ooliths can be seen. The Middle Calcareous Grit is probably present at depth in the Asenby–Coxwold Graben, but it has not been proved in boreholes, nor is it exposed in this area.

The presence of shell beds composed of *Myophorella hudlestoni*, together with *Rhizocorallium* burrows and cross-bedding, noted in exposures adjacent to the district, suggest a high-energy, shallow-marine environment of deposition (Hemingway, 1974). The unit probably belongs to the upper part of the Vertebrale Subzone and the lower part of the Maltonense Subzone (Table 9; Wright, 1980).

CORAL RAG MEMBER

The Malton Oolite Member (up to 20 m thick), which separates the Middle Calcareous Grit from the strati-graphically higher Coral Rag Member (Table 9; Wright, 1972), is not exposed in the district, but it is probably present at depth within the Asenby–Coxwold Graben. At the western end of this structure, the Coral Rag was formerly seen in a small inlier exposed by quarrying of the overlying

Upper Calcareous Grit at Snape Hill Quarry [508 787], but the exposure is now covered by quarry spoil. Fox-Strangways et al. (1886; p.367) recorded upto 1.4 m of Coral Rag ('crystalline limestone') with the coral *Thecosmilia an-nularis*, the echinoid *Hemicidaris florigemma* and the oyster *Lopha gregarea*. In the Hambleton Hills, to the east of the district, Twombley (1964) recognised a similar micrite–biomicrite facies rich in corals, echinoids and bivalves, which he interpreted as a back-reef facies that developed to the north of a reefal boundstone facies typically found in the Howardian Hills.

Upper Calcareous Grit Formation

The Upper Calcareous Grit crops out as an outlier within the Asenby–Coxwold Graben, where it is largely obscured by drift deposits. However, it forms a prominent feature at Snape Hill [50 78], where the formation was formerly quar-ried for lime. The formation is between 12 and 15 m thick, and consists of very fine- to fine-grained, highly calcareous, spiculitic sandstone and siltstone, with abundant beds of clayey, micritic limestone in the middle of the unit; the lowermost shaly beds (Fox-Strangways et al., 1886) are no longer exposed. The clayey carbonate facies is at least 6 m thick and is equivalent to the North Grimston Cementstone facies of Wright (1972; 1980) who assigned it to the Glosense Zone. The overlying siliciclastic members, defined by Wright (1972), comprise, in upward sequence, the Spaunton Sandstone and Snape Sandstone. The former consists of buff, thin-bedded, bioturbated, calcareous sandstone with abundant sponge spicules and siliceous nodules. The fauna includes belemnites and sparse bivalves. About 3.8 m of the Spaunton Sandstone are exposed in Snape Hill Quarry [5091 7868], but the full thickness in the district is unknown because the member is faulted against the overlying Snape Sandstone at this locality. Ammonites collected from the Spaunton Sandstone indicate that it belongs to the Glosense Zone (Wright, 1983; Sykes and Callomon, 1979). The Snape Sandstone Member, about 8 m thick, consists of buff, flaggy, cross-laminated siltstone and fine-grained sandstone with abundant ammonite fragments and, locally, bioclastic limestone. Ammonites collected from the Snape Sandstone indicate the Serratum Zone of the Upper Oxfordian (Wright, 1972; 1980). The boundary with the overlying Up-per Jurassic clays (equivalent to the Ampthill Clay and Kim-meridge Clay formations) is not exposed in the district but boreholes to the east record a burrowed, gradational boun-dary (Cox and Richardson, 1982). The Upper Calcareous Grit was deposited in a shallow-water, nearshore to offshore environment.

DETAILS

Snape Hill

The outcrop of the Upper Calcareous Grit lies close to the northern boundary fault of the Asenby–Coxwold Graben; minor faults associated with this structure and extensive drift cover obscure the stratigraphical relationships in this area. Variable dip directions are the result of fault-drag against the major fault.

The most complete section is in the main Snape Hill Quarry [5091 7868 to 5090 7876], where the calcareous beds were formerly

Bed
number

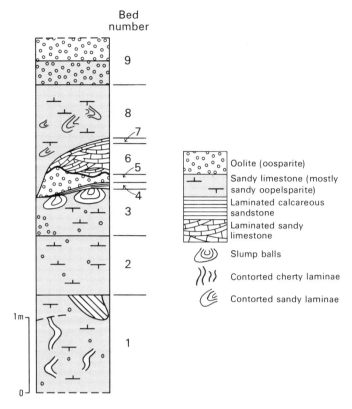

Oolite (oosparite)

Sandy limestone (mostly
sandy oopelsparite)

Laminated calcareous
sandstone

Laminated sandy
limestone

Slump balls

Contorted cherty laminae

Contorted sandy laminae

Figure 19 Generalised vertical section, Shaw's Gate Quarry. Bed numbers correspond to those in Plates 7 and 8.

quarried for lime. However, the section has deteriorated since Fox-Strangways et al. (1886) recorded a 14 m section in the Upper Calcareous Grit overlying the Coral Rag Member; the latter, and the lower shaly part of the Upper Calcareous Grit, are presently obscured by quarry spoil, but the upper part of the sequence is exposed as follows:

	Thickness m
UPPER CALCAREOUS GRIT	
Snape Sandstone Member	
Sandstone, buff, medium-bedded, and flaggy, thin-bedded, fine-grained, calcareous, spiculitic sandstone, with grey wispy laminae; cross-laminated in part; bivalves and small belemnites present; sparse burrows; gradational base	4.7
Faulted section	
Spaunton Sandstone Member	
Sandstone, buff, thin bedded, calcareous, cross-laminated in part, with abundant sponge spicules and siliceous nodules; abundant belemnites; sparse bivalves	3.8
North Grimston Cementstone Member	
Limestone, pale grey, flaggy-bedded, micritic, interbedded with harder beds of dark grey, clayey micrite; sparse ammonite fragments; irregular, undulating base	2.20
Limestone, dark grey, argillaceous; alternating harder, calcareous spiculite beds and flaggy argillaceous beds	2.90

Below these beds, Fox-Strangways et al., (1886) recorded 2.5 to 3.0 m of shaly beds (hidden by talus) overlying about 1.4 m of the Coral Rag Member (Coralline Oolite Formation).

On the south side of Snape Hill, a small disused quarry [5060 7841] exposes about 4 m of buff, thick-bedded, locally cross-bedded, calcareous sandstone exhibiting grey wispy laminae and ripple cross-lamination; small bivalve moulds and ammonite fragments are present. These beds are probably equivalent to the uppermost unit in the main quarry. Small overgrown quarries nearby, in Snape Wood, expose grey, flaggy, ripple cross-laminated, calcareous siltstones with sparse oysters [5075 7858] and grey, oolitic spiculitic limestone [5074 7870], but the stratigraphical relationship of these scattered exposures is obscure.

To the south-west of Snape Hill, fragments of dark grey siltstone and fine-grained sandstone with orange goethitic flecks, and buff calcareous sandstone with ammonite and bivalve fragments, are exposed as soil brash at a number of scattered localities [5074 7838; 5104 7863; 5107 7861]. These beds are stratigraphically higher than the uppermost beds exposed in Snape Hill Quarry and have yielded the ammonites *Amoeboceras* sp. and *Perisphinctes* sp., indicating the Glosense Zone; they are included in the Snape Sandstone Member.

To the north-west of Snape Hill, a small quarry [5114 7877] exposes mound-like masses (up to 1 m high) of rubbly bioclastic limestone (grainstone) consisting of abraded, subrounded fragments of spiculitic, oolitic limestone, along with bivalves, gastropods, ammonites and sparse lamellar corals. Many of the fossils are replaced by opaline silica which is also present both as fine veins and infilling calcite vugs; the silica is probably derived from disolution of sponge spicules. Beds infilling the area between the mounds comprise brown-orange, calcareous sandstone intercalated with grey siltstone containing sparse belemnite voids; these beds are draped against the margins of the mounds. This unique exposure probably represents small banks of carbonate debris eroded from the nearshore zone and transported offshore by storms. Subsequently, the slacks between the banks were infilled by siliciclastics during fair-weather sedimentation. Ammonites collected from the bioclastic limestone include *Amoeboceras* spp. (including *A.* cf. *regulare* Spath and *A. mansoni* Pringle) and *Perisphinctes* sp., together with *Dentalium* sp. and pectinid bivalves, indicating the Serratum Zone. These beds are included within the Snape Sandstone but their precise stratigraphical relationship with the beds exposed in Snape Hill Quarry is uncertain.

Ampthill Clay and Kimmeridge Clay formations (undifferentiated)

The **Kimmeridge Clay** is the youngest Jurassic formation in the district (Table 9) and it crops out in the east of the Asenby–Coxwold Graben, where it forms low ground largely covered by drift deposits. The formation is intermittently exposed below the till near Low Pasture House [5540 7830] and at Brink Hill [540 786], where soil brash consisting of dark grey, fissile mudstone with yellow-brown weathering, organic-rich laminae is exposed in the back-scars of small landslips (mud flows) [5420 7847; 5409 7844; 5419 7845; 5420 7863]. Abundant small "*Discinisca latissima*" and ammonite fragments are preserved in some beds. Comparison of this organic-rich fissile mudstone (oil shale) with the Kimmeridge Clay sequences recorded in boreholes in the Vale of Pickering and the southern North Sea (Cox et al., 1987) suggests that the beds at Brink Hill are younger than the Eudoxus Zone, but their precise age is uncertain.

The total thickness of the Kimmeridge Clay in the district is not certainly known, but a borehole at Low Pasture House [5521 7836] penetrated 121 m of the formation without reaching the base (Fox-Strangways et al., 1886). The Fordon No. 1 Borehole (Falcon and Kent, 1960), sunk about 50 km to the east of the district, proved 385 m of Kimmeridge Clay, but this figure has been questioned by Cox et al. (1987) who suggest that the total thickness of the formation in the Vale of Pickering, to the east of the district, is about 305 m.

In the Cleveland Basin, the Kimmeridge Clay was formerly thought to directly overlie the Upper Calcareous Grit (Corallian Group), but recent studies of outcrops and borehole cores from the western end of the Vale of Pickering (Institute of Geological Sciences, 1974; Pyrah, 1977; Cox and Richardson, 1982) demonstrate that mudstone with subsidiary beds and nodules of siderite (c.48 m thick), equivalent to the Ampthill Clay of southern England and spanning the Serratum, Regulare and Rosenkrantzi zones (Table 9; Upper Oxfordian), are present between the top of the Corallian Group and the base of the Kimmeridge Clay. A similar thickness of Ampthill Clay is probably present, at depth, in the Asenby–Coxwold Graben.

The marked change in lithofacies from shallow-water carbonates and nearshore siliciclastics, represented by the Upper Calcareous Grit, to offshore mudstones with thin carbonate beds and nodules passing upwards to organic-rich mudstones, represented by the Ampthill Clay and Kimmeridge Clay, respectively, reflects subsidence of the Cleveland Basin and deeper-water conditions during Late Oxfordian and Kimmeridgian times. Restricted circulation and high organic productivity in the Tethys Ocean during the late Kimmeridgian (post-Eudoxus Zone) led to deposition and preservation under anoxic bottom conditions of organic phytoplankton, which on later burial in the North Sea Basin generated hydrocarbons (Gallois, 1976).

SIX

Quaternary

About 80 per cent of the Thirsk district is mantled by Quaternary (drift) deposits, the bulk of which are of glacial origin and which were deposited during the late Devensian cold stage (approximately 18 000 to 10 000 years ago) (Penny, 1974; Rose, 1985; Bowen et al., 1986). Older (pre-Devensian) deposits may also be present in buried valleys. Flandrian sediments locally overlie the Devensian deposits and modify the postglacial topography.

The fluctuating advance and retreat of the Devensian ice sheet in the Vale of York resulted in a complicated sequence of glacial deposits (Table 10, Figures 20 and 21). As the ice sheet melted and retreated, it left behind associations of sub- and englacial facies such as till (boulder clay) and elongate ridges of glacial sand and gravel (eskers). Stillstands of the ice during its retreat resulted in associations of marginal facies, including terminal moraines (Figure 21). Fluvio-glacial terrace deposits (sandurs) and glacial lake deposits rest upon the earlier glacial deposits, which remained, in places, as emergent topographical features. Along the western margin of the district the picture is locally further complicated by deposits from the Yorkshire Dales glaciers which approached the main Vale of York ice sheet from the west.

The highest elevation of the glacial deposits in the district is about 230 m above OD. Consequently, most of the Hambleton Hills are free of glacial drift. The distribution of the glacial sediments indicates that the ice-sheet was diverted southwards around the foot of the escarpment, leaving the outliers of Woolmoor and Hood Hill (252 m above OD) above the ice sheet. South of Kilburn, the ice sheet moved south-eastwards towards the low ground of the Cox-south-eastwards towards the low ground of the Cox-wold–Gilling Gap and terminated at the Ampleforth moraine [57 77], at the western end of the Vale of Pickering (Penny 1974). Many Middle Jurassic outliers, such as Oldstead, Kilburn, Skipton Hill and Kirkby Knowle, are separated from the main escarpment by narrow, steep-sided valleys. These represent the sites of former marginal glacial channels, which were probably eroded by both the ice sheet and the marginal streams flowing between the stagnating ice and the escarpment.

The subdivision of drift deposits in the district is broadly based on their lithology, but, where possible, they are further subdivided by their morphology and/or stratigraphical position (Table 10; Figure 20). Thus, several generations of sand and gravel (pp.73–79) can be distinguished, even though they may be lithologically similar (Figure 20). The geology of the drift, particularly the sand and gravel deposits, is described in more detail in other BGS publications (Benfield, 1983; Cooper, 1983; Benfield and Cooper, 1983; Powell, 1983; Giles, 1982; Morigi and James, 1984; Strong and Giles, 1983).

Sand and gravel of unknown age (in buried valleys)

During the Devensian and earlier glaciations, the sea level was substantially lower than at present (Gaunt et al., 1974; Gaunt, 1981), resulting in fluvial erosion to well below Ordnance Datum. The rockhead contour map on the 1:50 000 scale map reveals a pattern of buried valleys, the deepest of which approximate to the present-day courses of the Rivers Ure and Swale.

Table 10 Outline of the classification of glacial deposits in the district.

Lithology	Deposit	Landform	Evironment of deposition
Till and sandy till (mixtite)	Till and sandy till (boulder clay)	Hummocky terrain and morainic ridges	Subglacial (lodgement till) and supraglacial (melt-out and flow tills)
Sand and gravel	Sand and Gravel of Unknown Age (in buried valleys)	Infilling buried valleys (proven in boreholes)	Fluvial? subglacial?
	Glacial Sand and Gravel	Elongate ridges (eskers)	Supra-, en- and subglacial streams
	Fluvioglacial Sand and Gravel	Broad spreads and ridges	Outwash fans, proglacial rivers draining to lakes and ice-marginal streams
	Glacial Lake Sand and Gravel	Very broad, flat spreads and low sand ridges	Shallow lakes and rivers entering lakes; dispersal by storm-generated currents and turbidity currents
	Fluvioglacial Terrace Deposits	Flat-topped terraces	Rivers in proglacial areas
Clay and silt (mostly laminated)	Laminated Clay closely associated with glacial deposits	Flat areas associated with eskers	Englacial ponds?
	Glacial Lake Clay	Flat or gently undulating	Deeper water, distal parts of lakes

Figure 20 Generalised temporal relationships of the Quaternary deposits in the Thirsk district.

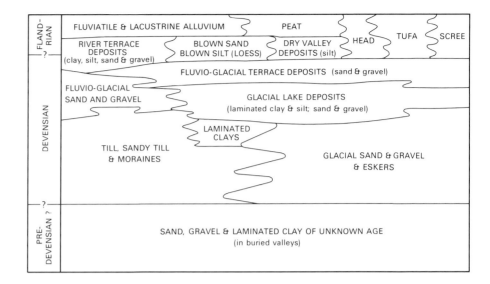

The buried valleys have a sinuous north-north-west–south-south-east trend (Figure 21) and are filled with sand and gravel, with subordinate lenses of faintly laminated silt and clay. These deposits are overlain by Devensian till, which, in samples from a borehole [4098 7604] west of Dalton, included clasts of the underlying laminated clay near the base. Such deposits predate the Devensian till, but are otherwise undated, although deposits of Ipswichian age have been recorded from similar buried valleys in the southern Vale of York (Gaunt et al., 1974).

In the Thirsk district, the sub-till deposits have been proved only in boreholes (Benfield, 1983; Cooper, 1983; Morigi and James, 1984); about 18 m of laminated clay, sand and gravel were recorded in a borehole west of Dalton [4098 7604]. The gravel clasts predominantly consist of Carboniferous sandstone and limestone, with sporadic clasts of chert and Triassic sandstone, which are locally abundant in basal deposits; Magnesian Limestone clasts are locally abundant in the west of the district. Buried-valley sand and gravel deposits in the 'proto'-Ure at Ripon (Figure 21) are proximal to lake deposits occurring further south, in the Harrogate district (British Geological Survey, 1987). The lakes were impounded when the eastward drainage of the 'proto'-Ure was blocked by the southerly advance of the Devensian ice sheet down the Vale of York (British Geological Survey, 1987). As the ice advanced further south, it overrode these earlier deposits which were subsequently buried by the Devensian till and sandy till.

Till, sandy till and moraines

In contrast to the Harrogate district, to the south (British Geological Survey, 1987), there are few lithofacies associations illustrating the advance of the Devensian ice sheet in the Thirsk district. The majority of the area is covered by a blanket of till and sandy till within which only features relating to the retreat of the Devensian ice sheet are distinguishable. The till sheet has a proved maximum thickness of 30 m at Low House [4446 8961], but is generally between 8 and 10 m thick. The base of the till is well exposed in only a few places. Generally, where the till rests on hard

rock, such as the Permian limestones or Middle Marl gypsum, the contact is sharp, but where it overlies soft mudstone and sandstone the junction is commonly diffuse. It rests on the Lower Magnesian Limestone at North Stainley [2852 7780], where the bedrock is grooved with glacial striae, suggesting ice movement towards the south-east.

Both till with a dominantly clay matrix and sandy till, in which the matrix ranges from very sandy clay to sand, occur in the district. However, due to their diffuse, gradational boundaries it has not been possible to map a boundary between them. Till is common over the more argillaceous types of bedrock, such as the Mercia Mudstone and the mudstones of the Lias Group, and the colour of the till matrix generally reflects that of the local bedrock. Red-brown, sandy till predominates where Sherwood Sandstone forms the bedrock.

The clasts in the till range in size from granules, through pebbles and cobbles, to boulders; they are commonly rounded to subrounded and show signs of glacial abrasion such as scratch marks, pitting and polishing. In the west of the district, the clasts mainly consist of Carboniferous limestone and some chert. Permian dolomite and dolomitic limestone is locally abundant, especially where the Magnesian Limestone forms the bedrock. Similarly, Triassic sandstone fragments are generally restricted to the sandy till where it overlies the Sherwood Sandstone bedrock. In the north-east of the district, the lithology of the erratics is more variable; they include Sherwood Sandstone, Jurassic limestones, sandstones (indeterminate), chert and ironstone; also Carboniferous limestone, which is relatively scarce. Far-travelled erratics of Shap Granite, tuff, basalt, haematite, jasper and metamorphic rocks are present sporadically throughout the district.

Much of the till and sandy till has an undulating to slightly hummocky topography, which reflects its depositional history as a complex of tills, some deposited as lodgement till during ice advance and others representing melt-out and flow tills derived from a stagnating ice sheet (Table 10). However, in some areas, marked topographical ridges of till, sandy till and glacial sand and gravel, which locally contain a high proportion of boulders, rise above the surrounding till plains and represent moraines. The approximate margins of

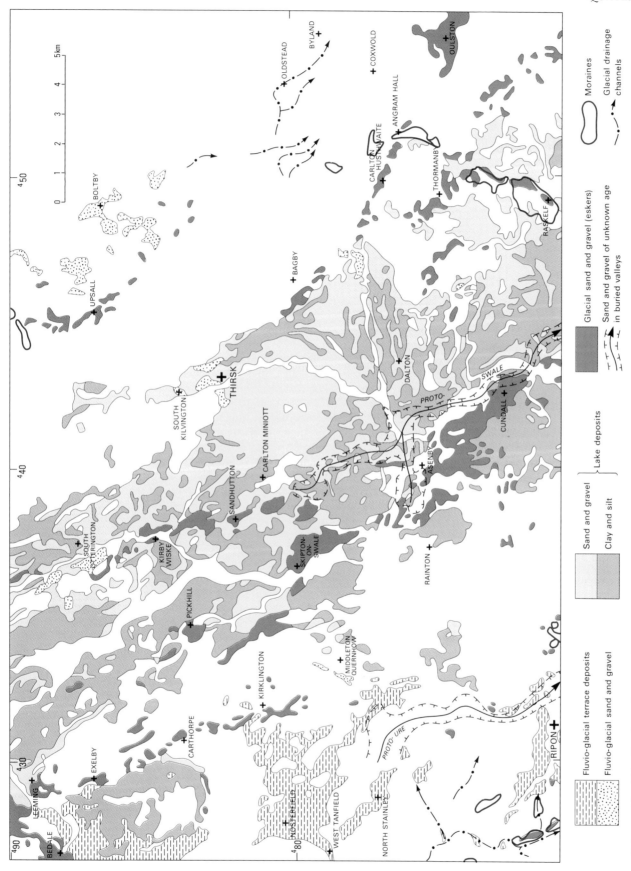

Figure 21   Distribution of exposed sand and gravel deposits of glacial origin. Based on Benfield (1983), Benfield and Cooper (1983), Cooper (1983) and Powell (1983a).

these landforms are outlined in green on the map and are shown in Figure 21. They are developed intermittently across the southern part of the district between Angram Hall [516 762] and Raskelf [490 710], around Copt Hewick [344 709] and between Low Lindrick [275 714] and Azerly Tower [266 741]. The moraines represent the products of deposition at the ice margin during stillstand phases as the Devensian ice sheet waned. Similar moraines cross the Harrogate (62) district to the south, and they trend broadly parallel to the main York and Eskrick moraines (Penny 1974). In the Thirsk district, lateral moraines west of Ripon are paralleled by deep valleys (some of them dry) marking former diversions of drainage around the edge of the Vale of York ice sheet (Figure 21) (Kendall and Wroot, 1924; British Geological Survey, 1987). Thieves Gill [275 741] was probably cut by diversion of the River Ure around the edge of the ice. The ice-marginal stream may have flowed south-westwards along the upper course of the Laver valley to join the marginal drainage system to the north of Harrogate (British Geological Survey, 1987). Alternatively, at a later stage, it may have been diverted eastwards from Ellington Banks along the present lower course of the Laver, in which case the glacial diversion of the 'proto'-Ure could have been responsible for the deposition of the fluvioglacial terrace deposits around the western edge of Ripon.

Similar marginal glacial channels are present along the foot of the Hambleton Hills escarpment, where the ice sheet scoured out a number of steep-sided channels to leave outliers such as Woolmoor, Skipton Hill, Hood Hill and Oldstead. Some of these channels were probably accentuated by fluvial erosion in streams flowing between the ice margin and the main escarpment. Incised valleys are present at Southwood Hall [5010 8440], near Rose Cottage [502 803], near Acre House [512 804] and between Oldstead [522 801] and Oldstead Hall [532 803].

Glacial sand and gravel

In the district, glacial sand and gravel, intimately associated with till, occurs in bodies ranging in size from small lenses to spreads up to several square kilometres in extent. However, the greater part of the glacial sand and gravel occurs within a series of south-south-east-trending eskers, which extend across the whole district (Figure 21). These commonly form steep-sided, sharp-crested ridges, slightly anastomosing in plan, which rise up 10 to 20 m above the surrounding country. The approximate boundaries of these landforms are shown edged in pink on the 1:50 000 map.

The lithology of the eskers mainly comprises moderately well-sorted, fine-grained sand, although all gradations from silt to boulder-gravel are present (Plate 9). The sand grades into, and interfingers with laminated clay. The lithological composition of the gravel clasts is similar to those of the till. In some 'shell and auger' boreholes "clayey" and "very-clayey" sands have been recorded (Morigi and James, 1984); it seems likely that these represent interbedded sands and clays which resulted from the marked variation in discharge typical of glacial streams.

The sands exhibit a wide range of sedimentary structures. Cross-stratification is common, and ripple marks, ripple cross-lamination, slumping and load casts also occur (Plate

9). The morphology and sedimentological characteristics of these deposits suggest deposition in a glaciofluvial environment, either within valleys cut into the surface of the ice sheet, or in tunnels under or within the ice (Banerjee and McDonald, 1975). Subsequent melting of the ice has largely inverted the topography, leaving the sand and gravel as upstanding ridges or eskers. Evidence for the removal of ice support comes from the disruption, slumping, minor faulting and tilting of bedding and other sedimentary structures (Plate 9).

The most westerly of these eskers extends southwards from the Northallerton district (Lovell, 1982), through Leeming [283 895], to Sutton Howgrave [321 800]. The 'beaded' ridges of sand and gravel are narrow (up to about 300 m wide and 1.5 km long). Near Carthorpe, a small pit [3130 8327] exposed beds of coarse gravel and boulders with channelled bases, interbedded with both ripple-marked and cross-laminated sand, and minor amounts of laminated clay, the whole totalling 3.5 m; the whole sequence shows signs of slumping and minor faulting, probably resulting from collapse due to the melting of supporting ice. The gravel component of this esker is dominantly of Carboniferous sandstone, though, in places, Carboniferous limestone forms almost half the pebble content; Permian limestone is also present but does not generally occur in the more easterly deposits (Giles, 1982; Benfield and Cooper, 1983).

The most extensive glacial sand and gravel deposits in the district occur within a major south-south-east-trending esker complex, which traverses the whole district from near Newby Wiske [362 897] in the north to Cundall [437 708] in the south (Figure 21). A western spur extends southwards from Leeming Airfield [310 885], where it is mainly covered by younger deposits, to join the main deposit near Asenby [397 754]. The lithology mainly comprises red-brown and red, fine- to medium-grained sand, with beds of coarse-grained sand and fine to coarse gravel; beds of red-brown laminated clay and sandy clay are interbedded with the sands. The gravel component of these deposits is mainly of Carboniferous sandstone, with between 10 and 50 per cent of Carboniferous limestone, and sporadic far-travelled pebbles. Cross-bedding and channelling are the most common sedimentary structures. Removal of ice support resulted in syn-sedimentary deformation such as slumping and micro-faulting. Further details of these deposits are given by Cooper (1983), Benfield (1983), Benfield and Cooper (1983) and Morigi and James (1984).

The Newby Wiske – Cundall esker is continuous with the Helperby – Aldwark Moor – Linton on Ouse belt of sand and gravel in the Harrogate district, to the south (British Geological Survey, 1987), which extends southwards into a well-developed esker-like ridge between the moraines at York and Eskrick. It is suggested that, as the Devensian ice sheet retreated, the main drainage route remained fairly constant through time, resulting in the creation of a linear esker complex over 55 km long, through several ice retreat stages.

In the east of the district, several minor sand and gravel deposits occur. The most northerly is situated at the margin of the thick drift of the Vale of York from near Altay Field Farm [451 892] to near Thirlby [491 835] (Powell, 1983). This deposit is generally poorly exposed, but a small pit near

Plate 9 Glacial sand and gravel exposed in an esker. Firtree Hill Gravel Pit, Cundall (L3085).

Thirlby revealed 2 m of mainly locally derived sandy gravel; the pebbles include Lias Group mudstones along with Jurassic sandstone, limestone and ironstone. Sporadic, exotic clasts such as basalt, tuff and Carboniferous crinoidal limestone also occur.

Similar broad tracts of red-brown sandy gravel, locally developed into esker-like ridges, occur around Oulston [545 745]. Thornton Hill Gravel Pit [5342 7465] is situated at the western end of an esker ridge and exposes about 6 m of red-brown, clayey sand with rounded to subrounded pebbles, cobbles and sparse boulders including quartzite, sandstone, chert, Jurassic limestone and Carboniferous limestone.

In the south-east of the district, scattered patches of glacial sand and gravel occur between Bagby [459 797] and Carlton Husthwaite [500 768], and also around Little Sessay [466 750] and Thormanby [491 750]. They largely consist of orange-brown, fine-grained sand with sparse pebbles (Benfield, 1983).

Some of the glacial sand and gravel deposits are associated with moraines; at Raskelf, a borehole [4969 7156] drilled on the crest of a moraine penetrated 4.4 m of sandy gravel. In other morainic complexes, for example at Low Lindrick [2755 7237], unbedded masses of pebbles, cobbles and boulders with a sandy clay matrix, similar to the local till, have been mapped as glacial sand and gravel, although, in sections, this type of deposit could be classed as gravelly till.

Laminated clay closely associated with glacial deposits

Dark yellowish brown to greyish brown, laminated clays with laminae of fine-grained sand and silt, and sporadic pebbles, occur within the main esker complex at Poplar Hill [404 747], Asenby, and south of Thornton Manor [430 715] (Benfield, 1983; Morigi and James, 1984). They were probably deposited in the same glacial environment as the glacial sand and gravel within the eskers, but at times when current flows diminished, probably due to winter freeze-up.

Glacial lake deposits (including penecontemporaneous fluviatile deposits)

Clays, silts and sands of glaciolacustrine origin occur largely in a broad south-south-east-trending tract in the central part of the district (Figure 21). They mainly formed during the late stagnation and melting stages of the Vale of York ice sheet and were deposited on the earlier glacial deposits in widespread glacial lakes impounded by the moraines to the south. Consequently, the deposits were laid down between and around areas of hummocky and undulating glacial drift; the result is an intricate patchwork of deposits which vary considerably in thickness over short distances. The glacial lake deposits generally have a distinctive flat morphology, but commonly rise gently upwards around the former lake margins. In some places, undulating areas of lake deposits attest to deposition over stagnant ice which subsequently melted.

The silt and clay, much of which is finely laminated, were deposited in the still water of relatively deep glacial lakes. Where meltwater drainage entered the lakes, fluvioglacial terrace deposits and deposits of fluvioglacial sand and gravel were formed; these pass distally into sand, then silt and clay of glacial lake origin. As lake levels fell, these streams introduced sand further into the lakes, so that it was ultimately spread across the former lake beds by a combination of lacustrine and fluviatile processes. The generally flat terrain of the lake deposits is sporadically broken by low sandy ridges whose topography has been emphasised by the effects of differential compaction.

Silt and clay form the bulk of the glacial lake sediments. They comprise dark grey, grey-brown and brown laminated clay in layers generally 1 to 4 mm thick, with laminae and, more rarely, very thin beds of silt and very fine-grained sand. These laminated sediments are typical of varved deposits, in which successive silt/clay units represent annual cycles of sedimentation, the silt deposited by the summer meltwater influx, the clay by the winter settling-out of the fine suspended material. The lamination is generally sub-horizontal, but may occur as drapes over irregularities such as the sporadic ripple-marked beds of fine-grained sand locally present in the sequence.

The silts and clays reach a thickness of 21.6 m in a borehole north-east of Brafferton [4439 7118] (Benfield 1983; Morigi and James, 1984), but are generally 3 to 8 m thick. A thick sequence of laminated silt and clay occupies the major bedrock depression of Snape Mires near Bedale (Giles, 1982), where boreholes proved up to 26 m of these deposits. This depression appears to have been caused by subsidence after the removal, by dissolution, of gypsum from the Middle and Upper Permian Marls. This was partly synchronous with the deposition of the laminated clays and silts, and, consequently, in the northern part of the Snape Mires, the lake deposits are not flat, but form a series of low ridges, commonly bounded by later peat deposits (chapter three; Cooper, 1986).

Glacial laminated silts and clays may present problems of poor ground conditions to foundation engineers. These deposits are generally evenly bedded and have a high water content. Their shear strength is low and they are highly compressible; thus problems of excessive settlement and bearing-capacity failure may occur. The common occurrence of interbedded, water-bearing, fine-grained sands may lead to instability at low angles of slope; these sands also run into excavations, which would require close shuttering. Heave, resulting from the unloading of these deposits at the base of deep excavations, or due to artesian water below thin clay, may also be a problem.

Sand and gravel commonly overlies the laminated silts and clays. In the north-east of the district, sand and gravel covers approximately 80 per cent of the area of glacial lake deposits (Figure 21) and comprises yellow or red-brown, fine- to medium-grained sand, locally with pebbly sand (Powell, 1983). The areal percentage of sand and gravel decreases to the south and west, so that in the Dalton and Pickhill areas it is about 50 per cent (Benfield, 1983; Benfield and Cooper, 1983), dropping to 15 per cent to the north-east of Ripon (Cooper, 1983).

Around Thirsk, there is a decreasing trend of both grain size and thickness to the south and west, ranging from pebbly coarse-grained sand overlying clayey fine-grained sand (total 8 m thick) to fine-grained clayey sand (about 2 m thick). The grain-size trend and the slightly hummocky morphology of some of the coarse-grained deposits suggests deposition from streams discharging sediment along a broad, south-westerly prograding lacustrine delta. The close spatial association of the coarser-grained deposits with ridges of fluvioglacial sand and gravel at Norby [425 825], north-west of Thirsk, suggests that there was a passage from fluviatile to lacustrine deposition across the area (Powell, 1983).

Less commonly, sand may be interbedded with, or lie below the lacustrine silts and clays. These occurrences may be the result of reworking and lakeward dispersal of proximal sand by either wave action or sediment-charged turbidity currents. In a few places, sand and gravel probably represents a local reworking of adjacent till or glacial sand and gravel at the lake margins. However, many of the sand bodies are isolated from an obvious source material and may have formed as penecontemporaneous fluviatile deposits laid down immediately after the glacial lakes drained.

Fluvioglacial sand and gravel

Fluvioglacial sand and gravel occurs in three slightly different settings across the district (Figure 21). First, in the north, around Middleton Quernhow [329 783] (Cooper, 1983; Morigi and James, 1984) and near Newby Wiske [363 885] (Benfield and Cooper, 1983) the deposits form broadly rounded, elongate ridges. These overlie, and clearly postdate the till or glacial sand and gravel; their steep-sided morphology suggests that they were laid down as streams of outwash in ice-bounded areas. These deposits comprise yellow-brown, fine-grained sand with small pebbles at Newby Wiske, and red and red-brown gravelly sand with abundant pebbles, cobbles and a few boulders around Middleton Quernhow.

The second occurrence of fluvioglacial sand and gravel, in the north-east of the district, is associated with the escarpment and steep-sided valleys of the Hambleton Hills (Powell, 1983). The deposits commonly have a sloping, roughly terrace-like form with steep sides, and their sedimentary structures include cross-bedding and upward-fining cycles. They comprise red-brown gravel with thin lenses of medium- and coarse-grained sand; the clasts are mainly of locally derived Jurassic sandstone, ironstone, limestone and siltstone, with a few pebbles of Carboniferous limestone and

Shap Granite. The grain size, lithology, sedimentary structures and morphology of the deposits suggest deposition from streams flowing in marginal channels between the degrading ice-sheet and the escarpment. The deposits near Kirby Knowle [470 875] and Boltby [490 866] are situated at valley-widening points, where sediment-laden streams may have debouched their bedloads because of the reduced current velocity (Powell, 1983).

The third occurrence is associated with glacial lake deposits on the northern outskirts of Thirsk [430 830], where fluvioglacial sand and gravel, marginal to glacial lake deposits, forms broad ridges of red-brown sandy gravel. The morphology of these deposits and evidence from a ditch section [4417 8230], where sandy gravel rests on glaciolacustrine sand, suggest deposition from streams flowing into a late-stage glacial lake (Powell, 1983). A similar mode of origin was suggested by Benfield (1983) for the deposit of orange-brown, pebbly, fine- to medium-grained sand and sandy gravel south of Thirkleby [472 776], which was probably laid down where a stream flowing south through the deep valley occupied by Thirkleby Beck debouched into a glacial lake. A small deposit south-west of Little Sessay [463 742] occurs in a valley between two areas of lake deposits and may have resulted from flow between the two lakes.

Fluvioglacial terrace deposits, undifferentiated

Fluvioglacial terrace deposits occur mainly in the west of the district, where drainage from the Pennine ('Dales') glaciers entered the Vale of York (Figure 21). This drainage system cut deep channels (many of which are now dry) where it interacted with the western margin of the Vale of York ice-sheet; it also deposited spreads of sand and gravel in the wider parts of the valleys and in front of the ice-sheet. These deposits are generally gravelly and form the highest, almost flat-topped terraces along the valleys. The marginal channels and fluvioglacial terraces show a progression northwards which follows the retreat stages of the ice sheet.

When the valley of the River Ure was blocked by the Vale of York ice sheet, water flowed southwards along Thieves Gill [275 742]; from here it probably drained south-west along the Laver Valley, south-east through Spa Gill, and then southwards past Sawley Hall to join the marginal drainage of the Harrogate district (Kendall and Wroot, 1924; Edwards, 1938; Cooper and Burgess, in press). The marked channel from near Galphay Mill, past Low Lindrick and through Studley Park to the Skell valley may also be part of this system; alternatively it may be a subglacial channel.

As the ice sheet retreated, it allowed the drainage in these marginal channels to escape eastwards into the Vale of York. Initially, the Skell valley was incised, and the sand and gravel terrace extending from Studley Roger [290 700] to Ripon was deposited at its mouth. Further regression of the ice and reopening of the Laver valley resulted in the deposition of the sand and gravel terraces extending southeastwards from Clotherholme Farm [285 720], through Ripon, to near Sharrow [325 715], where the Ure Valley was blocked by gravel deposits. These terraces are proximal to glacial lake deposits in the Harrogate district to the south (British Geological Survey, 1987) and may have also impounded a glacial lake to the north where laminated clay was deposited. The Laver and Skell fluvioglacial terrace deposits are sandy gravels in which Carboniferous limestone and sandstone are the predominant gravel components, although clasts of Magnesian Limestone are also common. Sections at Atkinsons Quarry [3065 7055] show abundant cross-bedding and channel structures, indicative of deposition in a braided-channel or sandur environment.

As the Vale of York ice sheet retreated further northwards, the marginal drainage abandoned the Laver and briefly escaped from Thieves Gill eastwards to Castle Dykes [292 757], where a small gravel terrace was deposited. This brief episode ended when the ice front retreated again, thereby unblocking the Ure Valley near West Tanfield. At the mouth of the Hack Fall Gorge, extensive outwash from the Ure was deposited around West Tanfield and Nosterfield [280 795] (Giles, 1982; Strong and Giles, 1983). This outwash was laid down in an area of undulating till where several elongate till ridges isolate ribbon-like terraces of sand and gravel. These terrace deposits are up to 9 m thick and extend as far east as Kirklington and south to Wath. Along much of the Ure Valley, the river has eroded the earlier terraces so that only small relict areas remain (Cooper, 1983; Morigi and James, 1984).

Lithologically, the Ure Valley deposits are similar to those of the Laver and Skell. Sections near West Tanfield [2763 7959; 2819 7945] show cross-bedding, channelling and probable ice wedges, suggesting deposition in a braided channel or sandur environment. At this time the Ure Valley was still blocked near Sharow [323 715] by the Laver and Skell gravels; consequently, the river bypassed the obstruction and cut a deep channel running eastwards past Sharow [328 716].

In the north-west of the district, between Snape [270 844] and Bedale [275 875], there is a flat sand and gravel terrace which skirts the west of Snape Mires and, adjacent to Bedale Beck, extends north-eastwards almost to Leeming [283 887] (Giles, 1982). A small area of the same fluvioglacial terrace is also present near Burneston [300 848] to the east of Snape Mires. The fluvioglacial terrace deposits of the Snape Mires area rest, in places, on glacial lake deposits, and formerly they probably extended over most of this area. However, much of the terrace has foundered due to the dissolution of gypsum in the Permian rocks below (chapter three), leaving only small relict outliers of sand and gravel, and depressions which later filled with lacustrine clay and peat (Giles, 1982; Cooper, 1986).

River terrace deposits, undifferentiated

As the Devensian glaciation drew to a close, the ice melted from the Vale of York and surrounding areas, the glacial lakes drained and the rivers established their present drainage pattern. This was largely controlled by both the existing bedrock and the glacial features. The River Swale flowed across, and incised into, the low-lying glacial lake deposits. These deposits, being largely of silt, sand and clay, were mainly eroded away and very few river terraces flank the river; the few that remain are of clayey and silty sand. Isolated terraces of clayey sand overlying clayey sand and gravel also occur along a tributary of the Swale, the Cod Beck, near Thornton-le-Street.

In contrast, the River Ure and its tributaries, the Laver and the Skell, cut down through extensive fluvioglacial terrace deposits. These rivers reworked pre-existing sand and gravel and redeposited it as extensive trains of terraces. These flank the river alluvium at various heights above the present floodplain, but at a lower level than the fluvioglacial terraces. The higher terraces of the Ure, Laver and Skell generally consist of sandy gravel, but in the lower terraces, up to 2 m of silt and clay, representing overbank deposits, rest on 5 m of sandy gravel.

Blown sand

Blown sand in the Thirsk district is largely associated with sand of glacial lake origin from which much of it was derived. Minor amounts are also associated with the Sherwood Sandstone outcrop and sandy till in the south of the district. Aeolian sand is most widespread along the east of the Vale of York, reflecting its transport by prevailing westerly winds. The blown sand varies from red-brown to yellow in colour, and is mostly well sorted; it is generally less than 2 m thick. Similar blown sand, to the south-east of the district at East Moor [608 640], overlies peat and organic-rich soil from which late Devensian to early Flandrian radiocarbon ages of 10 700 to 9950 years BP have been obtained (Matthews, 1970).

Blown silt (loess)

A small patch of structureless, yellow-brown silt resting on Hambleton Oolite occurs at the top of the Jurassic escarpment [499 898]. Its situation and grain-size characteristics suggest that this deposit is loess (windblown silt) (Catt et al., 1974); it was probably transported by the prevailing westerly winds, which picked up silt as they blew across the glacial deposits occupying the lower ground to the west. The following section was exposed in a forestry track on Dale Town Common [5001 8962]:

Peaty soil	0.03
Silt, yellow, mottled, slightly laminated, sandy at base	0.55
Silt, buff, with iron-stained laminae	0.09
Silt, pale buff, with clayey silt above	0.10
Sand, grey, brown, very fine-grained, mottled	0.13
Oolitic limestone bedrock	0.10

Scree

This deposit consists of angular fragments derived by weathering of exposed rock faces, probably under intense frost action, which have collected at the foot of steep slopes. It occurs most commonly below cliff faces at the top of the main Upper Jurassic escarpment, for example at Roulston Scar [511 826], but it is also found along the steep-sided valleys in the north-east of the district.

Since the Upper Jurassic Hambleton Oolite and Lower Calcareous Grit together form the majority of the steep scarp faces, debris from these formations make up most of the scree material. Scree has been mapped only where there is an appreciable thickness covering the bedrock. The most significant deposits are found at Plumpton Wood [5396 8867],

near Hawnby, Sunny Bank [5330 8888], Cliff Wood [5460 8876] and Wass House [5567 8996]. The deposits at Plumpton Wood and Wass House have been worked, locally, for road metal. Some of the scree is cemented by calcareous tufa, deposited by carbonated springs issuing from the base of the much fissured Lower Calcareous Grit.

Head

Head deposits comprise thin, heterogeneous, locally derived, stony and sandy clays which have moved downslope by solifluxion (periglacial freeze and thaw action). They form even-surfaced sheets on slopes and in valley bottoms. Due to poor exposure, however, many are commonly difficult to distinguish from local tills from which a large number of them are derived.

In the west of the district, head is found in the bottoms of dry valleys within the outcrop of the Lower Magnesian Limestone. Here, it consists of silt and clay with erratics and abundant local dolomite fragments. Similar solifluxion deposits consisting of silt and clay with erratics and fragments of Jurassic bedrock cover much of the Jurassic escarpment and the marginal valleys. Since most upland slopes in the North Yorkshire Moors have a thin veneer of solifluxion deposits, they have been mapped only where they are more than 1 m thick.

Alluvial fan deposits

A small area of gravel at Well [267 819], on the western margin of the district, has been mapped as an alluvial fan, which has been laid down at the mouth of an east-north-east-trending, steep-sided valley, now dry.

Calcareous tufa

Calcareous tufa is a low density, sponge-like, buff-coloured calcitic deposit, generally associated with springs; small deposits occur widely, both in the west and the east of the district on the Permian and Jurassic outcrops respectively. Extensive deposits are present at Snape Mill [2750 8409], near Mires House [2837 8499], and at the edge of Black Plantation [2906 8596]. The tufa forms mounds up to 100 m across, which are slightly elevated above the surrounding peat deposits; spring activity is prolific and marks the escape of highly carbonated artesian water from the Permian limestone and gypsum formations. These mounds are surrounded by peat, which contains extensive beds of shell marl or bog lime (buff, very soft, silt-grade calcite with abundant gastropod shells); similar tufa deposits associated with springs have been recorded by Norris et al. (1971) from the Burton Salmon area of West Yorkshire. At Ripon Parks [3070 7549], a spring-fed stream emanating from the gypsiferous beds has deposited terraces of calcareous tufa over a waterfall. In the Ure Valley, further south, calcareous spring activity is suggested by the presence of tufa-cemented gravels in boreholes [3165 7366; 3155 7268], which penetrated valley deposits (Morigi and James, 1984).

In the centre of the district, one small isolated patch of ferruginous, calcareous tufa occurs near Manor House Farm, Newsham [3888 8554], which is probably related to movement upwards of water along a fault. More abundant deposits are found in the east of the district, associated with the many springs, some of which occur along bedrock faults; for example, west of South Kilburn Park [498 782], a deposit of calcareous tufa over 300 m wide straddles the northern boundary fault of the Asenby–Coxwold Graben. The tufa deposits near Felixkirk [4635 8513] and Upsall [4505 8667] are being deposited where highly carbonated springs issue from the base of the Lower Jurassic Staithes Sandstone. The deposit near Upsall was formerly quarried for limestone. In a gravel pit near Boltby [4893 8710], calcareous tufa deposited from percolating groundwater has cemented some of the fluvioglacial deposits.

Dry valley deposits

Yellow-brown silt occurs in the bottoms of many of the dry valleys on the high ground in the north-east of the district. This deposit has a concave upper surface and was probably derived by solifluxion of loess or soil into the valley bottoms. It was not mapped where it is less than 1 m thick, since on the limestone plateau areas it cannot be distinguished from the pale brown, silty loam of the normal soil profile developed on the Hambleton Oolite bedrock.

The dry valleys form part of the drainage network which converges on the deeply incised, south-westerly draining River Rye. They were probably formed in late- or post-Devensian times when a vast amount of water was released by the melting of snowfields and permafrost on the moors.

Fluviatile and lacustrine alluvium

Fluviatile alluvial deposits flank most of the rivers and streams in the Thirsk district. The extensive deposits along the Rivers Ure and Swale extend to a kilometre in width, but the alluvium along the minor tributaries is generally less than a few hundred metres wide. All these areas are prone to flooding, except where artificial levees have been constructed. The alluvial floodplain deposits typically have a lower unit of sand and gravel deposited as meandering point bars or braided channels, and an upper unit of overbank floodplain deposits comprising thin-bedded to laminated silt and clay, with sporadic thin beds or lenses of fine-grained sand. Lacustrine alluvium is lithologically similar to these overbank deposits and was deposited where small streams were ponded-up in poorly drained areas.

The River Ure cuts through an area of extensive fluvioglacial and river terrace deposits, which consist mainly of sand and gravel, and redeposits them as alluvium in the lower reaches of the river. The gravelly alluvium is up to 8 m thick and is overlain by thin overbank deposits of silt and clay, commonly less than 1 m thick. The gravel fraction consists of pebbles and some cobbles, mostly of Carboniferous limestone and sandstone, but chert, Magnesian Limestone and traces of erratic rocks derived from the till are also present. The sand fraction is fine- to coarse-grained and composed mainly of quartz with some lithic fragments. The alluvial deposits of the Laver and Skell are similar to those of the Ure, and generally comprise sand and gravel up to 4 m thick, overlain by overbank deposits less than 1 m thick.

The alluvium of the River Swale is much finer grained than that of the River Ure; thick (up to 7.5 m) overbank deposits consisting of silt and clay overlie thin (up to 3.5 m) lag deposits of predominantly fine-grained sand. These lithologies broadly reflect the mainly till and lacustrine deposits of the local terrain, which have been reworked by the river.

Numerous ill-drained hollows also contain alluvial silt and clay, commonly associated with peat. The majority of these hollows are in areas mantled by till and some are typical kettle holes, formed by the melting of stagnant ice close to the surface of the till sheet, which subsequently created a depression. Other depressions, largely confined to areas underlain by Middle Marl, Upper Magnesian Limestone or Upper Marls, are subsidence hollows resulting from the removal by dissolution of gypsum from the marl formations (Cooper, 1987).

Bedded silty and clayey overbank deposits within fluviatile alluvium may give rise to similar engineering difficulties as the glacial laminated deposits (see p.78), but problems may be exacerbated by the presence of interbedded peats.

Peat

Peat is present in numerous low-lying and ill-drained flat areas throughout the district, where it forms flat boggy areas; it is also commonly associated with springs.

Widespread peat occurs in fluviatile alluvial deposits where it forms beds, lenses and pockets, commonly associated with abandoned channels. It is also common where the alluvium is poorly drained, such as in the area south of Boltby [491 866]. The thickest deposit in the district occurs nearby at Greendale [4988 8536], where 11 m of wet, "floating" peat occupies a channel which drained a former postglacial lake.

Enclosed hollows, many of which are kettle holes, and low-lying areas within the undulating glacial terrain are common sites for peat development. This is especially so around the Carrs, South Otterington [366 866], and within the hummocky terrain of the esker around Aram Grange [401 742].

In the west of the district, peat occurs in discrete subsidence hollows caused by foundering consequent upon the dissolution of Permian gypsum. Larger spreads of peat in foundered areas are also present, especially at Snape Mires [285 845] (Cooper, 1987) where it is associated with numerous springs, which issue from the Permian rocks, producing mounds of wet peat standing above the drained mire; the most striking example is at Pudding Pie Hill [2783 8446]. Throughout this area numerous beds of buff-coloured, calcareous tufa and bog-lime with gastropod shells are interstratified with the peat.

Peat has a high moisture content and a very low bearing capacity, and is highly compressible; it can, therefore, cause problems of uneven and considerable settlement in engineering works. Acidic groundwater associated with peat may be detrimental to buried and metallic services.

SEVEN

Structure

The structure of the Thirsk district is relatively simple. The area east of the Pennines, of which the district forms a part, has been subjected since the Caledonian earth movements (pre-Carboniferous) to gentle basin subsidence, uplift and predominantly tensional stresses. In the Pennines, to the west of the district, a group of faults initiated at the end of the Caledonian orogeny remained active during Carboniferous sedimentation (Kent, 1974), delineating the Askrigg Block from the Craven Basin (Figure 22). This major fault belt (Craven Faults) probably extends, at depth, into the district and may be manifested by subsequent faulting along the Asenby–Coxwold Graben in post-Jurassic times. In the Harrogate district, to the south, reactivation along this structural line resulted in the folding and faulting of Carboniferous rocks during the Hercynian orogeny (British Geological Survey, 1987). Post-Hercynian structures, expressed in the outcrop of the Permian, Triassic and Jurassic rocks, may also be related to renewed movement along these deep-seated structural trends and are associated with block faulting in the North Sea (Hallam and Sellwood, 1976). Inversion of the Cleveland Basin during the Tertiary (Hemingway and Riddler, 1982) resulted in eastward tilting of the rocks and the development of the Cleveland Anticline and associated subsidiary structures in the Jurassic strata north of the district. These structures do not, however, extend to the Hambleton Hills, in the north-east of the district, which show few structural features. Elsewhere in the district, the dominant structures are the east-west trending Asenby–Coxwold Graben, the north–south Borrowby–Knayton Graben and the small faults in the Thormanby–Oulston area (Figures 22 and 24).

GEOPHYSICAL SUMMARY AND CONCEALED PRE-PERMIAN GEOLOGY

Regional geophysical trends

Deep geological evidence for the pre-Permian basement rocks in the Thirsk area is confined to the British Coal Kirklington [3287 8091] and Sandhutton [3798 8157] boreholes (chapter two) and to a few boreholes located south and southeast of the district on the adjacent Harrogate (62) and York (63) sheets (Figure 24), i.e. at Ellenthorpe [4233 6703] (Wills, 1973; Falcon and Kent, 1960), Crayke [5616 6921] (Wills, 1973), Tholthorpe [468 669] and Farnham [3469 5996] (Burgess and Cooper, 1980) (Figure 24). A network of associated commercial seismic reflection data also exists, for example the Home Oil Company line adjacent to the Ellenthorpe Borehole (Allsop, 1985). These data provide evidence for the Carboniferous sequence in the adjacent area only, since all of the boreholes terminated in Carboniferous strata. The Crayke Borehole proved Yoredale facies (Viséan) of the Carboniferous Limestone, from 911 m to 1331 m below Ordnance Datum (OD); at Ellenthorpe, basinal shaly facies of the Carboniferous Limestone (Dinantian) was proved from 300 m to 1078 m below OD; and at Tholthorpe, the Millstone Grit (Namurian) was penetrated from 461 m to the bottom of the borehole at 901 m below OD. Both the Ellenthorpe and Cleveland Hills boreholes (Fowler, 1944), located about 25 km to the north of the district, penetrated shaly, basinal facies of the Carboniferous Limestone that were deposited east of the Askrigg Block during the Dinantian (Kent, 1966).

Geophysical logs from these commercial boreholes provide density and velocity information to assist in the interpretation of seismic reflection data and other types of geophysical surveys. Additional physical properties data are available from Parasnis (1951), Maroof (1973) and Entwisle (1984). The density of the Mesozoic rocks increases steadily with depth to the pre-Permian basement, with the exception of the Sherwood Sandstone which shows a reverse trend. The Coal Measures and Millstone Grit (predominantly sandstone, siltstone and mudstone) appear to possess similar density characteristics (2.55 Mg m^{-3}) in contrast to the higher density of the underlying Carboniferous Limestone (2.70 Mg m^{-3}). However, sonic velocity measurements show a steady increase with depth from the Mercia Mudstone Group (3.20 km s^{-1}) to the Carboniferous Limestone (6.10 km s^{-1}).

Regional Bouguer gravity data and aeromagnetic survey data (Smith and Royles, 1989) are shown in Figures 25 and 26 respectively. In general, the gravity field has been affected by basement structures, with the deeper trends superimposed on the more regional effect of the easterly dipping Permian and Mesozoic sediments. The Bouguer gravity field decreases from west to east, reflecting a general trend of increasing thickness of low-density Permian and Mesozoic

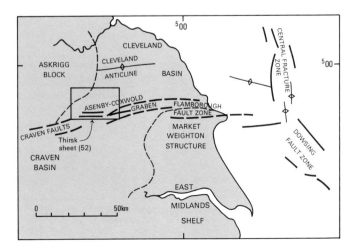

Figure 22   Major structural features of the region.

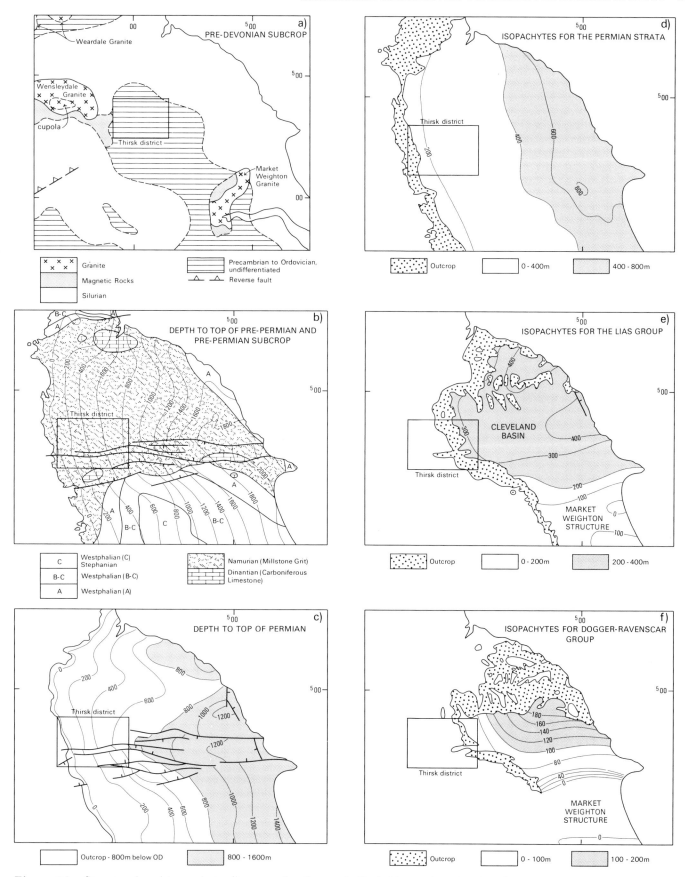

Figure 23   Structural and isopachyte diagrams for the north Yorkshire region showing the position of the Thirsk district in its regional context. From Whittaker (1985) with minor additions.

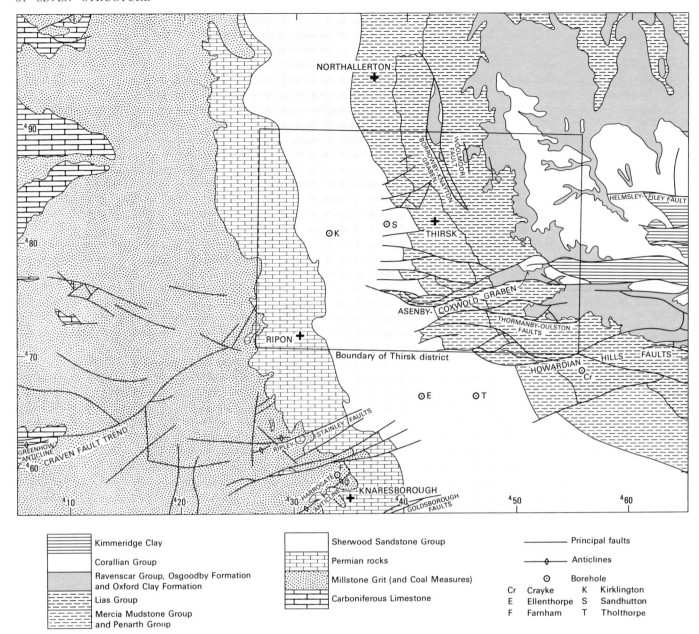

Figure 24 Major structural features and geological boundaries of the Thirsk district and surrounding area.

rocks away from the outcrop of the Carboniferous rocks in the west. West of the district the Bouguer gravity values again decrease towards the Askrigg Block reflecting the presence, at depth, of low-density Wensleydale granite (Dunham, 1974) (Figure 23A). Another influence on the gravity field is the Helmsley–Filey Fault and the associated Howardian–Flamborough Fault Belt (Figures 22 and 24), to the east of the district, which produce a strong north–south-trending gradient; similarly, an east–west trend of the gravity contours to the south-west of the district reflects the influence of the Craven Fault Belt, which flanks the southern margins of the Askrigg Block (Figures 22 and 24). West of the district, a positive gravity ridge to the north of, and parallel to, the gradient associated with the Craven Fault Belt, may represent the eastern extension of the Greenhow

Anticline (Figure 24), which has high-density Carboniferous Limestone in its core.

The aeromagnetic anomaly map (Figure 26) shows low-frequency, low-amplitude anomalies within the district; values decrease steadily to the north-east at an average rate of 5 nT km^{-1}. Depth calculations (Vacquier et al., 1951) indicate that the magnetic basement in this region is at least 5 km below ground level. A broad, but relatively higher frequency, aeromagnetic anomaly to the north of Ripon may be related to the small positive Bouguer gravity closures also present in this area (Figure 25).

Within the district and surrounding area there are a number of small positive Bouguer anomaly closures with small amplitudes ranging from 1 to 2 mGal (Figure 25).

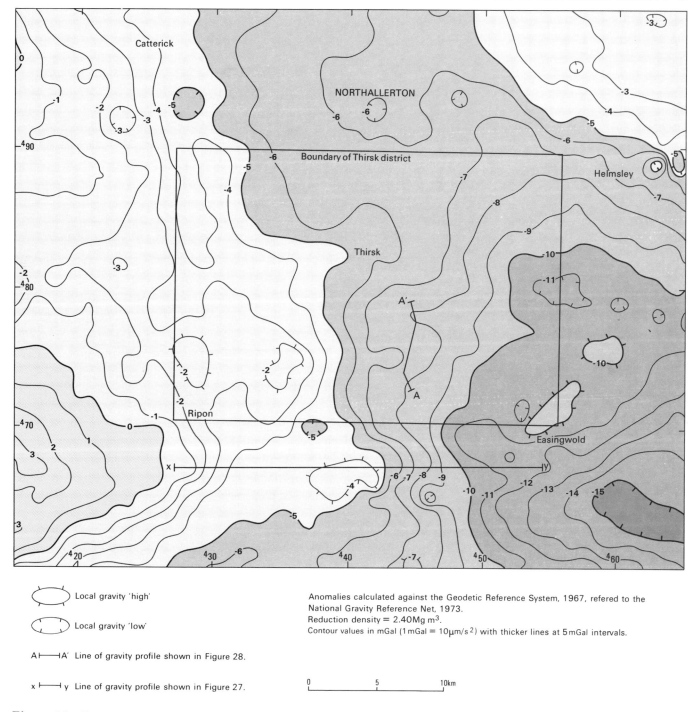

Figure 25 Bouguer gravity anomaly map of the Thirsk district and surrounding area.

Three of these closures have been previously investigated by Allsop (1985); two are located within the district, to the north-east and north-west of Ripon, and the third, to the south, is near the Ellenthorpe Borehole within the Harrogate (62) Sheet. The last was interpreted by Allsop (1985) as an upfaulted Carboniferous Limestone horst. This interpretation (Figure 27) was made on the basis of the geology proved in, and the physical properties measurements available from the Ellenthorpe Borehole, together with data available from a nearby seismic reflection line. The model was fitted to an

east–west gravity profile (X–Y in Figure 25) after corrections for the increase in the regional gravity field towards the North Sea and the removal of the effects of low-density Mesozoic rocks. The interpretation provided a detailed model for the horst structure first postulated by Wills (1973). The depth to the top of the horst is interpreted as 308 m below OD compared to the actual depth of 318 m below OD to the top of the Carboniferous Limestone proved in the Ellenthorpe Borehole, which is located on the flanks of the gravity anomaly. By analogy, two similar closures to the

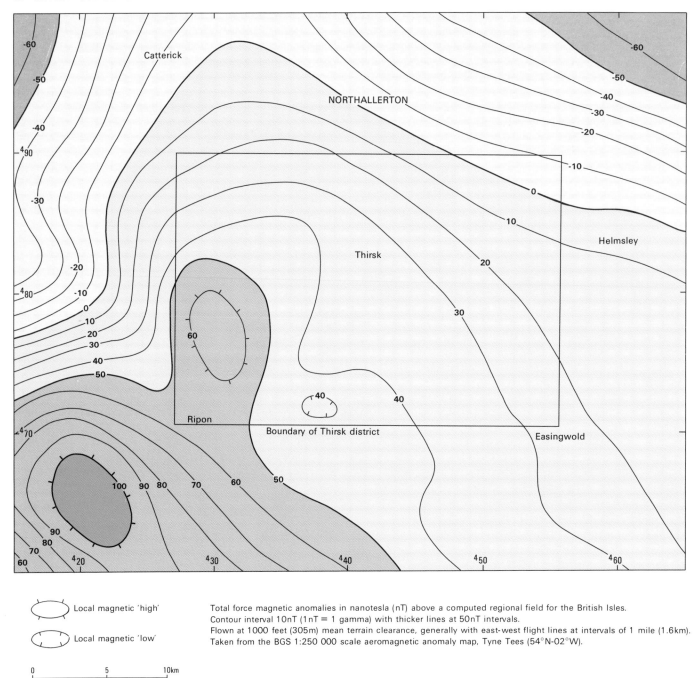

Local magnetic 'high'

Local magnetic 'low'

Total force magnetic anomalies in nanotesla (nT) above a computed regional field for the British Isles.
Contour interval 10nT (1nT = 1 gamma) with thicker lines at 50nT intervals.
Flown at 1000 feet (305m) mean terrain clearance, generally with east-west flight lines at intervals of 1 mile (1.6km).
Taken from the BGS 1:250 000 scale aeromagnetic anomaly map, Tyne Tees (54°N-02°W).

0   5   10km

Figure 26   Aeromagnetic anomaly map of the Thirsk district and the surrounding area.

north-east and north-west of Ripon, within the district, are considered to be caused by similar Carboniferous Limestone horst structures. However, north of Ripon there is a coincident positive aeromagnetic anomaly, first noted by Kent (1974), with an amplitude of 20 nT. Although the gravity interpretation indicates that the base of the Carboniferous Limestone horst is at a depth of 680 m below OD, the source of the magnetic anomaly is considerably deeper, with a relief of 914 m above the surrounding magnetic basement (c.5 km below ground level). The gravity and magnetic features are

probably related, the southern flank of the structure coinciding with the easterly extension of the Asenby–Coxwold Graben (Figure 24). The magnetic anomaly north of Ripon may be due to the effects of several horst structures within a general area of uplifted Carboniferous Limestone, which are manifested as a more widespread feature in the underlying magnetic basement, large enough to be detected by a regional aeromagnetic survey.

Regional gravity data show a small positive Bouguer gravity anomaly over the Asenby–Coxwold Graben 10 km

Figure 27 Two-dimensional computer interpretation of Bouguer gravity anomaly profile along section x–y in Figure 25.

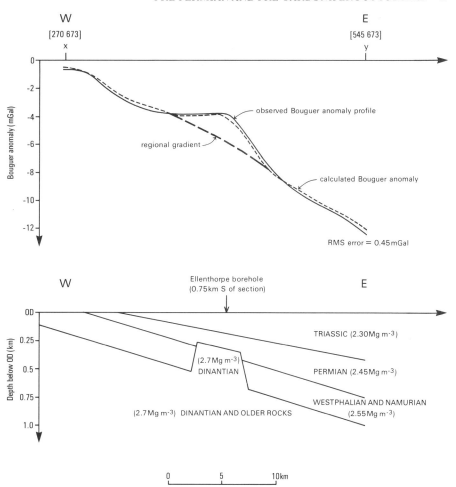

south of Thirsk [4425 4750] (Figure 25). Detailed gravity surveys, including two traverses, were undertaken across this anomaly in an attempt to define the extent and style of faulting present. Traverse A–A′ (Figure 25), considered here, is located perpendicular to the strike of the fault complex. Control data for this traverse include nearby seismic reflection lines and detailed information on the low-density lacustrine clays and till, and depth to bedrock (Figure 28a).

The observed gravity profile revealed a positive gravity anomaly with an amplitude of 1.5 mGal and an adjacent peak of 1 mGal. Laboratory measurements (Entwisle, 1984) on samples of overburden confirm an overall maximum density contrast with the underlying rocks of the Mercia Mudstone Group of -0.5 Mg/m^{-3}. The effect of the overburden (Figure 28b) has been removed from the observed profile, together with a general gradient reflecting the easterly dip of higher density rocks below the Mesozoic.

The resultant model (Chacksfield, 1985) shows the detailed structure across the graben (Figure 28c). Since the beds of the Mercia Mudstone are known to be almost horizontal (maximum dip = 3°), any abrupt density changes indicated by steep gravity gradients are likely to represent faulted junctions. A major fault (X in Figure 28c) on the northern flank of the graben is interpreted to have a vertical displacement of c.120 m at the mudstone/sandstone interface. Two further faults define the core of the graben (Y and

Z in Figure 28c) where the greatest thickness of mudstone occurs. However, in this central region, low-density Jurassic sediments also contribute to the local gravity field and therefore, in this two layer model, the thickness of mudstone at this point must be considered a minimum.

The additional detailed gravity data indicate that the core of the graben is about 2 km wide, trends east–west and is locally offset by north–south displacements. This is confirmed by the surface geological survey and shallow borehole data. The gravity anomaly decreases in amplitude towards the east where the effect of the sandstone/mudstone interface is masked by a thickening of Jurassic cover rocks.

PRE-PERMIAN AND PRE-CARBONIFEROUS SUBCROP

The pre-Permian geology and depth contours to the pre-Permian basement surface in the region are shown in Figure 23b. Lowermost Coal Measures crop out in the south-west of the district and have been proved, to a limited extent, in the west of the district below the Permian rocks (chapter two). To the north and east of the Carboniferous outcrop, Coal Measures strata have been removed by erosion and Namurian rocks underlie the Permian unconformity. The pre-Permian surface extends to a depth of c.850 m and

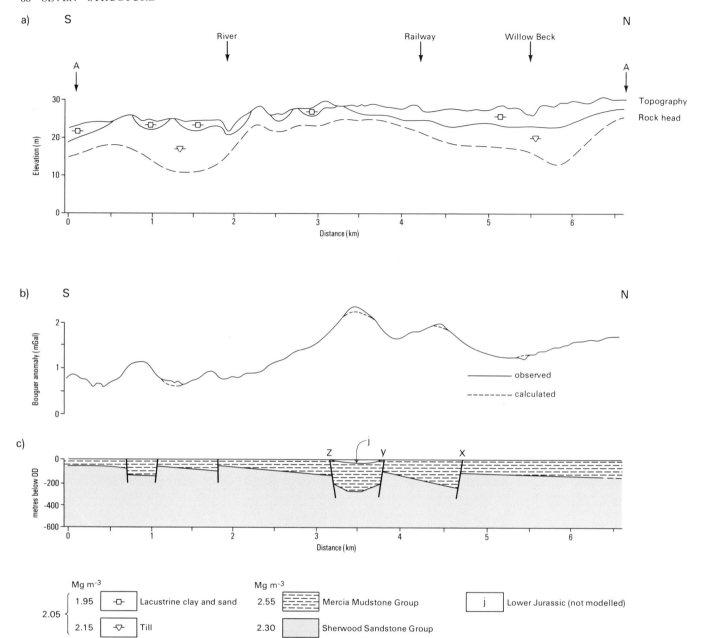

Figure 28 Gravity traverse and profile across the Asenby–Coxwold Graben (for line of section see Figure 25).

a) Section showing topography, drift deposits and depth to rockhead (Mercia Mudstone Group). b) Observed gravity profile with calculated model profile for comparison. c) Computed gravity model showing detailed structure across the graben; x, y and z are interpreted as faults (see text). Rock densities used for the interpretation are shown. Gravity observations are at approximately 44 m intervals.

c.5000 m in the north-eastern and south-eastern corners of the district respectively (Whittaker, 1985). The steady dip of the pre-Permian basement surface towards the east is disrupted only by the Asenby–Coxwold Graben and the Howardian–Flamborough Fault Zone. Coal Measures (Westphalian A and B) subcrop beneath the Permian strata a few kilometres outside the district near its south-east corner. Carboniferous Limestone has been proved to form a con-cealed inlier (horst) at the pre-Permian basement surface near Ellenthorpe, a few kilometres to the south of the district (Wills, 1973; Allsop, 1985) and a similar interpretation is postulated for the small positive gravity anomalies to the north-east and north-west of Ripon (Allsop, 1985).

The pre-Carboniferous geology within this area is un-proven and, therefore, can only be inferred from evidence outside the district; the thickness of the Carboniferous strata is also unknown in the district and adjacent area. The grav-ity evidence suggests that dense basement rocks underlie the

Carboniferous rocks. It is likely that Silurian rocks are present to the north and north-east, whereas older rocks, of possible Ordovician age, underlie the majority of the central/southern area (Figure 23a). Magnetic basement is, in general, deeper than 5 km and, therefore, it is only in the extreme west of the area that the magnetic basement rocks associated with the ?Ingletonian Group rise above the background level (Figure 23a). The magnetic rocks are likely to be similar to those proved in the Beckermonds Scar Borehole [SD 8635 8016], where a series of Ordovician, magnetite-rich siltstones, mudstones and greywacke sandstones underlie the Lower Carboniferous sediments (Wilson and Cornwell, 1982). These strongly magnetic sediments are draped over and around the Wensleydale Granite under the Askrigg Block, but their magnetic origin is unlikely to be directly associated with the emplacement of the granite. Depth estimates for these aeromagnetic anomalies suggest that a maximum depth to the magnetic basement in this western area has decreased to within 2 km ± 0.5 km of ground level. However, the method of depth calculation is usually applied to discrete magnetic bodies rather than to thick piles of sediments rich in disseminated magnetite; therefore, this estimate may be considered as a maximum. Data from the Masham sheet (British Geological Survey, 1985), west of the district, suggests that the magnetic ?Lower Palaeozoic rocks lie just below the base of the Carboniferous succession at about 800 m below ground level, thus confirming a possible overestimate of depth to magnetic basement in this case.

In the district the Carboniferous rocks represent an eastward extension of the Millstone Grit and Coal Measures exposed in the Pateley Bridge, Masham and Harrogate areas to the south and west (Figure 23b). The Harrogate Anticline and Ripley–Staveley Fault Belt (British Geological Survey, 1987), to the south of the district (Figure 24), represent a probable extension of the east-north-east-trending fold and fault zone at the southern margin of the Askrigg Block, further west. This Craven Fault Zone has been interpreted as a response to dextral (right-lateral shear) affecting the area from mid-Dinantian to early Namurian times (Arthurton, 1983). This structural line may pass into the Asenby–Coxwold Graben at depth, although there is evidence of a break in the trends of the two structures within the Permian outcrop in the Ripon area (Figure 24). If the structures are contiguous, it suggests renewed (late Jurassic–early Cretaceous) movement on the Asenby–Coxwold faults, along a zone of structural weakness initiated during the early Carboniferous.

The main uplift, folding, faulting and erosional phase of the Hercynian orogeny postdates the deposition of Westphalian (Coal Measures) strata, but the gentle deformation shown by the low-angle unconformity of the basal Permian rocks (Figure 23b) indicates that the district lay far to the north of the major Hercynian orogenic front. The postulated fault-bounded horsts of Carboniferous Limestone overlain unconformably by Permian strata, to the north-east and north-west of Ripon (Allsop, 1985 and pp.83, 87), probably formed during this deformation phase.

POST-PERMIAN STRUCTURES

The district formed part of the gently subsiding Yorkshire and East Midlands Shelf (Kent, 1974) during Permian times (Figure 23d). Permian rocks were deposited with progressive northwards overstep upon the Coal Measures and Millstone Grit, which had been reduced to a very low relief by subaerial erosion. Epeirogenic movements controlled sedimentation on the shelf during the Permian and Triassic; stratal thickness increases gradually to the east, and the rocks dip gently in the same direction. Subsequent dissolution of Permian gypsum beds near the outcrop has, however, resulted in a more complex structure-contour pattern in the west of the district (Figure 3).

The Market Weighton Structure, to the south-east of the district, developed as a major structural 'high' during the Jurassic (Figure 23e). It represents an area of low sedimentation rate, separating the gently subsiding East Midlands Shelf, to the south, from the rapidly subsiding Cleveland Basin, of which the district forms a part, to the north (Kent, 1974). The Market Weighton Structure did not affect sedimentation during deposition of the Sherwood Sandstone Group, but the Mercia Mudstone Group shows slight thinning across the structure (Kent, 1974). The Lias Group thins markedly from 271 m in the Felixkirk Borehole (Powell, 1984) to 173 m at Acklam, on the structure (Gaunt et al., 1980) (Figure 23e). Middle and Upper Jurassic rocks also thin southwards towards the structure (Figure 23f), but these attenuated strata were removed (along with early Cretaceous rocks) over the 'high' during pre-Chalk (pre-Cenomanian) erosion.

A number of intra-Jurassic earth movements are recorded in the district. The upper part of the Whitby Mudstone Formation was eroded during late Toarcian to Aalenian times, prior to deposition of the Dogger Formation. There is no evidence of subaerial erosion (weathered zones; soil horizons) in this district at the junction of the Alum Shales and the overlying Dogger Formation and, furthermore, water-worn phosphatised pebbles at the base of the latter suggest submarine erosion. In addition to basin-wide epeirogenic movements, which affected sedimentation during the Middle and Upper Jurassic, and caused many depositional breaks (chapter five), there is evidence of local intraformational faulting in the district, such as that postulated in Shaw's Gill, which abruptly terminates the south-eastern margin of the tilted Roulston Scar 'block' (Powell, 1982). Fault movement and tilting was post-Oxford Clay/pre-Lower Calcareous Grit, that is between the late Praecordatum and early Bukowski subzones (Lower Oxfordian). Local synsedimentary deformation of the Hambleton Oolite has been attributed to seismic shock resulting from coeval faulting (Hemingway and Twombley, 1963).

POST-JURASSIC STRUCTURES

Faults

The dominant structural features in the district are the faults which affect the Jurassic outcrop (Figure 24). These are:

(a) the Asenby–Coxwold Graben, and associated faults
(b) the Borrowby–Knayton Graben
(c) the Thormanby–Oulston faults
(d) minor north–south and north-east–south-west-trending faults on the western margin of the Hambleton Hills.

Asenby – Coxwold Graben

This structure is manifested as a zone of faulted blocks, bounded to the north and the south by generally east–west-trending boundary faults (Figures 24 and 28C). Although the relief within the graben is lower than that of the areas to the north and south, the strata within the structure are downthrown by as much as 350 m. The graben is largely obscured by drift deposits, but there is sufficient evidence from drift-free exposures, boreholes and geophysical surveys (Figure 28; Chacksfield, 1985) to define its form. Contrasting lithologies between the strata on each side of the major boundary faults enables the structure to be traced over most of the drift-covered terrain.

The structure is also known as, or is considered to form part of the Coxwold–Gilling faults (Kent, 1974), the Howardian Hills Fault Belt (Kent, 1980a) and the Vale of Pickering–Flamborough Head Fault Zone (Kirby and Swallow, 1987). Regionally, it forms part of a series of approximately east–west faults separating the Market Weighton Structure, to the south, from the inverted Cleveland Basin, to the north (Figures 22 and 23). The Helmsley–Filey Fault, north-east of the district, has a similar trend (Figures 22 and 23), and the Asenby–Coxwold Graben is also probably genetically related to a series of *en-échelon* faults in the Howardian Hills and the Yorkshire Wolds to the east, which displace Jurassic strata, but not the overlying, unconformable Chalk. Recent seismic traverses across the eastern extension of the Howardian Hills Fault Belt, at Flamborough Head, have demonstrated a complex history of faulting from late Jurassic (late Kimmeridgian) to early Cretaceous (Barremian) times (Kirby and Swallow, 1987).

The Asenby–Coxwold Graben is about 2.5 km wide at the eastern margin of the district, and narrows to 1 km near Asenby [398 753]. The northern boundary fault has a generally arcuate (concave-north) trace from Asenby to Kilburn Park [501 783]; east of the latter locality, the trace is irregular, marking a series of sharp 'dog-leg' curves. The southern boundary fault maintains a parallel concave-north trace from Asenby to Carlton Husthwaite [499 767], but east of here the trend is almost east–west. The strike of the beds within the graben is variable; it ranges from broadly north-west–south-east at the western end of the structure, with a small-scale synclinal fold near Barf Hill [4289 7526], to east–west at the eastern end, where there is evidence of structural foreshortening and block rotation. The curved trace of the northern bounding fault, and its 'dog-leg' arcuate trace between Kilburn Park and Byland Abbey [547 787] in areas of low topographical relief, indicate a low-angle fault plane, dipping to the south. This contrasts with the straighter trace of the southern boundary fault, which is probably a higher-angle, antithetic displacement. The area between these faults at the eastern end of the structure is oc-cupied by a complex pattern of rotated blocks of Jurassic strata ranging, at outcrop, from the Lias Group to the Kimmeridge Clay.

Dips at the western end of the structure are generally low (about 10°) towards the east. East of Thirkleby Barugh [477 771], the strike within the faulted blocks has a general north-north-westerly trend, with variable, high dips adjacent to the northern fault at Snape Hill [508 787], and northerly dips ranging from 15 to 23° at the southern margin of the structure. At Brink Hill [540 786], however, the Kimmeridge Clay is almost horizontal.

The graben faults cannot be traced with any confidence through the Permian strata in the west of the district; this may be because the throw on the faults decreases westwards, or because displacement is taken up along a single fault, or it may result from a decrease in the dip of the fault planes at structurally lower levels as they pass into listric (bedding-plane) faults within the Triassic–Jurassic sequence. Faults and half-grabens of a similar style have been documented in the Flamborough Head area (Kirby and Swallow, 1987) outside the district, at the eastern end of this series of structures. This may explain why such a major structure affecting the Jurassic rocks is not detectable on seismic traverses based on Permian (Magnesian Limestone) reflectors. Comparison with the structural style of the Flamborough Head Fault Zone (Kirby and Swallow, 1987) suggests a narrow, highly fractured, tensional fault zone, comprising tilted blocks with low-angle, listric bounding faults, at least along the northern boundary fault between Kilburn Park and Byland Abbey; the southern boundary fault appears to have a steeper dip.

The variable, high dips and strong jointing of the strata adjacent to the northern boundary fault (Snape Hill Quarry), folding in the Barf Hill area, and the east–west rotation of the strike in the eastern part of the structure suggest lateral deformation within the graben, possibly resulting from sinistral shear. This contrasts with the inferred dextral shear on the Craven Faults west of the district (Arthurton, 1983). Evidence against any marked transcurrent movement comes from the general continuity of the subdrift boundaries of both the Lias Group and the Ravenscar Group on either side of the graben, and the absence of minor drag folds adjacent to the structure.

The lower age limit of the Asenby–Coxwold Graben is post-Kimmeridge Clay. The upper age limit is uncertain since stratigraphical evidence is lacking in the district. Comparison of the structure with the Flamborough Head Fault Zone (Kirby and Swallow, 1987) suggests a lower Cretaceous (Barremian) age for much of the faulting, that is, prior to the deposition of the Chalk. Uplift and inversion of the Cleveland Basin during the Tertiary probably resulted in renewed tensional, vertical movement along some of the faults associated with the Asenby–Coxwold Graben, which lay along the hinge line between the Cleveland Basin (North Yorkshire Moors) and the Market Weighton Structure, to the south.

Borrowby – Knayton Graben

This north-west–south-east-trending, graben-like block (Figure 24) is the southerly termination of a north–south-trending structure which extends northwards for about 7 km outside of the district. In the north of the district, the structure throws down the Ravenscar Group against the Redcar Mudstone Formation with a maximum displacement of about 180 m between Borrowby and Knayton. East of Borrowby and south of Knayton, however, the Whitby Mudstone is faulted against the Redcar Mudstone. The width of the graben narrows southwards from about 1.5 km near Borrowby to about 0.5 km near South Kilvington. The southern topographical expression of the graben is less clearly defined because it is both drift covered and lacks lithological contrast. Primary Survey maps show the termination of the structure (below the drift) just south of Knayton [434 877], but it has been traced about 3 km to the south-east. The southwards extension is supported by the recognition of a topographic 'high' under the drift cover, and on the evidence of two critical sections. The first, in Spittle Beck [4400 8551], south of Kilvington Hall, exposes blue-grey, fissile, micaceous mudstone with small siderite nodules; the high dip (40°–50° SSW) suggests close proximity to a major fault. Micropalaeontological analysis of these beds indicates a late Pliensbachian to Toarcian age, demonstrating downthrow (c.100 m) of the Whitby Mudstone against Redcar Mudstone. At Broom Hill [4435 8487], orange-grey, fissile, organic-rich mudstone (Whitby Mudstone) is exposed, suggesting a fault displacement, of similar magnitude, to the east and west of the hill. The topographical feature, interpreted as a fault block, can be traced below the drift to Hag House [4475 8423], but it is not well defined further south. The north–south trend of this graben, at right angles to the Asenby–Coxwold structure, suggests a different genesis.

Extensional faults of a similar trend and associated with the Peak Trough, have been identified along the Yorkshire coast (Milson and Rawson, 1989). Movement along these faults is inferred to have occurred intermittently during Triassic, mid-Jurassic and late Jurassic–earliest Cretaceous times, and again in early Tertiary times. By analogy, movement along the bounding faults of the Borrowby–Knayton Graben during mid-Jurassic times may have influenced sedimentation in the area. Uplift of the present-day graben as a positive feature during the Middle Jurassic might account for the absence of transgressive marine units (Eller Beck Formation; Lebberston Member and Scarborough Formation) of the Ravenscar Group within the graben. Reverse movement (extensional north–south faulting) probably took place during inversion and uplift of the Cleveland Basin in early Tertiary times.

Thormanby–Oulston faults

A number of faults with east–west, north-east–south-west and north-west–south-east trends (Figure 24) affect the Lower and Middle Jurassic rocks in the south-east of the district; maximum throw is in the order of 40 m. The irregularly arcuate trend of the northernmost fault indicates a low-angle fault plane, in contrast to the straight trace of the approximately parallel, high-angle fault to the south. These structures represent the western termination of a series of *en echelon,* generally east–west-trending faults that extend east of the district across the Howardian Hills and beneath the unconformable Chalk cover of the Yorkshire Wolds, to Flamborough Head (Kirby and Swallow, 1987). Analogy

with faults in the latter area, suggests a lower Cretaceous age for the Thormanby–Oulston faults.

Minor faults

North-east–south-west-trending faults, near Abel Grange [4020 8420], are invoked to explain the marked offset of the Penarth Group subcrop between North Kilvington and South Kilvington. The faults are also supported by evidence from gravity anomalies and seismic traverses in the area (Allsop, 1985).

A north–south-trending fault north of Upsall [435 870] displaces the outcrops of a major sandstone of the Cloughton Formation and the Leberston Member about 20 m to the west. The fault may be tectonically related to the Borrowby structure since it has a similar orientation. A small fault with a similar trend forms a fault-scarp on the moor above Kirkby Knowle; it also offsets the Dogger in Storth Wood. The fault is projected south from here, below the till, to account for the Dogger being at a lower elevation on the eastern edge of the Felixkirk outlier [476 855] than on the western edge of the Housebrough outlier [481 857].

Superficial structures (landslips and cambers)

A large part of the major scarp face in the north-east of the district (Hambleton Hills), which comprises Middle and Upper Jurassic rocks, is affected by landslips and cambers. Landslips have also occurred on valley sides in the far north-east. The landslips appear to be inactive at present; however, they and the disturbed strata associated with cambers could give rise to engineering problems where the ground is disturbed by foundation or drainage works. Their degraded nature and some archaeological evidence, such as the presence of a late Bronze Age burial urn in the landslips that form Sutton Bank, suggest that little movement has taken place for a considerable period, probably thousands of years. It is likely, therefore, that most of the landslips occurred immediately after the stagnation and melting of the late Devensian ice sheet.

The ice sheet probably eroded the softer beds such as the Oxford Clay, the Scalby Formation and the Whitby Mudstone Formation along the base of the scarp and oversteepened the scarp face. Meltwater from the ice sheet, and water released from snowfields or from permafrost on the plateau, acting through frost-widened joint spaces, increased the pore water pressure in the mudstone and siltstone units below the more permeable, competent beds such as the Lower Calcareous Grit, Kellaways Rock, Scarborough Formation and Saltwick Formation. As a result, the scarp face became unstable and a series of landslips, with mudflows at their toes, moved downslope.

The landslips take the form of rotational slips, block slides and mudflows, but all three types may be present at one site. Rotational slips initiated within the Whitby Mudstone Formation and involving the overlying Ravenscar Group occur at lower levels on the scarp face. The most spectacular is at Brockholes, near Kirkby Knowle [4740 8775], where the Scarborough Formation and the Cloughton Formation are exposed in the back scar. Movement occurred as a series of rotational slips, with mudflows at the toes of the slips. A little to the south, at Wind Egg [4740 8704], the edge of the escarpment has moved downslope as a single block; nearby at Birk Bank [474 867], much of the base of the Ravenscar Group is obscured by shallow rotational slips.

Small slips are also present at the base of the Dogger, or the Saltwick Formation where the Dogger is absent. These mass movements usually constitute mudflows, and many have developed from near-surface solifluxion movements in the underlying mudstones. Examples can be seen at Skipton Hill [495 842], Osgodby Hall [494 810], Felixkirk [469 847] and near Grange Farm [457 896].

Higher in the scarp face, rotational slips at the level of the Lower Calcareous Grit occur almost continuously from Low Paradise [5017 8817], south to Roulston Scar and then south-east to Byland Abbey. The most spectacular, with concave back scars, are those below Boltby Scar [504 863], in South Wood [505 847], below Whitestone Cliff [506 837] and at Sutton Bank [513 827].

Block slides and cambers are present along the scarp face, but are particularly common in the narrow valleys which cut the dip slope of the escarpment in the north-east of the district. The principal mechanism here appears to have been erosion of softer, impermeable beds along spring lines (par-

ticularly at the base of the Lower Calcareous Grit); this caused cambering of the scarp face as the impermeable beds were eroded and/or plastically deformed. Subsequently, deep camber gulls opened at the edge of the escarpment or at the tops of valley slopes, and blocks either hinged downwards or became detached and slid downslope. Examples of this style of landslip are found at Sneck Yate Bank [504 875] (Plate 10), Limperdale Gill [537 867] and Peak Scar [530 883]. At these localities, the detached or hinged blocks dip at about 30° to 35° towards the valley.

Most of the edge of the main escarpment and the sides of the interior valleys are cambered to some degree; a notable exception is Roulston Scar, probably because of the absence in this area of the less competent Oxford Clay between the Osgodby Formation and the Lower Calcareous Grit. The maximum extent of camber is generally within 250 m of the edge of the scarp face, although larger areas may be involved at valley spurs. Spectacular camber gulls are present between High Barn [507 867] and Sneck Yate Bank [504 875] (Plate 10). The gulls (up to 6 m deep) are arranged *en échelon* along the edge of the escarpment, and the blocks between each pair of gulls dip at between 10° and 35° into the valley. The approximate north–south orientation of these struc-

Plate 10   Deep camber-gulls at the edge of the Hambleton Hills escarpment. Sneck Yate Bank (L3044).

tures suggests that they are associated with the widening of a set of major joints; such a joint set was observed in Boltby Scar Quarry, some 700 m further south. Other hinged, but attached blocks can be seen at Sled Hill [5210 8720] and at Limperdale Rigg [5230 8654].

Block falls represent another type of downslope mass movement related to major joint development. At Roulston Scar [511 826], earlier rotational slips initiated in the Scalby Formation are now covered with large blocks of Lower Calcareous Grit. These block falls were triggered by the widening of the major joints near the edge of the escarpment. At Whitestone Cliff [506 837], such falls have occurred in historical times, and one was witnessed by John Wesley in the 18th century.

EIGHT

Economic geology

MINERALISATION

Mineralisation is present in small amounts in the Lower Magnesian Limestone (Cadeby Formation) of the district. Near West Tanfield [SE 283 782], a vein of baryte and galena with associated fluorspar, up to 4 cm wide, was recorded by Lamming and Robertson (1968). The BGS Sleningford Mill Borehole [2778 7841] also proved galena in numerous breccias, and sphalerite in vughs (Appendix 2); sphalerite associated with dolomite in vughs is also present in the dolomitic limestone outcrop nearby, along the banks of the River Ure. To the north of this locality, at Well Quarry [267 812], minor veins of baryte and galena were recorded during the resurvey, and an unusual occurrence of diagenetic baryte in a hydraulic breccia pipe was also recorded by Harwood (1981).

LIMESTONE AND DOLOMITE

Permian limestone and dolomite

The Lower Magnesian Limestone (Cadeby Formation) (see chapter three and Figure 2) has been extensively quarried in the district. Details of both the abandoned and working quarries, and the lithological variation and aggregate potential are given by Cooper (1987) and Bridge and Murray (1983) respectively. The Lower Magnesian Limestone consists mainly of dolomite, but sporadic beds of calcitic dolomite are also present. There are two working quarries in the district (Harris et al., 1988): at Potgate Farm, North Stainley [278 757], where the upper part of the Lower Magnesian Limestone is extracted mainly for use as aggregate; and at Sutton Grange [285 744], where the upper part of the formation, which is generally soft and heavily dolomitised, is quarried for use as agricultural lime. The presence of magnesium carbonate in the lime is beneficial because modern agricultural practices tend to result in land with magnesian deficiencies (Harris, 1982).

The Upper Magnesian Limestone (Brotherton Formation) is generally a harder and more calcitic dolomite than the Lower Magnesian Limestone. The exception is around Chapel Hill, Thornborough [293 793], where it is heavily dolomitised, soft and friable. Since the formation is both thin and extensively drift covered, it offers little potential as an aggregate source. Details of the disused quarries in the Upper Magnesian Limestone are given in chapter three and by Cooper (1987).

Jurassic limestone and calcareous sandstone

The Upper Jurassic Corallian Group, which crops out in the north-east of the district, contains large resources of limestone and calcareous sandstone (chapter five). The principal sources are the Lower Calcareous Grit, the Hambleton Oolite and its sandy facies, the Birdsall Calcareous Grit. Only the Hambleton Oolite provides a pure, or nearly pure calcium carbonate rock; the other units have a variable silica content in the form of quartz sand grains and chalcedonic silica (sponge spicules).

The Lower Calcareous Grit has been worked for lime, road metal and building stone at a number of small quarries close to the edge of the escarpment [5167 8124; 5182 8165; 5269 8154]. Beds and concretions ('Ball Beds') of grey, sparsely oolitic limestone were selectively exploited for the production of lime, and the calcareous sandstone beds were used for walling stone or for buildings. Some of the quarries in the formation lie within large landslipped areas below the main outcrop, for example near Roulston Scar [5115 8112] and at Sutton Bank [5124 8274].

The Hambleton Oolite was formerly exploited in hundreds of small, shallow quarries on the moors, along the escarpment and on valley sides; its thin-bedded, flaggy nature made it an ideal walling stone. Much of the stone was burnt locally to produce lime for use on the acidic soils of the Corallian 'Grits' and the Ravenscar Group. Between 1940 and 1950, the Birdsall Calcareous Grit and the lower leaf of the Hambleton Oolite were extensively worked at Cleave Dyke Quarry [5075 8626], near Boltby Scar (Frontispiece and Plate 6). The quarry face was about 13 m high and the material was transported by aerial ropeway some 1200 m to the village of Boltby, 170 m below.

Other limestone beds within the Middle Jurassic Ravenscar Group that were formerly exploited for lime include the Dogger at Cleaves Bank Quarry [4965 8275] and Kennycow Quarry [5007 8252], the Lebberston Member near High Rigg [5044 8305], south-east of Husthwaite [5174 7450; 5408 7587] and at Oulston Quarry [5494 7305], and the Brandsby Roadstone near High Ground Barns [5030 8075], at Boar's Gill [5185 8071] and near Oldstead [5348 8006].

GYPSUM

Permian gypsum deposits

Thick beds of gypsum are present in both the Middle Marl (Edlington Formation) and the Upper Marl (Roxby Formation). The gypsum is secondary, resulting from the groundwater hydration of anhydrite near the surface; it extends downdip from the outcrop to its transition to anhydrite (see chapter three for details). The gypsum belt (Figure 3) is generally about 4 to 5 km wide.

Interaction between the gypsum and groundwater eventually causes its dissolution, resulting in subsidence and foundering of the overlying strata (see chapter three). Widespread subsidence east and north of Ripon, and around

Snape Mires, together with the existence of considerable groundwater flow into the deep, preglacial buried valley at the former locality, suggest that gypsum is unlikely to be workable in these areas. Between Nosterfield [278 805] and Kirklington [318 813], however, features such as a bedrock high, with thick Middle and Upper Marls and no evidence of extensive groundwater flow or subsidence, suggest that the gypsum beds here may be of economic importance.

Triassic gypsum deposits

Although gypsum beds occur at three horizons within the Mercia Mudstone Group (see p.21), they are commonly covered by thick drift deposits. Borehole evidence indicates that the gypsum occurs as thin beds and nodules. Only the uppermost horizon, some 20 m below the top of the group, has been exploited, and only at a single locality, Little Sessay [467 746], where shallow pits, now degraded, provided small supplies for local use. In the north of the outcrop, a number of boreholes were drilled around Beal House [3669 8663] to explore the potential of the same horizon, but the deposits did not prove worthy of exploitation. Neither of the two lower horizons within the Mercia Mudstone Group has been worked within the district.

IRONSTONE

In north Yorkshire, Jurassic ironstones have been worked at four stratigraphical horizons: the Cleveland Ironstone Formation, the Dogger Formation, the Eller Beck Formation and the Kellaways Rock. In the Thirsk district, only the ironstones of the Dogger Formation have been exploited to any extent.

Although the Cleveland Ironstone Formation is present throughout the district (see p.31), the ironstone seams are fewer and thinner than in north Cleveland, where they have been worked extensively (Hemingway, 1974). In addition, much of their outcrop is covered with drift, and, although a trial borehole [4705 8488] was sunk at Mount St John (Phillips, 1858) in the last century, no development has been attempted in the district.

Ironstone of the Dogger Formation has a maximum thickness of 3 m (p.38) and was formerly worked in the district, principally in the Kirby Knowle area. Four adit shafts [4698 8818; 4723 8798; 4749 8670; 4780 8640] have been located along the escarpment between Kirby Knowle and Storth Wood. The largest spoil-tip is adjacent to a collapsed entrance [4749 8670] at Birk Bank. To the north of Kirby Knowle, an adit and spoil tip have been located near Brickshed Cottage [4687 8866]. The ore consists of sideritic, berthierinitic, oolitic ironstone; the ooliths are mostly berthierine and the matrix predominantly siderite, although diagenetic sideritisation of the berthierine ooliths is also present. Records show that these mines were abandoned in 1921. Fox-Strangways et al. (1886) recorded another adit near Boltby, which is presumed to have been adjacent to a small exposure [4860 8653] west of the village. Iron-rich furnace slag was found close to the Dogger outcrop near Cowesby Hall [4747 8964].

The basal ironstone bed (Ingleby Ironstone) of the Eller Beck Formation has not been worked in this district; it is thinner and more sandy than at outcrop in north Cleveland, where it was formerly mined (Hemingway, 1974).

There is some evidence that the highest iron-rich horizon, the Kellaways Rock, has been worked on a small scale. Ironstone slag was found in a small tip adjacent to a stream near Hawnby Bridge [5412 8919]. The partly smelted ironstone rock includes berthierinitic ooliths in a sandy matrix. The ore may have been obtained from goethite bands or berthierinitic sandstone in the locally exposed Kellaways Rock.

COAL

Coals within the Middle Jurassic Ravenscar Group were widely exploited in north Yorkshire in the 18th and 19th centuries. Most worked seams lay within the Saltwick or Cloughton formations (Hemingway, 1974), but in the Thirsk district seams within the Scalby Formation were also exploited.

A seam, 0.4 m thick, in the Cloughton Formation (see p.45) was worked in the former Newburgh Park Colliery [5538 7572], probably located south of Hurst House near the eastern boundary of the district. A section of the strata penetrated by the 'Engine Pit' at this colliery is given by Fox-Strangways et al. (1886). These authors also referred to coal workings at Coxwold but gave no precise details; a possible location is the outcrop of the Cloughton Formation south-west of the village.

Higher in the succession, coal seams in the upper part of the Moor Grit Member (Scalby Formation) outcrop north and north-west of Oldstead. Exposures north-east of Acre House [5164 8032] and at Common Wood [5320 8065] reveal seams 0.10 to 0.40 m thick, consisting of silty coal of low rank, which may have been worked at surface. A nearby bell-pit [5187 8085], adjacent to Boar's Gill, which probably worked the same seams, is accompanied by a small spoil tip which includes fragments of soft, shiny, laminated coal, indicating that the coal may be of better quality at depth.

More extensive workings of two seams, either within or just above the Moor Grit Member, occur within the Asenby–Coxwold Graben around Burtree House [4828 7680], north of Birdforth. The sites of four shafts were located during the resurvey, one of which was probably the main shaft of former Birdforth Colliery, which ceased production in 1798 (Owen, 1970). Fox-Strangways et al. (1886) reported that the lower of the two seams at this colliery was said to have been 0.9 to 1.2 m thick. In addition, two areas with shallow pits are indicated on Primary Survey maps.

Exploration of the Birdford Colliery area as a potential opencast coal site in 1944 showed that there were indeed two seams, but that their thinness, lack of continuity and relatively poor quality militated against any modern development.

AGGREGATE

Sand and gravel

Sand and gravel is widespread in the Thirsk district (Figure 21). Reports analysing the potential resources have been prepared for most of the district (Benfield, 1983; Benfield and Cooper, 1983; Cooper, 1983; Powell, 1983). More intensive resource studies by the BGS Industrial Minerals Assessment Unit, involving drilling and grading of samples, have been made of areas in the north-west (Giles, 1982), the south-west (Strong and Giles, 1983) and south central (Morigi and James, 1984) parts of the district.

In summary, the principal resources and locations of sand and gravel for use as aggregate, for which details can be found in the references cited above, are:

	Approximate maximum thickness (m)
(a) *Sand and gravel of unknown age* (in buried valleys)	
Pickhill [3433 8322]	18
Topcliffe [3841 7578]	8–10
Topcliffe Parks [4017 7713]	6
Dalton Bridge [4098 7604]	18
Ure Valley [30 76] to [32 70]	16

at depth

(b) *Glacial sand and gravel*	
Bedale [28 90] to [27 88]	6
Burneston–Kirklington [30 85] to [31 82]	9
Sutton Howgrave [32 80]	4
Gatenby [32 87]	7
Pickhill [34 83]	14
Sinderby-Skipton on Swale [34 82] to [37 80]	3
Newby Wiske–Busby Stoop [36 90] to [39 80]	9
Skipton on Swale [37 79] to [37 78]	19
Asenby [38 76] to [43 72]	17
Upsall–Thirlby [45 89] to [49 83]	2
Topcliffe–Brafferton [40 76] to [43 70]	22
Bagby [45 80] to [46 79]	2
Little Sessay [46 75]	2
Carlton Husthwaite [48 78] to [49 76]	2
Thormanby [48 75]	2
Raskelf [50 72] to [48 70]	5
Oulston [53 74] to [55 74]	6

(c) *Fluvioglacial sand and gravel*	
Newby Wiske [36 88] to [37 86]	4
Sutton Howgrave–Middleton Quernhow [33 79] to [33 78]	5
Cowesby, Kirkby Knowle, Boltby, Tang Hall [47 89] to [49 84]	4
Thirkleby Bridge [47 78]	4
Little Sessay [46 74]	2
Bedale-Snape [28 88] to [27 83]	8

(d) *Fluvioglacial terrace deposits*	
Wath [30 79] to [33 76]	4
Ripon [32 73] to [30 70]	6
Kirklington [30 80] to [32 82]	5
Nosterfield [27 81] to [30 80]	12
North Stainley [29 77] to [29 80]	3

(e) *River terrace deposits*	
River Ure (N Nunwick) and (Sleningford Mill) [32 74] to [28 78]	7
Rivers Laver and Skell (Ripon) [30 70] to [33 70]	9

(f) *River alluvium*	
River Ure [27 78] to [32 70]	8
River Swale [32 89] to [43 70]	8

Glacial sand and gravel deposits are currently (1988) worked at Firtree Hill Gravel Pit, Cundall [4142 7425] as are fluvioglacial terrace deposits at three pits near Nosterfield [277 797] and at West Tanfield [281 791]. Alluvial sand and gravel of the River Ure are also periodically worked at at North Stainley [299 769]. Sandy till and sand of glacial lake deposits are not good mineral prospects because they usually contain a high percentage of clayey fines, and are generally interbedded with clay. The sand of glacial lake deposits was formerly worked in shallow pits in the district, often in conjunction with the associated laminated clays, but it is generally too thin to justify commercial extraction. Addresses of the working sand and gravel pits in the district are given in Harris et al. (1988).

Scree

Scree deposits in the Hawnby area have been worked for aggregate, principally for local use as hard core and road metal. It consists of angular fragments of oolitic limestone, calcareous sandstone and chert, ranging in size from 0.02 to 0.10 m. Up to 6 m of this deposit has been worked in pits near Plumpton Wood [5396 8867] and Wass House [5567 8996], but it may be as much as 10 m thick. Some of the deposit is not workable because of irregular patches of calcareous cement.

CLAY

Both solid and drift deposits have been used in the past to provide the raw material for brick and tile manufacture. Of the former, the Whitby Mudstone Formation was once worked in shallow pits [467 886] north of Kirkby Knowle and in pits [493 810] near Osgodby Hall. Siltstone and mudstone in the Middle Jurassic Scalby Formation were worked on Boltby Moor [494 882].

However, the extensive deposits of glacial-lake laminated clays provided the more important and more widely worked sources of raw material within the district. In the north of the district, the larger pits included those near Bridge Grange Farm [283 873], south-east of Bedale, and south-west of Solberge Hall [350 886]; a small pit was dug at Brickyard Farm, Carthorpe [294 837]. To the north-west and west of Thirsk, extensive pits were excavated near Avenue Grange [391 844], at Carlton Miniott Brick and Tile Works [404 819] and nearby at Carlton Lodge [398 816]. Further west, smaller brickyards existed south-east of Maunby [367 859], north of Melmerby [337 775], south of Baldersbey [358 781] and at Barugh House, Nunwick [339 745]. To the south-east, Hutton Sessay Brick and Tile Works [457 765] was a major development, and former clay pits [461 729 to 464 726] occur widely around Pilmoor Hall. Finally, in the south-east of the district, the Raskelf Brick and Tile Works [476 715] was of a significant size.

JET

Jet is diagenetically altered, araucarian wood (Hemingway, 1974), which probably formed by compression of water-logged wood in coaly swamps; the wood was subsequently transported offshore and finally deposited in anoxic conditions on the sea floor during the Toarcian stage. Its occurrence in the Jet Rock Member (Whitby Mudstone Formation) is sporadic, and the hard, shiny, semiprecious mineral was formerly extracted from exposures on the Yorkshire coast for use in the production of jewellery. A number of trial pits [5090 7948] for jet have been identified near Kilburn, where the largely drift-covered Jet Rock Member is intermittently exposed; fragments of jet were found in the spoil tips, but the area is presently degraded and overgrown. The date of the trial workings is not known.

SILICA SAND

Silica sand is used in the manufacture of refractory bricks and linings, as moulding sand, and for glass making. Sand from the Moor Grit was formerly worked for these purposes outside the district at Commondale [NZ 66 10] and Whitby (Smith, 1974); within the district, the Moor Grit, where exposed in quarries, is a fine- to medium-grained, almost pure orthoquartzite which could provide abundant silica sand.

Sand for glass making has been extracted outside the district from the Scalby Formation near Malton, and from the Kellaways Rock at Burythorpe [SE 79 64] (Smith, 1974). Ample reserves are available from these formations within the district, although the Kellaways Rock probably contains too many iron impurities to be of exploitable quality.

HYDROCARBONS

The Cleveland Basin has been the subject of considerable exploratory activity for hydrocarbons over many decades. However, only limited success has been achieved to date, with the discovery of a number of minor gas fields. The petroleum geology of the basin has been reviewed by Kirby et al. (1987), Scott and Colter (1987) and Fraser et al. (1990); the western margin of the basin has received much less attention than elsewhere. No exploratory wells have yet been drilled within the Thirsk district, and only restricted seismic reflection surveys, using both dynamite and vibroseis sources, have been carried out. Deep boreholes in adjacent districts have yielded only minor gas shows.

Potential source rocks of Jurassic and Carboniferous age are present within the district. Organic-rich, oil-prone source rocks occur in the Lias Group, particularly the Whitby Mudstone Formation, and in the Kimmeridge Clay, but these are immature (Barnard and Cooper, 1983; Kirby et al., 1987). This, and their restricted and relatively shallow occurrence, precludes the possibility of economic accumulations being derived from such sources in the district. Comparison with neighbouring areas suggests that the concealed Carboniferous rocks are dominantly gas prone, despite the near complete absence of coal-bearing Westphalian (Coal Measures) rocks. It can be inferred that such rocks in the district will be within the oil window (vitrinite reflectance values between 1.0 and 1.5 per cent), at levels of organic maturity below peak gas generation. Oil-prone late Brigantian–Namurian shales of prodelta facies, which sourced the

oilfields of the East Midlands, are believed to be absent in North Yorkshire (Fraser et al., 1990). However, as so little is known of the Carboniferous rocks beneath the district, and of their sedimentary and structural controls, the presence of oil-prone sources cannot yet be totally discounted.

Although local sources of hydrocarbons are therefore unlikely to be present, westerly migration of gas from Carboniferous rocks in the deeper parts of the Cleveland Basin is probable (Kirby et al., 1987). Unfortunately, suitable trapping structures may be absent in the Permian and Mesozoic rocks of the district. In the Cleveland Basin, gas accumulations occur typically in the Kirkham Abbey and Brotherton formations where thick halite sections form tight seals. In the Thirsk area, the Kirkham Abbey Formation is thin and not separated from the Edlington Formation, and the district is to the west of halite deposition and preservation. It must be doubted whether the marginal Permian clastic rocks of the Edlington and Roxby formations can form suitable seals even in closed structures. Structural or even stratigraphical traps in Carboniferous rocks cannot be discounted, given the present lack of detailed knowledge of these rocks. The reservoir properties of Carboniferous sandstones in the Cleveland Basin are generally poor because of the effects of the two phases of deep burial and inversion that they have undergone (Kent, 1980b). However, around the basin margins as in the Thirsk district, such effects are likely to be less severe and more favourable porosity and permeability may have been preserved.

It must be concluded that on present evidence the prospects of finding major hydrocarbon accumulations within the district do not seem great. However, as no detailed study has yet been carried out, and so little is known of the Carboniferous strata of the district, this conclusion may yet prove premature.

HYDROGEOLOGY AND WATER SUPPLY

The district lies within Hydrometric Area 27, and the water resources are administered by the Yorkshire Region of the National Rivers Authority. The principal drainage comprises the Rivers Swale and Ure with their tributaries; the River Rye crosses the extreme north-east corner of the sheet.

The mean annual rainfall varies from more than 760 mm over the higher ground to about 660 mm upon the lower ground. Mean annual losses due to evapotranspiration are of the order of 350 to 400 mm. Rivers tend to be moderately flashy, the mean flows of the Swale and the Ure being around 20 cubic metres per second (m³/sec) against peak flows of the order of 200 m³/sec. The base flow index is generally of the order of 0.4 to 0.5 (Anon, 1988).

Surface water supplies and springs

Within the district, surface water supplies from river and stream intakes are licensed for an annual take of 1576 thousand cubic metres (m³); these supplies are almost wholly used for agricultural purposes, comprising irrigation and livestock. In addition, numerous fairly small springs are used for the same purposes to a licensed annual total of 169 thousand m³; these springs issue from various formations including superficial deposits. A number of generally more substantial springs are used for public supply, notably the Kilburn and Oldstead springs [535 814] issuing from the Osgodby Formation and licensed for 500 thousand cubic metres per annum (m³/a), and the Melmerby springs [340 755] which appear to issue from glacial sands and gravels and are licensed for 81 thousand m³/a. The total licensed take for public supply from springs is 832 thousand m³/a. The upper reaches of the Lunshaw Beck have been impounded to form the small Boltby Reservoir [496 886].

Groundwater

Some previous work on groundwater has been carried out. The eastern half of the district is covered by a well catalogue (Oakley, Bush and Toombs, 1944). The water resources were evaluated by the Yorkshire Ouse and Hull River Authority (1969). A summary of the groundwater resources, obtained from the Yorkshire Water Authority, was published by the European Economic Community (Monkhouse and Richards, 1982). Details of groundwater level fluctuations in observation wells in the Magnesian Limestone and the Sherwood Sandstones have been published in Hydrological Data UK (Anon, 1988).

The major aquifers within the district are the Lower and Upper Magnesian Limestones and the Sherwood Sandstone Group. Whereas supplies for domestic use and agricultural applications are drawn from almost all the formations in the area, public water supplies are pumped only from the two major aquifers. The aquifers are described below in upward stratigraphical order. Licensed abstractions by aquifer and usage are given in Table 11, and chemical analyses of groundwater from three sources are given in Table 12.

The outcrop of the **Millstone Grit** is restricted to a small area in the west of the district. Groundwater can be obtained from the sandstones within this unit, the flow being predominantly through fissures, with a limited additional intergranular storage. Failure to intersect fissures results in a well with little or no yield. Some 37 thousand m³/a are licensed for abstration, all for small agricultural and domestic requirements averaging 5 thousand m³/a. The groundwater quality is usually good, with a total hardness of less than 250 milligrammes per litre (mg/l) as $CaCO_3$. The concentrations of chloride and sulphate are also usually low, but occasional

problems occur with high levels of iron (more than 0.3 mg/l) and more rarely, manganese.

The **Lower** and **Upper Magnesian Limestones** are relatively high-yielding aquifers. The Lower Magnesian Limestone (including the Basal Breccia) is probably more important than the Upper. Infiltration over the outcrop is hindered by an extensive cover of till (boulder clay), but the average is probably of the order of 160 mm annually. Much of the resources within this aquifer come from infiltration to the outcrop west of the district.

The licensed abstraction of groundwater from the Lower and Upper Magnesian Limestones in this district amounts to just under one million m³/a. Of this, 25 per cent is for public supply, 40 per cent for industrial usage, and the rest for domestic, agricultural and other purposes. Agricultural abstractions are usually fairly small, of the order of 10 to 15 thousand m³/a, although some spray irrigation schemes use over 60 thousand m³/a. Public supply and industrial sources are rather larger, generally about 300 thousand m³/a. Table 11 shows the distribution of licensed abstraction.

The matrix of the Lower and Upper Magnesian Limestones is essentially impermeable, and groundwater flow is through extensive fissure systems which are occasionally cavernous. The aquifer characteristics of the Lower Magnesian Limestone have been determined at very few places. Pumping tests at the Lightwater Farm site [286 756], involving three separate boreholes, suggested transmissivities varying from 1000 to 3000 square metres per day (m²/d) and a coefficient of storage of about 1×10^{-4}. A statistical analysis of borehole performance suggests that a borehole of 300 mm diameter penetrating 20 m of saturated aquifer would have a mean yield of the order of 520 m³/d for a drawdown of 10 m; there would be approximately a 20 per cent chance that the yield would be less than 125 m³/d for the same drawdown. Reducing the borehole diameter to 150 mm would reduce these figures to 350 and 85 m³/d respectively.

In the areas where the Lower and Upper Magnesian Limestones crop out or are covered only with a few metres of thickness of drift, the groundwater quality is usually good. The total hardness varies from 200 to 350 mg/l, mostly carbonate hardness. The chloride ion concentration rarely exceeds 40 mg/l, while the levels of iron and manganese are generally low. The water is of the calcium-bicarbonate type. A typical analysis is given in Table 12. Where the aquifer is

Table 11 Licensed abstractions by aquifer and usage in the Thirsk district. Units are in thousands of cubic metres per annum.

Aquifer	Public supply	Agricultural and domestic	Industrial	Other
Drift	—	453	—	—
Lias Group	—	29	—	—
Mercia Mudstone Group	—	8	—	—
Sherwood Sandstone Group	206	966	19	32
Magnesian Limestones	333	250	402	13
Millstone Grit	—	37	—	—
Totals:	539	1743	421	45

Overall total: 2748 thousand cubic metres per annum

Table 12
Chemical analyses
of groundwater
from the Thirsk
district. Units in
mg/l except where
otherwise stated.

Source	1	2	3
Source	Galphey Lane	RAF Leeming	Leckby
Grid reference	288 716	316 890	412 740
Aquifer	Mg Lst	SSG	SSG
Analyst	Yorkshire Water	Government Chemist	Yorkshire Water
Data of analysis	June 1979	March 1985	June 1976
Total hardness (as $CaCO_3$)	236	180	264
Carbonate hardness (as $CaCO_3$)	236	180	232
pH (pH units)	7.57	7.4	
Calcium (as Ca)	61.7	91	88
Magnesium (as Mg)	19.9	27	11
Sodium (as Na)	44.6	12	14
Potassium (as K)	3.7	< 1	2.2
Bicarbonate (as HCO_3)	301.3	220	283
Sulphate (as SO_4)	42.3	45	31
Chloride (as Cl)	22	90	21
Nitrate (as NO_3)	3.4	3.9	1.3
Iron (as Fe)	0.05	0.02	0.19
Manganese (as Mn)	0.02	0.33	0.34

Mg Lst = Magnesian Limestone   SSG = Sherwood Sandstone Group

confined beneath the overlying Triassic strata, the degree of mineralisation is much greater. The total hardness rises to values above 1000 mg/l, very largely non-carbonate hardness, while sulphate in particular may exceed 800 mg/l (as SO_4). The water tends towards the calcium-magnesium-sulphate type.

The role of the Middle and Upper Permian Marls is uncertain. The Middle Marl does not always appear to act as an aquiclude, and so allows for some degree of hydraulic continuity between the upper and lower limestones. The Upper Marl, however, does appear to seal off the base of the Sherwood Sandstones. Undoubtedly, the presence of gypsum in these marls contributes to the high levels of sulphate encountered in the confined limestone aquifers.

The **Sherwood Sandstone Group** forms the second major aquifer in the district. Due to the rather extensive drift cover, infiltration is restricted, but probably ranges from about 165 mm per annum beneath the thicker drift to nearly 200 mm where the drift is thin and sandy.

The licensed abstraction from the Sherwood Sandstone amounts to just under 1.2 million m^3/a; of this, 17 per cent is for public supply, 2 per cent for industrial usage, and the rest for domestic, agricultural and other purposes. The mean licensed take for agricultural purposes is about 20 thousand m^3/a, but for spray irrigation 30 to 50 thousand m^3/a are more usual. Yields from public supply sites are generally less than is the case with the Magnesian Limestone, the maximum being of the order of 136 thousand m^3/a.

The transmissivity of the sandstones is somewhat variable, usually being in the range of 30 to 500 m^2/d. This may to some extent be explained by the presence of fissuring which, being developed locally to a greater or lesser extent, controls the rate of groundwater flow. Intergranular flow does take place, and the intergranular storage is substantial. Where the sandstone outcrop is capped by permeable sands and gravels, the apparent transmissivity, as determined by pumping tests on boreholes, may be much greater and may exceed 1000 m^2/d. The storage coefficient appears generally to be in the range of 1×10^{-3} to 3×10^{-2}. A statistical analysis of borehole performance suggests that a borehole of 300 mm diameter penetrating 50 m thickness of saturated aquifer would have a mean yield of 600 m^3/d for a drawdown of 15 m; there would be approximately a 20 per cent chance that the yield would be less than 60 m^3/d for the same drawdown. Reducing the diameter to 150 m would theoretically reduce these values to 460 to 45 m^3/d respectively.

Groundwaters in the unconfined Sherwood Sandstone aquifer are normally of the calcium-bicarbonate type. The total hardness appears to range from 150 to 300 mg/l, mostly carbonate hardness. The chloride ion concentration is usually less than 30 mg/l although, locally, concentrations approaching 100 mg/l have been recorded. The concentration of the sulphate ion is usually low, less than 50 mg/l, while the levels of iron are generally less than 0.2 mg/l, and manganese can be surprisingly high, concentrations above 0.3 mg/l (as Mn) being recorded. Where the aquifer is confined beneath the Mercia Mudstones, the degree of mineralisation tends to increase. The total hardness may exceed 600 mg/l, largely non-carbonate hardness, and the concentration of sulphate may be more than 600 mg/l. The chloride ion concentration would also be expected to increase, but there is little evidence for this.

The **Mercia Mudstone Group** (with which, hydrogeologically, the Penarth Group is included) is not generally regarded as an aquifer. Nonetheless, some groundwater is often obtainable from the sandstone beds interbedded with the mudstone. In other parts of the outcrop, particularly in the Midlands, numerous sources have been developed for domestic and similar small requirements. However, in the Thirsk district, there is only one licensed source which is for 8 thousand m^3/a. Cavernous horizons associated with the partial dissolution of gypsum beds formerly provided a useful groundwater supply for the Thirsk laundry.

The **Jurassic strata** are little used for groundwater supply from wells and boreholes. There are four licensed sources in the outcrop of the Lias Group, with a total licensed take of under 30 thousand m³/a. Most of the water seems to be taken from the Staithes Sandstone Formation and from the limestone beds (Calcareous Shales) of the Redcar Mudstone Formation. There is insufficient information to permit any analysis of borehole yields. The groundwater appears to vary from soft (total hardness less than 50 mg/l) to hard (hardness more than 550 mg/l), the harder waters apparently being in the Calcareous Shales. The concentration of iron may exceed 3.0 mg/l while the sulphate ion concentrations may be high in the harder waters.

The sandstones and limestones of the Ravenscar Group have some potential as aquifers, although groundwater flow is restricted by numerous, interbedded, thin mudstone aquicludes. However, there are only a few shallow wells in use for domestic supplies. One well of 30 m depth, located in the Scalby Formation beyond the eastern margin of the sheet, yielded 130 m³/d. High concentrations of iron have been recorded, although the groundwater is otherwise generally of good quality.

The Corallian Group might be considered to have a significant potential as an aquifer with generally high permeabilities due largely to fissure flow through joints and bedding planes. However, the strata are deeply incised by the River Rye and its tributaries; consequently, the aquifer is drained by many springs, the potentiometric surface is lowered over large areas to near river level, and the storage capacity of the aquifer is much reduced. Additionally, the population density on the moors is low, the demand on groundwater is very small, and few wells have been constructed.

The Kimmeridge and Ampthill Clays have little hydrogeological significance in this district.

There are 10 licensed groundwater sources located within the **drift** (superficial deposits). Abstraction is mainly from the glacial sands and gravels. The total licensed abstraction is for 453 thousand m³/a, almost all for agricultural use. The mean licensed figure is for 45 thousand m³/a, but the maximum for a single site is for 270 thousand m³/a near Nosterfield [276 801]. There is little available information on groundwater quality, but it would be expected that local concentrations of iron and nitrate could be high. Drift aquifers are also susceptible to pollution from surface sources, and are consequently of doubtful use for domestic supply.

REFERENCES

Most of the references listed below are held in the Library of the British Geological Survey at Keyworth, Nottingham. Copies of the references can be purchased subject to the current copyright legislation.

ABRAHAM, D A. 1981. The sand and gravel resources of the country west of Boroughbridge, North Yorkshire. Description of the 1:25 000 resource sheet SE36. *Mineral Assessment Report, Institute of Geological Sciences,* No. 78.

ALLEN, J R L. 1963. The classification of cross-stratified units, with notes on their origin. *Sedimentology,* Vol. 2, 93 – 114.

ALLSOP, J M. 1985. Geophysical indications of the sub-Permian geology beneath the Ripon area, Northern England. *Proceedings of the Geologists' Association,* Vol. 96, 161 – 169.

ANDERTON, R, BRIDGES, P H, LEEDER, M R, and SELLWOOD, B W. 1979. *A dynamic stratigraphy of the British Isles: A study in crustal evolution.* (London: Allen and Unwin.)

ANON. 1988. Hydrological Data UK: Hydrometric Register and statistics 1981 – 85. (Wallingford: Institute of Hydrology.)

ARKELL, W J. 1933. *The Jurassic system in Great Britain.* (Oxford: Clarendon Press.)

— 1945. The zones of the Upper Jurassic in Yorkshire. *Proceedings of the Yorkshire Geological Society,* Vol. 25, 339 – 359.

ARTHURTON, R S. 1980. Rhythmic sedimentary sequences in the Triassic Keuper Marl (Mercia Mudstone Group) of Cheshire, northwest England. *Geological Journal,* Vol. 15, 43 – 58.

— 1983. The Skipton Rock Fault – an Hercynian wrench fault associated with the Skipton Anticline, northwest England. *Geological Journal,* Vol. 18, 105 – 114.

— JOHNSON, E W, and MUNDY, D J C. 1988. Geology of the country around Settle. *Memoir of the British Geological Survey,* Sheet 60 (England and Wales).

ASHTON, M. 1977. Stratigraphy and carbonate environments of the Lincolnshire Limestone Formation, eastern England. Unpublished PhD thesis, University of Hull.

BAIRSTOW, L. 1969. Lower Lias. 24 – 37 in *William Smith bicentenary field meeting in north-east Yorkshire.* HEMINGWAY, J E (editor) (limited circulation).

BANERJEE, I, and McDONALD, B C. 1975. Nature of esker sedimentation. 132 – 154 in Glaciofluvial and glaciolacustrine sedimentation. JOPLIN, A V, and McDONALD, B C (editors). *Special Publication of the Society of Economic Palaeontologists and Mineralogists,* No. 23.

BARNARD, P C, and COOPER, B S. 1983. A review of the geochemical data related to the northwest European Gas Province. 19 – 33 in *Petroleum geochemistry and exploration of Europe.* BROOKS, J (editor). *Special Publication of the Geological Society of London,* No. 12.

BARROW, G. 1877. On a new marine bed in the Lower Oolites of East Yorkshire. *Geological Magazine,* Vol. 4, 552 – 556.

BATE, R H. 1964. Middle Jurassic ostracoda from the Millepore Series, Yorkshire. *Bulletin of the British Museum (Natural History), Geology,* Vol. 11, 75 – 133.

— 1967. Stratigraphy and palaeoecology of the Yorkshire Oolites and their relationships with the Lincolnshire Limestone. *Bulletin of the British Museum (Natural History), Geology,* Vol. 14, 111 – 141.

BATHURST, R B C. 1975. *Carbonate sediments and their diagenesis* (2nd enlarged edition). (Amsterdam: Elsevier.)

BENFIELD, A C. 1983. *The geology of the county around Dalton, North Yorkshire, with particular reference to sand and gravel deposits: description of 1:25 000 sheet SE 47.* (Keyworth, Nottingham: Institute of Geological Sciences.)

— and COOPER, A H. 1983. *The geology of the country around Pickhill, North Yorkshire, with particular reference to sand and gravel deposits: description of 1:25 000 sheet SE 38.* (Keyworth, Nottingham: Institute of Geological Sciences.)

— and WARRINGTON, G. 1988. New records of the Westbury Formation (Penarth Group, Rhaetian) in North Yorkshire, England. *Proceedings of the Yorkshire Geological Society,* Vol. 47, 29 – 32.

BLACK, M. 1929. Drifted plant-beds of the Upper Estuarine Series of Yorkshire. *Quarterly Journal of the Geological Society, London,* Vol. 85, 389 – 437.

— 1934. A synopsis of the Jurassic rocks of Yorkshire. *Proceedings of the Geologists' Association,* Vol. 45, 247 – 306.

BOWEN, D Q, ROSE, J, McCABE, A M, and SUNDERLAND, D J. 1986. Correlation of Quaternary glaciations in England, Ireland, Scotland and Wales. *Quaternary Science Reviews,* Vol. 5, 299 – 340.

BRIDGE, D Mc C and MURRAY, D W. 1983. The lithological variation and aggregate potential of the Magnesian Limestone, north of Ripon, North Yorkshire (1:25 000 sheets SE 27, 28 and 37). *Open-file Report of the Institute of Geological Sciences.*

BRITISH GEOLOGICAL SURVEY. 1985. Masham. England and Wales Sheet 51. Solid. 1:50 000. (Southampton: Ordnance Survey for British Geological Survey.)

— 1987. Harrogate. England and Wales Sheet 62. Solid. 1:50 000. (Southampton: Ordnance Survey for British Geological Survey.)

BUCKMAN, S S. 1915. A palaeontological classification of the Jurassic rocks of the Whitby district; with a zonal table of Lias ammonites. 59 – 102 in Geology of the country between Whitby and Scarborough. FOX-STRANGWAYS, C E, and BARROW, G. *Memoir of the Geological Survey of England and Wales* (2nd edition).

BURGESS, I C, and COOPER, A H. 1980. The Farnham (IGS) Borehole near Knaresborough, North Yorkshire. *Report of the Institute of Geological Sciences,* No. 81/1, 12 – 17.

CATT, J A, WEIR, A H, and MADGETT, P A. 1974. Loess of eastern Yorkshire and Lincolnshire. *Proceedings of the Yorkshire Geological Society,* Vol. 40, 23 – 29.

CHACKSFIELD, B C, 1985. Detailed gravity survey of the Asenby – Topcliffe Graben: Thirsk. *Report of the Regional Geophysics Research Group, British Geological Survey, Keyworth,* No. 162.

CHOWNS, T M. 1968. Environmental and diagenetic studies of the Cleveland Ironstone Formation of north-east Yorkshire. Unpublished PhD thesis, University of Newcastle upon Tyne.

CLARK, D N. 1980. The diagenesis of Zechstein carbonate sediments. *Contributions to Sedimentology*, Vol. 9, 167–203.

COOPER, A H. 1983. *The geology of the country north and east of Ripon, North Yorkshire, with particular reference to the sand and gravel deposits: description of 1:25 000 sheet SE 37.* (Keyworth, Nottingham: Institute of Geological Sciences.)

— 1986. Subsidence and foundering of strata caused by the dissolution of Permian gypsum in the Ripon and Bedale areas, North Yorkshire. 127–139 in The English Zechstein and related topics. HARWOOD, G M, and SMITH, D B (editors). *Special Publication of the Geological Society of London*, No. 22.

— 1987. *The Permian rocks of the Thirsk district; geological description and local details of 1:50 000 Sheet 52 and component 1:10 000 sheets SE27 SE/NE, SE 28 SE/NE, SE 37 SW/NW and SE 38SW.* (Keyworth, Nottingham: British Geological Survey.)

— 1988. Subsidence resulting from the dissolution of the Permian gypsum in the Ripon area; its relevance to mining and water abstraction. 387–390 in Engineering geology of underground movements. BELL, F G, CULSHAW, M G, CRIPPS, J C, and Lovell, M A (editors). *Engineering Geology Special Publication of the Geological Society of London,* No. 5.

— 1989. Airborne multispectral scanning of subsidence caused by Permian gypsum dissolution at Ripon, North Yorkshire. *Quarterly Journal of Engineering Geology, London,* Vol. 22, 219–229.

— and BURGESS, I C. 1992. Geology of the country around Harrogate. *Memoir of the British Geological Survey*, Sheet 62 (England and Wales).

COPE, J C W. 1974. New information on the Kimmeridge Clay of Yorkshire. *Proceedings of the Geologists' Association*, Vol. 85, 211–221.

— GETTY, T A, HOWARTH, M K, MORTON, N, and TORRENS, H S. 1980. A correlation of Jurassic rocks in the British Isles. Part One: Introduction and Lower Jurassic. *Special Report of the Geological Society of London*, No. 14.

COLTER, V S, and REED, G E. 1980. Zechstein 2 Fordon Evaporites of the Atwick No. 1 borehole, surrounding areas of NE England and the adjacent southern North Sea. *Contributions to Sedimentology*, Vol. 9, 115–129.

COX, B M, and RICHARDSON, G. 1982. The ammonite zonation of Upper Oxfordian mudstones in the Vale of Pickering, Yorkshire. *Proceedings of the Yorkshire Geological Society*, Vol. 44, 53–58.

— LOTT, G K, THOMAS, J E, and WILKINSON, I P. 1987. Upper Jurassic stratigraphy of four shallow cored boreholes in the UK sector of the southern North Sea. *Proceedings of the Yorkshire Geological Society*, Vol. 46, 97–109.

CURTIS, C D, and SPEARS, D A. 1968. The formation of sedimentary iron minerals. *Economic Geology,* Vol. 63, 257–270.

DAVIS, A G. 1967. The mineralogy and phase equilibrium of Keuper Marl. *Quarterly Journal of Engineering Geology, London*, Vol. 1, 25–38.

DUNHAM, K C. 1974. Granite beneath the Pennines in north Yorkshire. *Proceedings of the Yorkshire Geological Society*, Vol. 40, 191–194.

EDWARDS, W. 1938. The glacial geology. 333–343 in The geology of the country arround Harrogate. *Proceedings of the Geologists' Association*, Vol. 49, 293–352.

—1951. The concealed coalfield of Yorkshire and Nottinghamshire. *Memoir of the Geological Survey of Great Britain* (3rd edition).

— 1967. Geology of the country around Ollerton. *Memoir of the Geological Survey of Great Britain* (2nd edition).

ELLIOTT, R E. 1961. The stratigraphy of the Keuper Series in southern Nottinghamshire. *Proceedings of the Yorkshire Geological Society*, Vol. 33, 197–234.

ELLIOTT, T. 1978. Clastic shorelines. 143–175 in *Sedimentary environments and facies.* READING, H G (editor). (Oxford: Blackwell Scientific Publications.)

ENTWISLE, D C. 1984. Density and moisture content determinations on three samples from Thirsk, North Yorkshire. *BGS Engineering Geology Report*, No. 84/5.

FALCON, N L, and KENT, P E. 1960. Geological results of petroleum exploration in Britain 1945–57. *Memoir of the Geological Society of London*, No. 2.

FISHER, M J, and HANCOCK, N J. 1985. The Scalby Formation (Middle Jurassic, Ravenscar Group) of Yorkshire: reassessment of age and depositional environment. *Proceedings of the Yorkshire Geology Society*, Vol. 45. 293–298.

FORBES, B G. 1958. Folded gypsum of Ripon Parks, Yorkshire. *Proceedings of the Yorkshire Geological Society*, Vol. 31, 351–358.

FOWLER, A. 1944. A deep bore in the Cleveland Hills. *Geological Magazine*, Vol. 81, 193–206.

FOX-STRANGWAYS, C. 1892. Jurassic rocks of Britain, Vols. 1 and 2, Yorkshire. *Memoir of the Geological Survey of Great Britain*.

— 1908. The geology of the country north and east of Harrogate. *Memoir of the Geological Survey of Great Britain* (2nd edition).

— and BARROW, G. 1915. The geology of the country between Whitby and Scarborough. *Memoir of the Geological Survey of Great Britain* (2nd edition).

— CAMERON, A G, and BARROW, G. 1886. The geology of the country around Northallerton and Thirsk. *Memoir of the Geological Survey of England and Wales*.

FRASER, A J, NASH D F, STEEL, R P, and EBDON, C C. 1990. A regional assessment of the intra-Carboniferous play of northern England. 417–439 in Classic petroleum provinces. BROOKS, J (editor). *Special Publication of the Geological Society of London*, No. 50.

FUZESY, L M. 1980. Origin of nodular limestones, calcium sulphates and dolomites in the Lower Magnesian Limestone in the neighbourhood of Selby, Yorkshire, England. *Contributions to Sedimentology*, Vol. 9, 35–44.

GALLOIS, R W. 1976. Coccolith blooms in the Kimmeridge Clay and origin of North Sea oil. *Nature, London*, Vol. 259, No. 5543, 473–475.

GAUNT, G D. 1981. Quaternary history of the southern part of the Vale of York. 82–97 in *The Quaternary of Britain*. NEALE, J and FLENLEY, J (editors). (Oxford: Permagon Press.)

— BARTLEY, D D, and HARLAND, R. 1974. Two interglacial deposits proved in boreholes in the southern part of the Vale of York and their bearing on contemporaneous sea levels. *Bulletin of the Geological Survey of Great Britain*, No. 48, 1–23.

— IVIMEY-COOK, H C, PENN, I E, and Cox, B M. 1980. Mesozoic rocks proved by IGS boreholes in the Humber and Acklam areas. *Report of the Institute of Geological Sciences*, No. 79/13, 1–34.

— FLETCHER, T P, and WOOD, C J. 1992. Geology of the country around Kingston upon Hull and Brigg. *Memoir of the British Geological Survey*. Sheets 80 and 89 (England and Wales).

GEOLOGICAL SURVEY OF GREAT BRITAIN. 1874. Harrogate. England and Wales Sheet 62. Drift. (Chessington: Ordnance Survey for Geological Survey.)

— 1884. Thirsk. England and Wales Sheet 52. Drift. (Chessington: Ordnance Survey for Geological Survey.)

GILES, J R A. 1982. The sand and gravel resources of the country around Bedale, North Yorkshire: description of 1:25 000 sheet SE 28. *Mineral Assessment Report, Institute of Geological Sciences*, No. 119.

GLENNIE, K W. 1983. Lower Permian Rotliegend desert sedimentation in the North Sea area. 521–541 in *Eolian sediments and processes, developments in sedimentology*, Vol. 38, BROOKFIELD, M E, and AHLBRANDT, T S (editors). (Amsterdam: Elsevier.)

— and EVANS, G. 1976. A reconnaissance of Recent sediments of the Ranns of Kutch, India. *Sedimentology*, Vol. 23, 625–647.

GRAY, D A. 1961. The hydrology of the Vale of York. *Unpublished Report of the Geological Survey of Great Britain*, WD/52/1.

— 1974. Water resources and supply. 373–384 in *The geology and mineral resources of Yorkshire*. RAYNER, D H, and HEMINGWAY, J E (editors). (Leeds: Yorkshire Geological Society.)

HALLAM, A. 1967. An environmental study of the Upper Domarian and Lower Toarcian in Great Britain. *Philosophical Transactions of the Royal Society*, B, Vol. 252, 393–445.

— 1975. *Jurassic environments.* (Cambridge: Cambridge University Press.)

— and SELLWOOD, B W. 1976. Middle Mesozoic sedimentation in relation to tectonics in the British area. *Journal of Geology*, Vol. 84, 301–321.

HANCOCK, N J, and FISHER, M J. 1981. Middle Jurassic North Sea deltas with particular reference to Yorkshire. 186–195 in *Petroleum geology of the continental shelf of north-west Europe*. ILLING, L V, and HOBSON, G D (editors). (London: Institute of Petroleum.)

HARRIS, P M. 1982. Limestone and dolomite. *Mineral Dossier, Mineral Resources Consultative Committee*, No. 23.

— HIGHLEY, D E, and BENTLEY, K R (compilers). 1988. Directory of mines and quarries 1988 (2nd edition). (Keyworth, Nottingham: British Geological Survey.)

HARRISON, W (editor). 1892. Ripon Millenary. A record of the festival also a history of the city arranged under its wakeman and mayors from the year 1400. (Ripon: W Harrison.)

HARWOOD, G M. 1980. Calcitized anhydrite and associated sulphides in the English Zechstein first cycle carbonate (EZ1 Ca). *Contributions to Sedimentology*, Vol. 9, 61–72.

— 1981. Baryte mineralisation related to hydraulic fracturing in English Permian Z1 carbonates. 379–387 in *Proceedings of the International Symposium on Central European Permian, Warsaw.*

— 1986. The diagenetic history of the Cadeby Formation carbonate (EZ1 Ca), Upper Permian, eastern England. 75–86 in The English Zechstein and related topics. HARWOOD, G M, and SMITH, D B (editors). *Special Publication of the Geological Society of London,* No. 22.

HEDBERG, H B (editor). 1976. *Internation stratigraphic guide: a guide to stratigraphic classification, terminology and procedure.* (New York: Wiley.)

HEMINGWAY, J E. 1949. A revised terminology and subdivision of the Middle Jurassic rocks of Yorkshire. *Geological Magazine*, Vol. 86, 67–71.

— 1974. Jurassic. 161–223 in *The geology and mineral resources of Yorkshire*. RAYNOR, D H, and HEMINGWAY, J E (editors). (Leeds: Yorkshire Geological Society.)

— and KNOX, R W O'B. 1973. Lithostratigraphical nomenclature of the Middle Jurassic strata of the Yorkshire Basin of north-east England. *Proceedings of the Yorkshire Geological Society*, Vol. 39, 527–535.

— and OWEN, J S. 1975. William Smith and the Jurassic coals of Yorkshire. *Proceedings of the Yorkshire Geological Society*, Vol. 40, 297–308.

— and RIDDLER, G P. 1982. Basin inversion in north Yorkshire. *Transactions of the Institute of Mining and Metallurgy, Section B*, Vol. 91, 175–186.

— and TWOMBLEY, B N. 1963. Convolution phenomena in the Hambleton Oolite. *Transactions of the Leeds Geological Association*, Vol. 7, 139–150.

HOWARD, A S. 1985. Lithostratigraphy of the Staithes sandstone and Cleveland Ironstone formations (Lower Jurassic) of north-east Yorkshire. *Proceedings of the Yorkshire Geological Society*, Vol. 45, 261–275.

HOWARTH, M K. 1955. Domerian of the Yorkshire coast. *Proceedings of the Yorkshire Geological Society*, Vol. 30, 147–175.

— 1973. The stratigraphy and ammonite fauna of the upper Liassic grey shales of the Yorkshire coast. *Bulletin of the British Museum (Natural History), Geology*, Vol. 24, 238–277.

INGRAM, R L. 1954. Terminology for the thickness of stratification and parting units in sedimentary rocks. *Bulletin of the Geological Society of America*, Vol. 65, 937–958.

INSTITUTE OF GEOLOGICAL SCIENCES. 1974. *Annual report for 1973.* (London: Institute of Geological Sciences.)

— 1976. IGS Boreholes 1975. *Report of the Institute of Geological Sciences*, No. 76/10.

— 1978. Bouguer gravity anomaly map (Tyne-Tees). 1:250 000 series. (London: Institute of Geological Sciences.)

— 1981. Magnetic anomaly map (Tyne-Tees). 1:250 000 series. (London: Institute of Geological Sciences.)

— 1983. IGS boreholes 1982. *Report of the Institute of Geological Sciences*, No. 83/11.

IVIMEY-COOK, H C, and POWELL, J H. 1991. Late Triassic and early Jurassic biostratigraphy of the Felixkirk Borehole, North Yorkshire. *Proceedings of the Yorkshire Geological Society*, Vol. 48, 367–374.

JAMES, A N, COOPER, A H, and HOLLIDAY, D W. 1981. Solution of the gypsum cliff (Permian, Middle Marl) by the River Ure at Ripon Parks, North Yorkshire. *Proceedings of the Yorkshire Geological Society*, Vol. 43, 433–450.

KALDI, J G. 1980a. Aspects of the sedimentology of the Lower Magnesian Limestone (Permian) of Eastern England. Unpublished PhD thesis, University of Cambridge.

— 1980b. The origin of nodular structures in the Lower Magnesian limestone (Permian) of Yorkshire. *Contributions to Sedimentology*, Vol. 9, 45–60.

— and GIDMAN, J. 1982. Early diagenetic dolomite cements: examples from the Permian Lower Magnesian Limestone of England and the Pleistocene carbonates of the Bahamas. *Journal of Sedimentary Petrology*, Vol. 52, 1073–1085.

KENDALL, P F, and WROOT, H E. 1924. The geology of Yorkshire. (Vienna: printed privately.)

KENT, P E. 1966. The structure of the concealed Carboniferous rocks of north-eastern England. *Proceedings of the Yorkshire Geological Society*, Vol. 35, 323–352.

— 1974. Structural history. 13–28 in *The geology and mineral resources of Yorkshire*. RAYNOR, D H, and HEMINGWAY, J E (editors). (Leeds: Yorkshire Geological Society.)

— 1980a.   *British regional geology: eastern England from the Tees to the Wash* (2nd edition).   (London: HMSO for Institute of Geological Sciences.)

— 1980b.   Subsidence and uplift in East Yorkshire and Lincolnshire: a double inversion.   *Proceedings of the Yorkshire Geological Society*, Vol. 42, 505–524.

KIRBY, G A, SMITH, K, SMITH N J P, and SWALLOW, P W. 1987.   Oil and gas generation in eastern England.   171–180 *Petroleum geology of north west Europe.* BROOKS, J, and GLENNIE, K W (editors). (London: Graham and Trotman.)

KIRBY, G A, and SWALLOW, P W. 1987.   Tectonism and sedimentation in the Flamborough Head region of north-east England.   *Proceedings of the Yorkshire Geological Society*, Vol. 46, 501–509.

KNOX, R W O'B. 1969.   Sedimentological studies of the Eller Beck Bed and Lower Deltaic series in north-east Yorkshire. Unpublished thesis, University of Newcastle Upon Tyne.

— 1970.   Chamosite ooliths from the Winter Gill Ironstone (Jurassic) of Yorkshire (England).   *Journal of Sedimentary Petrology*, Vol. 40, 1216–1225.

— 1973.   The Eller Beck Formation (Bajocian) of the Ravenscar Group of NE Yorkshire.   *Geological Magazine*, Vol. 110, 511–534.

— 1984.   Lithostratigraphy and depositional history of the late Toarcian sequence at Ravenscar, Yorkshire.   *Proceedings of the Yorkshire Geological Society*, Vol. 45, 99–108.

LAMMING, P D, and ROBERTSON, D K. 1968.   Galena in Magnesian Limestone at West Tanfield, Yorkshire.   *Transactions of the Leeds Geological Association*, Vol. 7, 310–314.

LEEDER, M R. 1982.   Upper Palaeozoic basins of the British Isles–Caledonide inheritence versus Hercynian plate margin processes.   *Journal of the Geological Society of London*, Vol. 139, 479–491.

— and NAMI, M. 1979.   Sedimentary models for the non-marine Scalby Formation (Middle Jurassic) and the evidence for late Bajocian/Bathonian uplift of the Yorkshire Basin.   *Proceedings of the Yorkshire Geological Society*, Vol. 42, 461–482.

LIVERA, S E, and LEEDER, M R. 1981.   The Middle Jurassic Ravenscar Group ('Deltaic Series') of Yorkshire: recent sedimentological studies as demonstrated during a field meeting, 213 May, 1980.   *Proceedings of the Geologists' Association*, Vol. 92, 241–250.

LOVELL, J H. 1982.   The sand and gravel resources of the country around Caterick, North Yorkshire: description of 1:25 000 resource sheet SE 29.   *Mineral Assessment Report Institute of Geological Sciences*, No. 120.

MAROOF, S I. 1973.   Geophysical investigations of the Carboniferous and pre-Carboniferous formations of the East Midlands of England.   Unpublished thesis, University of Leicester.

MARR, J E. 1921.   The rigidity of north-west Yorkshire. *Naturalist*, 63–72.

MASSON SMITH, D, HOWELL, P M, and ABERNETHY-CLARK. 1974.   The National Gravity Reference Net 1973. (NGRN '73).   *Ordnance Survey Professional Papers, New Series*, No. 26.

MATTHEWS, B. 1970.   Age and origin of aeolian sand in the Vale of York.   *Nature, London*, Vol. 227, 1234–1236.

MILSON, J, and RAWSON, P F. 1989.   The Peak Trough—a major control on the geology of the North Yorkshire coast. *Geological Magazine*, Vol. 126, 699–705.

MONKHOUSE, R A, and RICHARDS, H J. 1982.   *Groundwater resources of the United Kingdom.*   (Hanover: The Schaefer GmbH, for Commission of the European Communities.)

MORIGI, A N, and JAMES, J W C. 1984.   The sand and gravel resources of the country north-east of Ripon, North Yorkshire: description of 1:25 000 resource sheet SE 37 and part of SE 47. *Mineral Assessment Report, British Geological Survey*, No. 143.

MOSSOP, G D, and SHEARMAN, D J. 1973.   Origins of secondary gypsum rocks.   *Transactions of the Institution of Mining Metallurgy, Section B: Applied Earth Sciences*, Vol. 82, B146–B154.

NAMI, M, and LEEDER, M R. 1978.   Changing channel morphology and magnitude in the Scalby Formation (M. Jurassic) of Yorkshire, England.   431–440 in Fluvial sedimentology. MIALL, A D (editor). *Memoir of the Canadian Society of Petroleum Geologists*, No. 5.

NORRIS, A, BARTLEY, D D, and GAUNT, G D. 1971.   An account of the deposit of shell marl at Burton Salmon, West Yorkshire.   *Naturalist*, 57–63.

OAKLEY, K P, BUSH, E R, and TOOMBS, H A. 1944.   Water supply from underground sources of East Yorkshire–North Lincolnshire District.   *Wartime Pamphlet of the Geological Survey of England and Wales*, No. 12, Part 1.

OLIVE, W W. 1957.   Solution–subsidence troughs, Castile Formation of Gypsum Plain, Texas and New Mexico.   *Bulletin of the Geological Society of America*, Vol. 68, 351–358.

OWEN, J S. 1970.   The moor coal of North Yorkshire: the Thirsk area.   *Buelletin of the Cleveland Teeside Local History Society*, Vol. 8, 1–12.

PAGE, K N. 1989.   A stratigraphical revision for the English Lower Callovian.   *Proceedings of the Geologists' Association*, Vol. 100, No. 3, 363–382.

PARASNIS, D S. 1951.   A study of rock densities in the English Midlands.   *Monthly notes of the Royal Astronomical Society Journal, Geophysical Supplement*, Vol. 6, No. 5, 252–271.

PARSONS, C F. 1977.   A stratigraphic revision of the Scarborough Formation.   *Proceedings of the Yorkshire Geological Society*, Vol. 41, 203–222.

— 1980.   Aalenian and Bajocian correlation chart.   3–21 in A correlation of Jurassic rocks in the British Isles. Part 2. Middle and Upper Jurassic. COPE, J C W, et al. (editors). *Special Report of the Geological Society of London*, No. 15.

PATTISON, J. 1978.   Upper Permian palaeontology of the Aiskew Bank Farm Borehole, North Yorkshire.   *Report of the Institute of Geological Sciences*, No. 78/14.

— SMITH, D B, and WARRINGTON, G. 1973.   A review of late Permian and early Triassic biostratigraphy in the British Isles. 220–260 in The Permian and Triassic systems and their mutual boundary. LOGAN, A V, and HILLS, L V (editors). *Memoir of the Canadian Society of Petroleum Geologists*, No. 2.

PENNY, L F. 1974.   Quaternary.   245–264 in *The geology and mineral resources of Yorkshire.* RAYNOR, D H, and HEMINGWAY, J E (editors). (Leeds: Yorkshire Geological Society.)

PHILLIPS, J. 1829.   *Illustrations of the geology of Yorkshire, or a description of the strata and organic remains. Part 1. The Yorkshire Coast.*   (York: privately printed.)

— 1858.   On some comparative sections in the Oolite and Ironstone Series of Yorkshire.   *Quarterly Journal of the Geological Society, London*, Vol. 14, 84.

POWELL, J H. 1982.   Hambleton Hills; description of field meeting, 19–20 September, 1981.   *Proceedings of the Yorkshire Geological Society*, Vol. 44, 213–216.

— 1983. *The geology of the country around Thirsk, North Yorkshire, with particular reference to the sand and gravel deposits: description of 1:25 000 sheet SE 48.* (Keyworth, Nottingham: Institute of Geological Sciences.)

— 1984. Lithostratigraphical nomenclature of the Lias Group in the Yorkshire Basin. *Proceedings of the Yorkshire Geological Society*, Vol. 45, 51–57.

— 1992. *Gyrochorte* burrows from the Scarborough Formation (Middle Jurassic) of the Cleveland Basin, and their sedimentological setting. *Proceedings of the Yorkshire Geological Society*, Vol. 49.

— and RATHBONE, P A. 1983. The relationship of the Eller Beck Formation and the supposed Blowgill Member (Middle Jurassic) of the Yorkshire Basin. *Proceedings of the Yorkshire Geological Society*, Vol. 44, 365–373.

PURDY, E G. 1963. Recent calcium carbonate facies of the Great Bahama Bank. 2. Sedimentary facies. *Journal of Geology*, Vol. 71, 472–497.

PYRAH, B J. 1977. An exposure of Upper Oxfordian clays in the Vale of Pickering, Yorkshire. *Proceedings of the Yorkshire Geological Society*, Vol. 41, 197–198.

RAYMOND, L R. 1955. The Rhaetic beds and Tea Green Marl of North Yorkshire. *Proceedings of the Yorkshire Geological Society*, Vol. 30, 5–23.

RAMSBOTTOM, W H C. 1974. Namurian. 73–87 in *The geology and mineral resources of Yorkshire.* RAYNOR, D H, and HEMINGWAY, J E (editors). (Leeds: Yorkshire Geological Society.)

REEVES, M J, PARRY, E L, and RICHARDSON, G. 1978. Preliminary evaluation of the groundwater resources of the western part of the Vale of Pickering. *Quarterly Journal of Engineering Geology*, Vol. 11, 253–262.

RICHARDSON, L. 1912. The Lower Oolitic Rocks of Yorkshire. *Proceedings of the Yorkshire Geological Society*, Vol. 17, 184–215.

RIDING, J B, and WRIGHT, J K. 1989. Palynostratigraphy of the Scalby Formation (Middle Jurassic) of the Cleveland Basin, north-east Yorkshire. *Proceedings of the Yorkshire Geological Society*, Vol. 47, 349–354.

ROSE, J. 1985. The Dimlington Stadial/Dimlington Chronozone: a proposal for naming the main glacial eqisode of the Late Devensian in Britain. *Boreas*, Vol. 14, 225–230.

SCOTT, J, and COLTER, V S. 1987. Geological aspects of current onshore Great Britain exploration plays. 95–107 in *Petroleum geology of north west Europe.* BROOKS, J, and GLENNIE, K W (editors). (London: Graham and Trotman.)

SEDGWICK, A. 1829. On the geological relations and internal structure of the Magnesian Limestone, and the lower portions of the New Red Sandstone series in their range through Nottinghamshire, Derbyshire, Yorkshire and Durham to the southern extremity of Northumberland. *Transactions of the Geological Society of London*, Series 2, 3, 37–124.

SELLWOOD, B W. 1970. The relation of trace fossils to small scale sedimentary cycles in the British Lias. 489–504 in *Trace fossils.* CRIMES, T R, and HARPER, J C (editors). *Geological Journal, Special Issue*, No. 3.

— and HALLAM, A. 1974. Bathonian volcanicity and North Sea rifting. *Nature, London*, Vol. 252, 27–28.

SENIOR, J R. 1975. The Middle and Upper Jurassic succession at Boltby Moor, near Thirsk, Yorkshire. *Proceedings of the Yorkshire Geological Society*, Vol. 40, 289–295.

SMITH D B. 1968. The Hampole Beds—a significant marker in the Lower Magnesian Limestone of Yorkshire, Derbyshire and Nottingham. *Proceedings of the Yorkshire Geological Society*, Vol. 36, 463–477.

— 1970a. Permian and Trias. 66–91 *in* The geology of Durham County. JOHNSON, G A L, and HICKLING, G (editors). *Transactions of the Natural History Society, Northumberland*, Vol. 41, No. 1.

— 1970b. The palaeogeography of the British Zechstein. 20–23 in *Third symposium on salt*, Vol. 1. RAU, J L, and DELLWIG, L F (editors). (Northern Ohio Geological Society.)

— 1972. Foundered strata, collapse breccias and subsidence features of the English Zechstein. 255–269 in UNESCO geology of saline deposits. *Proceedings of the Hannover Symposium (Earth Sciences*, No. 7).

— 1974a. Permian. 115–144 in *The geology and mineral resources of Yorkshire.* RAYNER, D H, and HEMINGWAY, J E (editors). (Leeds: Yorkshire Geological Society.)

— 1974b. The stratigraphy and sedimentology of the Permian rocks at outcrop in North Yorkshire. *Journal of Earth Sciences, Leeds,* Vol. 8, 365–386.

— 1980. The evolution of the English Zechstein basin. *Contributions to Sedimentology*, Vol. 9, 7–34.

— 1989. The late Permian palaeogeography of north-east England. *Proceedings of the Yorkshire Geological Scoiety*, Vol. 47, 285–312.

— BRUNSTROM, R G W, MANNING, P I, SIMPSON, S, and SHOTTON, F W. 1974. A correlation of Permian rocks in the British Isles. *Special Report of the Geological Society of London*, No. 5.

— HARWOOD, G M, PATTISON, J, and PETTIGREW, T. 1986. A revised nomenclature for Upper Permian strata in eastern England. 9–17 in The English Zechstein and related topics. HARWOOD, G M, and SMITH, D B (editors). *Special Publication of the Geological Society of London*, No. 22.

SMITH, E G. 1974. Constructional materials and miscellaneous mineral products. 361–371 in *The geology and mineral resources of Yorkshire.* RAYNER, D H, and HEMINGWAY, J E (editors). (Leeds: Yorkshire Geological Society.)

— and WARRINGTON, G. 1971. The age and relationships of the Triassic rocks assigned to the lower part of the Keuper in north Nottinghamshire, north-west Lincolnshire and south Yorkshire. *Proceedings of the Yorkshire Geological Society*, Vol. 38, 201–227.

— RHYS, G H, and GOOSSENS, R F. 1973. Geology of the country around East Retford, Worksop and Gainsborough. *Memoir of the Geological Survey of Great Britain.*

SMITH, I F, and ROYLES, C P. 1989. The digital aeromagnetic survey of the United Kingdom. *British Geological Survey Technical Report*, No. WK/89/5.

SMITHSON, F. 1931. The Triassic sandstones of Yorkshire and Durham. *Proceedings of the Geologists' Association,,* Vol. 42, 125–156.

STANCZYSZYN, R. 1982. The sand and gravel resources of the country around Tholthorpe, North Yorkshire: description of 1:25 000 resource Sheet SE 46. *Mineral Assessment Report Institute of Geological Sciences*, No. 88.

STEWART, F H. 1963. The Permian Lower Evaporites of Fordon, Yorkshire. *Proceedings of the Yorkshire Geological Society*, Vol. 34, 1–44.

STRÖBEL, W. 1973. Der Grundgips im Raum Stuttgart als Modell für Gipsauslaugung und Bildung von Erdfällen. 1–8 in Proceedings of a symposium on sink-holes and subsidence, Hanover. Deutsche Gesellschaft fur Erd und Grunbau Essen, T1-G.

STRONG, G E, and GILES, J R A. 1983. The sand and gravel resources of the country around West Tanfield, North Yorkshire: description of 1:25 000 sheet SE 27. *Mineral Assessment Report, British Geological Survey*, No. 135.

SYKES, R M, and CALLOMON, J H. 1979. The *Amoeboceras* zonation of the Boreal Upper Oxfordian. *Palaeontology*, Vol. 22, 839–903.

TATE, R, and BLAKE, J F. 1876. *The Yorkshire Lias*. (London: John Van Voorst.)

TAYLOR, B J, BURGESS, I C, LAND, D H, MILLS, D A C, SMITH, D B, and WARREN, P T. 1971. *British regional geology: northern England* (4th edition). (London: HMSO for Institute of Geological Sciences.)

TAYLOR, J C M, and COLTER, V S. 1975. Zechstein of the English sector of the southern North Sea basin. 249–263 in *Petroleum and the continental shelf of north-west Europe*, Vol. 1, Geology. WOODLAND, A W (editor). (Barking: Applied Science Publishers.)

TUTE, J S. 1868. On certain natural pits in the neighbourhood of Ripon. *Geological Magazine*, Vol. 5, 178–179.

— 1870. On certain natural pits in the neighbourhood of Ripon. *Proceedings of the Geological and Polytechnic Society of Yorkshire*, Vol. 5, 2–7.

TWOMBLEY, B N. 1964. Environmental and diagenetic studies of the Corallian rocks in Yorkshire, west of Thornton Dale. Unpublished PhD thesis, University of Newcastle upon Tyne.

VACQUIER, V, STEENLAND, N C, HENDERSON, R G, and ZEITZ, I. 1951. Interpretation of aeromagnetic maps. *Memoir of the Geological Society of America*, No. 47.

VAN BUCHEM, F S P, and McCAVE, I N. 1989. Cyclic sedimentation patterns in Lower Lias mudstones of Yorkshire (GB). *Terra Nova*, Vol. 1, 461–467.

WARREN, J K, and KENDALL, C G St C. 1985. Comparison of sequences formed in marine sabkha (subaerial) and saline (subaqueous) settings—modern and ancient. *Bulletin of the Association of American Petroleum Geologists*, Vol. 69, 1013–1023.

WARRINGTON, G. 1974a. Les évaporites du Trias britannique. *Bulletin de la Société géologique de France*, (7), Vol. XVI, n°6, 708–723.

— 1974b. Trias. 145–160 in *The geology and mineral resources of Yorkshire*. RAYNER, D H, and HEMINGWAY, J E (editors). (Leeds: Yorkshire Geological Society.)

— AUDLEY-CHARLES, M G, ELLIOTT, R E, EVANS, W B, IVIMEY-COOK, H C, KENT, P E, ROBINSON, P L, SHOTTON, F W, and TAYLOR, F M. 1980. A correlation of Triassic rocks in the British Isles. *Special Report of the Geological Society of London*, No. 13.

WHITTAKER, A (editor). 1985. *Atlas of onshore sedimentary basins in England and Wales. Post-Carboniferous tectonics and stratigraphy.* (Glasgow & London: Blackie for British Geological Survey.)

— HOLLIDAY, D W, and PENN, I E. 1985. Geophysical logs in British stratigraphy. *Special Report of the Geological Society of London*, No. 18.

WILLS, L J. 1973. A palaeogeological map of the Palaeozoic floor below the Permian and Mesozoic formations in England and Wales with inferred and speculative reconstructions of the Palaeozoic outcrops in adjacent areas in Permo-Triassic times. *Memoir of the Geological Society of London*, No. 7.

WILSON, A A, and THOMPSON, A T. 1965. The Carboniferous succession in the Kirkby Malzeard area, Yorkshire. *Proceedings of the Yorkshire Geological Society*, Vol. 35, 203–227.

— and CORNWELL, J C. 1982. The Institute of Geological Sciences Borehole at Beckermonds Scar, North Yorkshire. *Proceedings of the Yorkshire Geological Society*, Vol. 44, 59–88.

WILSON, V. 1933. The Corallian rocks of the Howardian Hills (Yorkshire). *Quarterly Journal of the Geological Society of London*, Vol. 89, 480–509.

WOOLLAM, R, and RIDING, J B. 1983. Dinoflagellate cyst zonation of the English Jurassic. *Report of the Institute of Geological Sciences*, No. 83/2.

WRIGHT, J K. 1968. The stratigraphy of the Callovian rocks between Newtondale and the Scarborough Coast, Yorkshire. *Proceedings of the Geologists' Association*, Vol. 79, 363–399.

— 1972. The stratigraphy of the Yorkshire Corallian. *Proceedings of the Yorkshire Geological Society*, Vol. 39, 225–266.

— 1977. The Cornbrash Formation (Callovian) in North Yorkshire and Cleveland. *Proceedings of the Yorkshire Geological Society*, Vol. 41, 325–346.

— 1978. The Callovian succession (excluding Cornbrash) in the western and northern parts of the Yorkshire Basin. *Proceedings of the Geologists' Association*, Vol. 89, 259–261.

— 1980. Oxfordian correlation chart. 61–76 *in* A correlation of Jurassic rocks in the British Isles. Part 2: Middle and Upper Jurassic. COPE, J C W, et al. (editors). *Special Report of the Geological Society of London*, No. 15.

— 1983. The Lower Oxfordian (Upper Jurassic) of North Yorkshire. *Proceedings of the Yorkshire Geological Society*, Vol. 44, 249–281.

YORKSHIRE OUSE AND HULL RIVER AUTHORITY. 1969. *Water Resources Act 1963 Section 14: Survey of water resources*. (Leeds: Yorkshire Ouse and Hull River Authority.)

ZIEGLER, P A. 1982. *Geological atlas of Western and Central Europe*. (Maatschappij: Elsevier for Shell International Petroleum.)

APPENDIX 1

Boreholes and shafts

The appendix lists, by 1:10 000 quarter-sheet, those boreholes and shafts in the district that are of particular geological interest. Shafts of which only the site is known are omitted, as are most water, motorway, and site investigation boreholes.

The primary source of information on sinkings before 1886 is the Geological Survey Memoir 'Geology of the country around Northallerton and Thirsk', (Fox-Strangways et al., 1886).

The sites and brief abstract logs of most of the boreholes listed are shown on the six-inch geological maps.

The following abbreviations are used:

Chronostratigraphical units

D	Drift
J	Jurassic
T	Triassic
P	Permian
P-T	Permo-Triassic
C	Carboniferous

References

FS	Fox-Strangways et al., 1886
Rep IGS	Report of the Institute of Geological Sciences
MA	Mineral Assessment Report, Institute of Geological Sciences

BGS registered number	Name	National Grid ref.	Surface level	Total depth	Chronostratigraphical unit	Reference
SE 27 NE						
1b	Potgate Farm	2778 7553	c. 76	60.96	P,C	
2	Musterfield Farm	2713 7608	c. 97	107.59	P,C	
3	Sleningford Grange	2851 7753	c. 43	41.15	D,P	
5	North Stainley Council Houses	2882 7726	c. 41	27.43	D,P	
6	Wood Farm	2888 7531	c. 70	108.81	D,P,C	
22	Lightwater Farm No. 2	2871 7643	49	40	D,P	
23	Lightwater Farm No. 3	2863 7641	50	40	D,P,C	
24	West Tanfield	2746 7912	45.4	14.5	D,P	MA No.135
26	Back Lane	2967 7986	41.8	12.5	D,P	MA No.135
35	Rushwood Hall	2973 7789	36.6	17.5	D,P	MA No.135
48	Sleningford Mill	2778 7841	45	40.67	D,P,C	
SE 27 SE						
1	Doublegates Quarry	2943 7142	c. 45	40.54	D,P,C	
2	School of Military Engineering	2957 7184	c. 50	46.63	D,P	
8	Thieves Gill Farm	2734 7399	c. 94	36.57	D,P,C	
11	High Lindrick Farm	2722 7035	c.106	94	D,P,C	
26	Galphay Lane	2876 7161	53	62.5	D,P,C	
27	Galphay Lane	2876 7159	53	66	D,P,C	
21	Sunley Raynes	2900 7139	47	17.7	D,P	MA No.135
23	Studley Roger	2954 7026	44.3	12.0	D,P	MA No.135
SE 28 NE						
1	Watling Gate Cottages	2944 8933	c. 32	28.96	D,T	
2	Newhouse	2934 8686	c. 40	25.60	D,P	
4	Scar Cottage	2891 8989	c. 33	30.48	D,T,P	
5	Leeming Bar	2859 8989	c. 32	43.59	D,T,P	
35	Exelby	2950 8680	37.1	10.20	D,T	MA No.119
SE 28 SE						
5	Well Quarry	2673 8128	c. 80	76.2	P,C	
18	Salmon House	2730 8360	43.2	19.0	D	MA No.119
24	Upsland	2990 8109	c. 37.0	13.5	D,P	MA No.119
25	Flask Lane	2805 8078	42.8	16.0	D,P	MA No.119
26	Lady Bridge	2911 8099	41.8	11.5	D,P	MA No.119
27	Three Hills	2917 8014	42.3	14.5	D	MA No.119

BGS registered number	Name	National Grid ref.	Surface level	Total depth	Chronostratigraphical unit	Reference
SE 37 NW						
1	Norton Conyers Hall	3199 7628	c. 38	216	D,P,C	
3	Parkfield House	3220 7798	c. 39.6	35.6	D,T,P	
4	Grange Farm	3228 7697	c. 33.8	32.9	D,P	
6	Middleton Quernhow	3330 7852	c. 36.6	27.4	D,T	
8	Bedale Hunt Inn	3439 7911	c. 35.4	25.9	D,T	
12	The Manor	3345 7831	c. 37	43.3	D,T	
13	Coldstone Lodge	3347 7839	c. 37	30.6	D,T	
14	Coldstones Farm	3345 7985	c. 37.8	95.1	D,T,P	
24	The Old House	3344 7825	c. 37	30.48	D,T	
27	Melmerby Road	3431 7538	c. 39.6	60	D,P,T	
34	Upsland Farm	3078 7984	38.7	6	D,P	MA No.143
38	Middleton Quernhow	3320 7894	c. 37.0	12.5	D,T	MA No.143
50	North Parks Farm	3003 7642	33.5	20.7	D	MA No.143
51	Norton Conyers	3171 7607	30.1	18.0	D,P	MA No.143
52	North Lawn, Norton Conyers	3202 7680	31.7	7.8	D,P	MA No.143
56	Whinny Hills	3207 7555	27.7	7.3	D,P	MA No.143
58	Manor Farm	3413 7813	c. 36.6	60.96		
79	Home Farm	3231 7650	c. 32	45.72		
SE 37 NE						
2	Catton Hall	3727 7862	c. 27.4	37.2	D,T	
3	Baldersby St. James	3633 7682	c. 35.1	93	D,T	
4b	Park House Farm	3868 7553	31.1	36.57	D,T	
5	Park Nurseries	3841 7577	c. 31.1	38.1	D,T	
6b	Asenby	3980 7532	28	77.1	D,J,T	
16	Topcliffe	3998 7594	25.9	45.7	D,T	
17	Rainton	3724 7508	31.1	91.4	D,T	
18	Bridge End Farm	3615 7983	24.4	45.72	D,T	
19	Topcliffe Fields	3959 7605	22.2	45.72	D,T	
34	Skipton on Swale	3719 7966	c. 29.6	19.1	D,T	MA No.143
50	Park House	3856 7532	34.3	23.0	D,T	MA No.143
53	Rush House Farm	3917 7963	c. 26	76.2	D,T	
SE 37 SW						
35	South Park Farm	3080 7414	c. 46.0	36.88	D,P	
40	Hutton Hall	3342 7406	39.62	44.81	D,P	
41	Sharow Hall	3301 7165	39.6	45.72	D,P	
43	Ripon Gasworks	3153 7157	c. 22.9	58.2	D,P	
45	Copt Hewick Hill	3453 7183	54.9	42.67	D,T	
46	Blois Hall	3455 7253	c. 71.9	65.53	D,T	
47	White Swan Laundry	3106 7120	c. 30.5	182.88	D,P,C	
91	Home Farm	3222 7328	c. 39.6	66.44	D,T,P	
93	Ripon City Golf Club	3071 7292	c. 46.3	34	D,P	
96	Manor Farm	3278 7349	c. 44.2	76.81	D,T,P	
97	Hutton Hill	3263 7273	c. 54	92	T,P	
100	Hall Garth Hill	3160 7488	24.5	15.4	D,P	MA No.143
106	Ure Bank	3155 7268	c. 22.5	21.4	D	MA No.143
128	Dallamires Lane	3198 7059	c. 24.4	68	D,P,T	
SE 37 SE						
1	Windmill Cafe	3623 7424	c. 48.8	39.6	D,T	
2	The Bungalow	3657 7260	c. 50.9	30.5	D,T	
4	RAF Dishforth	3867 7158	c. 32.0	76.8	D,T	
7	Windmill Cafe	3620 7417	c. 48.8	45.7	D,T	
10	Lingham Lane Farm	3947 7296	22.86	60.96	D,T	
12	Guy Reed Farms	3883 7434	c. 35	60	D,T	
17	Cana Barn	3639 7175	c. 61	91.44	D,T	
40	The Carrs	3796 7398	26.2	15.1	D,T	MA No.143
42	Primrose Hill	3985 7464	26.1	25.0	D,T	MA No.143
45	Dishforth	3877 7341	27.7	19.2	D,T	MA No.143
81	Dishforth Sewage treatment works	3845 7335	c. 28.6	76.2	D,T	

BGS registered number	Name	National Grid ref.	Surface level	Total depth	Chronostra-tigraphical unit	Reference
SE 38 NW						
4	Milton House	3022 8746	40.5	36.5	D,T	
6	Fairholme Farm	3276 8956	c. 29.9	36.88	D,T	
10b	Far Fairholme	3216 8904	c. 26	10.10	D,T	
21a	Leeming Airfield	3117 8902	c. 27	16.1	D,T	
SE 38 NE						
14	Wathstones	3641 8836	c. 31.1	46	D,T	
SE 38 SW						
1	Kirklington Gravel Pits	3142 8184	c. 41	52.43	D,P	
3	Street House Farm Cottage	3317 8160	36	24.69	D,T	
8	Pasture (Barn) House Farm	3322 8321	30.8	42.67	D,T	
9	Haw Transport Cafe	3344 8123	c. 39.6	24.38	D,T	
10	High Ness Farm	3338 8384	32	25.3	D,T	
11	Church House	3463 8380	c. 27.4	36.58	D,T	
12	Pickhill Post Office	3461 8343	c. 29	27.43	D,T	
14	Crab Tree Inn	3397 8008	36	25.91	D,T	
17b	Pickhill	3433 8321	c. 31.8	46.8	D,T	
18	Low Ness Farm	3272 8427	c. 29	27.43	D,T	
19b	Kirklington Hall	3152 8130	c. 39.6	28	D,T,P	
27	New Filling Station	3379 8064	38.7	30.48	D,T	
29	Sinderby Filling Station	3369 8054	c. 39.6	30.48	D,T	
33	Red House Farm	3011 8108	c. 41.1	39.62	D,P,T	
34	Berry Hill Farm	3307 8050	36.6	54.86	D,P,T	
38	Kirklington	3287 8091	33.76	298.48	D,T,P,C	
42	High Ness Farm	3311 8370	c. 29	60.96	D,T	
45	Street Farm	3285 8148	c. 35	60.96	D,T,P	
46	Mount Pleasant Farm	3090 8395	46.0	39.01	D,T,P	
SE 38 SE						
1	Howe	3586 8026	c. 23.2	26.82	D,T	
5	Sand Hutton Schools	3816 8227	c. 31.4	27.43	D,T	
6	Scarboro' House Farm	3596 8334	c. 24.38	36.58	D,T	
7	Castle Farm	3765 8423	28.96	31.09	D,T	
8	Mowbray House	3923 8206	c. 29.2	45.72	D,T	
9d	Sandhutton	3939 8202	26.5	121.9	D,T	
13	Cowland Lane	352 808	c. 24.4	70	D,T	
SE 47 NW						
1	Topcliffe	4020 7643	27.51	39.62	D,T	
3	Dalton	4201 7505	c. 18.3	35.4	D,T	
7	Dalton	4330 7636	c. 24.4	91.4	D,T	
8	Topcliffe	4018 7713	c. 24.4	58.2	D,T	
19	Dalton Airfield	4225 7561	c. 19.8	45	D,T	
20	Thirsk Bypass No. 76	4234 7958	c. 31	18.0	D,T	
49d	Asenby-Topcliffe Bypass	4000 7516	c. 24	7.4	D,J	
65	Common House	4100 7688	24.3	19.7	D,T	MA No.143
73	Scaife Shay Bridge	4472 7646	c. 27.0	7.7	D,J	MA No.143
79a	Dalton West Bridge	4098 7604	c. 17	33.7	D,T	
SE 47 NE						
24	Thirkeby Bridge	4734 7743	c. 35	7.3	D	
28	Crowtree House	4616 7679	c. 27	15.3	D,T	
32	Quarry Hill Farm	4790 7726	c. 35	20.1	D,J	
SE 47 SW						
1	Cundall Village	4242 7263	c.100	60.06	D,T	
3	Norton-Le-Clay	4018 7113	c. 21.9	32.92	D,T	
6	Ray Bank	4388 7133	c. 18.3	60.96	D,T	
12	Studforth Farm	405 725	c. 17.1	92	D,T	
13	Highfield Farm	4386 7008	c. 21.9	51.82	D,T	
14	Leckby	4115 7401	20.4	44.19	D,T	
17	Leckby Grange	4138 7472	20.4	12.0	D,J	
31	Park Hill	4231 7101	22.3	19.0	D,T	MA No.143
39	Studforth	4018 7276	c. 58	90	D,T	
40	Cundall Sewage Works	421 725	c. 60	76.2	D,T	

BGS registered number	Name	National Grid ref.	Surface level	Total depth	Chronostra-tigraphical unit	Reference
SE 47 SE						
2	Sessay	4781 7404	c.103	30.48	J	
3	Brafferton	4514 7071	c. 16.5	53.04	D,T	
4	Pilmoor	462 721	c. 24.4	65.53	D,T	
16	Raskelf	4903 7101	c. 31	20.00	D,J	
17	Royston Hills	4847 7052	c. 26	19.70	D,T	
SE 48 NW						
6	Low Farm Cowesby	4447 8962	c. 97.5	37.49	D,J	
8	Thirsk-Northallerton Golf Course	4202 8502	c. 39.6	95.09	D,J,T	
SE 48 NE						
2	Felixkirk	4835 8576	185	299.15	J,T	Rep. IGS No. 83/11
SE 48 SW						
3	Marr & Co's Brewery	4272 8209	c. 36	109.9	D,T	F S
4	Carlton Minniott	402 814	c. 28.3	45.72	D,T	
19	Woodhead & Bray	4274 8210	c. 37.2	74.37	D,T	
21	Auction Mart	4207 8179	c. 34.7	45.41	D,T	
SE 48 SE						
1	Mount St. John	471 848	c.168	6.1	D,J	F S
SE 57 NE						
3	Low Pasture House	5521 7836	c. 56	121.31	D,J	F S
5	Newburgh Park Coll.	5538 7572	c.121	15.2	J	F S
SE 57 SW						
4	Oulston Well	5470 7438	121.92	30.78	D,J	
7	Springfield Farm	5141 7212	30.2	45.72	D,J	

APPENDIX 2

Selected borehole logs

Aiskew Bank Farm Borehole: BGS Ref SE 28 NE/9; SE 2667 8888]; surface level 40 m above OD.

This borehole was sunk in 1974 by the Geological Survey to prove the Permian and Namurian succession in the north-east corner of the Masham (51) district; it is situated near Bedale, a few hundred metres west of the Thirsk district. The borehole was logged by Drs A A Wilson and D B Smith and the Permian fossils identified by Mr J Pattison (Table 3; Pattison, 1978). Carboniferous fossils were identifed by Drs W C H Ramsbottom and A A Wilson.

	Thickness m	Depth m
Soil	0.20	0.20
Pleistocene and Recent		
Clay, reddish brown, with pebbles and cobbles, mainly of sandstone	22.97	23.17
Clay and silt, brown, generally stoneless	12.23	35.40
Clay, grey, silty, with pebbles of sandstone and Carboniferous limestone	0.54	35.94
Clay, khaki, stoneless	1.06	37.00
Clay, grey, becoming brown with depth, silty, with pebbles of dolomite, limestone and sandstone; abrupt base at rockhead	8.20	45.20
LOWER MAGNESIAN LIMESTONE (see Table 3, for palaeontology)		
Dolomite, yellow and buff, very fine sand and silt grade, largely reduced to a powder; 40 per cent recovery	15.58	60.78
Dolomite, buff, silt-grade, with stellate groups of platy calcite crystals after gypsum; stylolitic contacts and calcite-filled vughs	6.09	66.87
Dolomite, buff and brown, silt grade, porous, with vughs; stylolitic bedding contacts	3.68	70.55
Dolomite, grey, silt grade, with relict ooliths and a few vughs; abundant foraminifera	3.37	73.92
Dolomite, grey, silt grade, with relict ooliths and abundant shelly fossils; a few stylolites with pyrobitumen	1.88	75.80
Dolomite, grey, with relict ooliths and peloids; foraminifera and shelly fossils	2.38	78.18
Dolomite, grey, silt to very fine sand grade, with relict ooliths and pellets; stylolitised bedding planes; 0.004 m dark grey mudstone at base	0.86	79.04
Dolomite, grey, silt to very fine sand grade, with calcite pods that have dolomite aureoles; stylolitised with pyrobitumen; numerous mudstone and dolomitic mudstone laminae towards base	6.51	85.55
Dolomite, grey, with ooliths and oncoids, and an abundant shelly fauna; some stylolitic contacts	1.97	87.52
Dolomite, grey, laminated, with mudstone and dolomitic mudstone laminae; scattered shelly fossils	3.35	90.87
Dolomite, grey, calcareous, with coquinoid beds; oolitic, with an abundant shelly fauna	0.63	91.50

	Thickness m	Depth m
Dolomite, grey, calcareous, with scattered dark grey oncoliths, up to 0.001 m across, and several layers rich in glauconite; abundant shelly fauna	0.90	92.40
MARL SLATE		
Mudstone, grey, with scattered nodular pellets of mudstone up to 0.001 m across, possibly of algal origin	0.10	92.50
BASAL BRECCIA		
Breccia conglomerate, comprising grey, calcareous sand with abundant grey clasts of dolomitised Carboniferous limestone, and sporadic sandstone, chert and siltstone fragments. The angular to subangular fragments, up to 0.2 by 0.004 m across, are plate-like with scattered traces of crinoid columnals and corals, largely obliterated by recrystallisation. Desert varnish is present on some clasts	2.78	95.28
Breccia conglomerate, grey, with pale grey, subangular, dolomitised Carboniferous limestone clasts and several calcareous bands up to 0.005 m thick with a few clasts	1.17	96.45
Unconformity		
LOWER FOLLIFOOT GRIT		
Sandstone, grey, fine- to medium-grained, coarse near base, feldspathic and cross-bedded; carbonaceous debris on several bedding planes; chalcopyrite in nests at 97.40 to 97.55 m; sporadic micaceous bedding planes	3.65	100.10
Sandstone, pale grey, fine-grained, with a 0.005 m-thick feldspathic purple mudstone band at 104.95 m	5.00	105.10
Sandstone, pale grey, medium-grained, with blotchy cementation of baryte in patches up to 1 cm across	0.35	105.45
Sandstone, pale grey, fine- to medium-grained, mainly feldspathic, with micaceous partings and some cross- bedding	4.33	109.78
Mudstone and siltstone, grey, mainly laminated, with abundant laminae and thin beds of fine-grained sandstone up to 0.002 m thick; some beds are bioturbated and many of the sandstones show groove-cast bases and flame structures	25.50	135.28
Mudstone, grey, silty, with *Anthracoceras* sp., fish scales and teeth, and a bivalve fragment; phosphatic nodules near base; passing down into	0.81	136.09
Sandstone, fine- and medium-grained, clayey, with phosphatic nodules; passing down into quartzite with rootlets (seatearth?) and aggregates of pyrite	0.61	136.70

	Thickness m	Depth m
Sandstone, fine-grained, micaceous, with cross-lamination and groove casts	1.02	137.72
Limestone, grey, very silty, with podded texture	0.06	137.78
Mudstone, grey, with crinoid columnals and a prolific fauna including: *Antiquatonia costata*, *Productus s.s.*, orthotetoids, spiriferoids, orthocones, productoids with spines attached, spiriferoids, *Lingula*, *Orbiculoidea*, archaeocidarid spines, *Limipecten*, *Sulcatopinna*? and a fenestellid	1.08	138.86
Limestone, silty, with crinoid debris	0.03	138.89
Mudstone, grey, with productoids, *Avonia* sp., *Lingula* sp., spiriferoid, *Leiopteria* sp, *Limipecten* sp., *L. dissimilis*, crustacean, *Donaldina* sp., archaeocidaroid spines, bryozoa, *Parallelodon* sp., nuculoid, *Coleolus* sp., orthotetoids, chonetoids, *Schuchertella* sp., pectinoids, *Edmondia*? and *Retispira striata*	2.69	141.58
Sandstone, grey, fine- and very fine-grained, laminated and thin-bedded, with abundant siltstone laminae; sporadic cross-lamination in sandstone beds; gradational, interbedded base with mudstone below	5.27	146.85
Mudstone, grey and dark grey, silty, with *Lingula*; plant debris near base	4.35	151.20

COLSTERDALE MARINE BEDS

	Thickness m	Depth m
Mudstone, grey to dark grey, with sporadic clay ironstone beds and nodules; *Planolites* near top of unit; abundant fauna, including *Anthracoceras* sp. productoids, orthocone nautiloids, *Posidonia corrugata*, *Palaeoneilo* juv., *Solemya primaeva*, *Posidoniella variabilis*, *Nuculopsis gibbosa*, *Polidevcia attenuata*, *Crurithyris* sp., *Rugosochonetes* sp., *Lingula* sp., *Spiriferellina* sp. and *Glabrocingulum* sp.	18.34	169.54
Mudstone, grey to dark grey, with sporadic clay ironstone beds and nodules; abundant fauna, including *Posidonia corrugata*, *Cravenoceras holmesi* (three dimensional), *Anthracoceras* sp., *Glabrocingulum* sp., *Polidevcia attenuata*, *Nuculopsis gibbosa*, *Spiriferellina* sp.	3.73	173.27
Sandstone, very fine-grained, orthoquartzitic	1.03	174.30
Coal, dense, with low-angled calcite veins (dip 27°); true thickness 0.075 m	0.09	174.39
Seatearth mudstone, dark grey with 0.04 m seatearth sandstone at top	0.61	175.00
Mudstone, grey and dark grey (dip 3–7°), with pyrite and coprolites?, *Lingula* sp., fish scales and shelly fragments	1.60	176.60

RED SCAR GRIT

	Thickness m	Depth m
Sandstone, fine- to medium-grained, quartzitic, with some cross-lamination	2.17	178.77

Well Quarry Borehole: BGS Ref SE 28 SE/5; [2673 8128]; surface level c.80 m above OD. Water borehole in quarry.

	Thickness m	Depth m
LOWER MAGNESIAN LIMESTONE		
Limestone	25.30	25.30
"Marl"	5.80	31.10

Unconformity

CARBONIFEROUS STRATA

	Thickness m	Depth m
Shale with coarse-grained sandstone beds	24.70	55.80
Coarse-grained sandstone	8.50	64.30
Shale	1.50	65.80
Fine-grained sandstone	10.40	76.20

Felixkirk Borehole: BGS Ref SE 48NE/2; [4835 8576]; surface level 185 m above OD.

This borehole was drilled near Houseborough Farm in 1982 to provide a complete cored sequence through the Lias Group in the west of the Cleveland Basin and to investigate the nature of the Lias Group – Penarth Group junction. Due to collapse of the hole, drilling was terminated close to the base of the Penarth Group.

The following geophysical logs were run to a depth of about 270 m: Gamma, LS Density and 3-arm Caliper, Multi-Channel Sonic, Neutron-Neutron, Self Potential and Resistivity, and Focussed Electric. Down-hole temperatures were also recorded.

The core was logged on site by Dr J H Powell. Following further detailed logging of the core, some of the unit boundaries have been slightly revised from those given in Report of the Institute of Geological Sciences, 1983. Fossils listed here were identified by Dr H C Ivimey-Cook; palynomorphs from the Penarth Group section (Figure 7, p.24) were determined by Dr G Warrington.

	Thickness m	Depth m
Ravenscar Group		
SALTWICK FORMATION		
Mudstone, yellow-brown, silty (poor recovery)	5.10	5.10
Sandstone, yellow-orange, green-grey where unweathered, quartzose, micaceous, medium-to coarse-grained, cross-laminated, with sparse carbonaceous plant fragments; bioturbated in part, with subvertical, circular burrows; laminae and intraclasts of siderite mudstone	10.07	15.17
DOGGER FORMATION		
Ironstone, yellow-orange, consisting of sideritic mudstone, weathering to limonite; scattered chamosite ooliths; rare small phosphatic pebbles (0.002 to 0.005 m diameter); shell fragments and bivalves, including oysters, locally abundant	2.72	17.89
Limestone, green-grey, shelly (biosparite); small disseminated shell fragments; argillaceous micrite at base	0.20	18.09
Lias Group		
WHITBY MUDSTONE FORMATION		
Alum Shale Member		
Mudstone, medium grey, fissile; silty in part, micaceous, with scattered brachiopods and bivalves, including *Lingula* sp. and pectinids; also belemnites and ammonites of the *bifrons* Zone	13.21	31.30
Jet Rock Member		
Mudstone, medium to dark grey, fissile, micaceous and silty in part; calcitic and pyritised fossils include bivalves (particularly inoceramids in shell laminae), gastropods, and ammonites of the *falciferum* Zone (proved to 49.01 m)	14.21	45.51

	Thickness m	Depth m

Mudstone, dark grey, fissile, silty, with brown organic-rich laminae ; calcitic and pyritised fossils include abundant ammonites and shell laminae; thin beds of finely laminated (upward-fining), micaceous, calcareous siltstone and silty mudstone (47.10 to 47.60 m; 48.94 to 49.80 m and 55.00 to 55.40 m); black coaly wood fragments (jet) at 46.81 m and 47.92 m; green-grey calcareous concretions up to 0.01 m diameter from 49.80 to 50.63 m; ammonites of the *falciferum* and *tenuicostatum* zones — 10.50 — 56.01

Grey Shale Member

Mudstone, medium grey, micaceous, silty, with sparse, thin, pale grey siltstone laminae (upward-fining); buff to green-grey calcareous nodules (up to 0.10 m diameter); disseminated pyrite and septarian cracks at 58.48 m, 59.00 m, 60.20 m and 61.00 m; fossils include bivalves and belemnites, and ammonites of the *tenuicostatum* Zone (to 60.94 m) — 4.99 — 61.00

CLEVELAND IRONSTONE FORMATION

Siltstone, pale grey, calcareous, passing down to extensively bioturbated, fine-grained sandstone with horizontal and subvertical burrows including *Chondrites*; silty mudstone with sparsely oolitic (berthierine ooliths), calcareous siltstone bands from 61.22 to 61.29 m — 0.29 — 61.29

Sandstone, pale grey, calcareous, micaceous, very fine- to fine-grained and siltstone; extensively bioturbated, including *Diplocraterion* and *Chondrites* burrows; bivalves include *Pseudopecten* sp. and *Pholadomya* sp.; brown, organic-rich silty mudstone laminae with upward-fining pulses from 61.88 to 62.03 m (?Sulphur Band) — 1.26 — 62.55

Ironstone, calcareous, sideritic, with berthierine ooliths; oolitic intraclasts and scoured erosion surfaces; thin sandstone laminae; sharp base (**Main Seam**) — 0.35 — 62.90

Mudstone and silty mudstone, finely laminated, with small siderite concretions, *Chondrites* burrows and small bivalves and ammonite fragments — 2.24 — 65.14

Ironstone, pale green-grey, calcareous, sideritic, with berthierine ooliths and siderite intraclasts; fossils include thick-shelled bivalves and belemnites; bioturbated in part; silty mudstone parting (**Avicula Seam**) — 0.42 — 65.56

Sandstone, pale grey, very fine-grained, micaceous, and siltstone; extensively bioturbated, including *Chondrites* burrows; siderite concretions; bivalves locally abundant; silty mudstone from 68.38 to 70.10 m — 4.16 — 69.72

Ironstone, pale grey, calcareous, sideritic, with sparse berthierine ooliths and mudstone intraclasts; sideritc mudstone in part; bivalves and burrows present; sharp base (**Osmotherly Seam**) — 0.38 — 70.10

STAITHES SANDSTONE FORMATION

Sandstone, pale to medium grey, calcareous,

	Thickness m	Depth m

very fine- to medium-grained, micaceous, ripple cross-laminated and cross-bedded; extensively bioturbated, including *Chondrites, Diplocraterion* and indeterminate horizontal and subvertical burrows, which destroy primary lamination; sharp erosive scours with sandstone intraclasts; sideritic matrix in part; thin beds of grey siltstone (c.0.20 to 0.80 m thick) with silty mudstone laminae; shell beds with thick-shelled bivalves, including oysters — 14.93 — 85.03

Siltstone, sandy, with thin beds of pale to medium grey, calcareous, micaceous, fine-grained sandstone; ripple cross-laminated; extensively bioturbated; scoured erosional bases; siderite nodule at 90.14 to 90.23 m — 5.02 — 90.05

Sandstone, as for beds at 70.10 to 85.03 m; gradational base from 94.14 to 94.85 m; ammonites of the *ibex* Zone at 94.14 m — 4.80 — 94.85

REDCAR MUDSTONE FORMATION

"Ironstone/Pyritous Shales"

Mudstone, grey, silty, with thin beds of pale grey siltstone; small (0.001 m) pyrite nodules; siltstone beds show upward-fining laminae; overall upward-coarsening sequence; siderite nodules common down to 158.07 m; glauconite peloids present in cross-laminated siltstone from 109.62 to 109.64 m, and from 128.95 to 129.63 m; pyrite-filled burrows common; fossils abundant at some horizons, including bivalves (*Pinna* sp., *Plicatula* sp.), belemnites. brachiopods, crinoid columnals and pyritised ammonites of the *ibex* and *jamesoni* zones; *Chondrites* burrows locally common — 69.53 — 164.38

"Siliceous Shales"

Mudstone, grey, silty, micaceous; interbedded with thin beds of pale grey, calcareous, fine-grained sandstone and siltstone; coarser beds commonly have erosively scoured bases with occasional shell lags, and show upward-fining rhythms; sparse siderite nodules; small limonite peloids from 192.65 to 192.75 m and from 194.85 to 194.98 m; bioturbation common, particularly in coarser beds, where *Chondrites* produces diffuse lower boundaries; *Diplocraterion* and *Rhizocorallium* also present; abundant fossils include bivalves and belemnites, and ammonites of the *raricostatum, oxynotum, obtusum* and *turneri* zones — 35.28 — 199.66

"Calcareous Shales"

Mudstone, grey, silty, micaceous, calcareous in part; interbedded with thin beds (c.0.20 to 1.00 m) of pale grey, calcareous siltstone, calcareous sandstone and sandy bioclastic limestone; coarser beds are cross-laminated in part and commonly have erosively scoured bases with occasional shell lags, and show upward-fining pulses; cross-laminated, shallow scours common; sparse, ovate siderite nodules; sparse limonite ooliths in

	Thickness m	Depth m

limestone beds; coarser beds are extensively bioturbated, with abundant *Chondrites, Diplocraterion* and *Siphonites* burrows; pyrite-filled burrows also present; shelly fauna in coarse beds comprises disseminated shell fragments, including crinoid ossicles, echinoid fragments, abundant thick-shelled oysters, including *Gryphaea arcuata, Modiolus* sp., *Protocardia* sp. and *Pteromya* sp., rhynchonellid brachiopods (*Calcirhynchia calcaria*) and gastropods; shell fragments are commonly highly abraded; sparse ammonites prove the *turneri, semicostatum, bucklandi, angulata, liasicus* and *planorbis* zones; base of *planorbis* Zone at 278.68 m   79.02   278.68

Mudstone, dark grey, silty, laminated, and thin beds of shelly limestone and calcareous siltstone; fissile mudstone from 282.60 to 282.97 m, abundant bivalves from 278.68 to 283.00 m, including *Astarte* sp., *Cardinia* sp., *Liostrea hisingeri, Lucina, Meleagrinella* sp., *Modiolus hillanoides, M. minimus, Protocardia rhaetica, Pseudolimea* sp. and *Pteromya tatei*; sparse bivalves below, including *M. minimus, P. tatei, Gervillia praecursor, Meleagrinella fallax,* and *P. rhaetica*; pyrite-filled burrows from 282.64 to 288.87 m   10.19   288.87

Penarth Group

LILSTOCK FORMATION

Cotham Member
Mudstone, grey-green, soft (soapy texture), with thin upward-fining, siltstone laminae (0.001 to 0.004 m); the latter show ripple cross-lamination and shallow, erosive scours; pyrite-filled burrows; fish fragments; abundant *Euestheria minuta*; sharp base   5.71   294.58

WESTBURY FORMATION
Mudstone, dark grey to black, organic-rich, bioturbated, with thin beds and laminae of pale grey, fine-grained, pyritic sandstone and siltstone; convolute laminae and contorted slump balls from 294.58 to 295.16 m; occasional small siderite nodules; extensively bioturbated, including *Diplocraterion* burrows and horizontal and sub-vertical circular burrows; scattered fish fragments; abundant bivalves, including *Chlamys valoniensis, Eotrapezium concentricum, E. ewaldi, Lyriomyophoria postera, Protocardia rhaetica, Rhaetavicula contorta* and *Tutcheria cloacina* above 297.0 m, and *E. concentricum, E. germari, Modiolus sodburiensis, R. contorta* and *P. rhaetica*, and the gastropod *Natica* sp., from 297.0 to 298.96 m   4.57   299.15
End of borehole

Kirklington NCB Borehole: BGS Ref SE 38 SW/38; [SE 3287 8091]; surface level 33.76 m above OD.

This borehole was sunk by the NCB (British Coal) in 1978 to prove the Triassic, Permian and Carboniferous sequences. It was cored from a depth of 36.52 m.

	Thickness m	Depth m

Pleistocene and Recent
| Clay with pebbles and sand (till) | 18.00 | 18.00 |

Triassic

Sherwood Sandstone Group
| Sandstone (from chippings) | 18.52 | 36.52 |
| Sandstone, red-brown, fine-grained, micaceous, with mudstone and siltstone laminae | 15.48 | 52.00 |

UPPER MARL
Siltstone, red-brown with sporadic green sandstone beds; scattered small gypsum crystals throughout	6.25	58.25
Sandstone and siltstone, red-brown, with ripple marks and fibrous gypsum veins	2.32	60.57
Siltstone and mudstone, red-brown, with numerous fibrous gypsum veins; nodules and lenses of gypsum and anhydrite	9.25	69.82
Anhydrite (Billingham Main Anhydrite), grey with red mottling at top, becoming massive and translucent below 76.68 m; patches of gypsum in bottom 0.5 m	9.30	79.12

UPPER MAGNESIAN LIMESTONE
| Limestone, grey-buff, thin-bedded, with mudstone partings and laminae; algal mat laminations at top | 9.70 | 88.82 |

MIDDLE MARL
Mudstone, grey, with a few fibrous gypsum veins	2.32	91.14
Breccia of red and grey mudstone with gypsum veins	1.01	92.15
Mudstone, grey with sporadic thin beds of anhydrite and muddy anhydrite	6.23	98.38
Limestone, dolomitic (Kirkham Abbey Formation), with beds of grey anhydrite and mudstone	2.65	101.03
Anhydrite, grey, with thin limestone beds, passing down into massive nodular anhydrite	1.77	102.80
Breccia of mudstone and anhydrite	0.49	103.29
Anhydrite (Hayton Anhydrite), bluish grey, massive and nodular, with sporadic mudstone lenses and partings; lenses and stringers of dolomite towards base; subordinate alteration to gypsum in middle and base of unit	29.06	132.35

LOWER MAGNESIAN LIMESTONE
Limestone, grey and buff, dolomitic, with abundant gypsum-filled vughs	13.63	145.90
Limestone, slightly dolomitic, cross-bedded in 3 to 10 cm units	3.98	149.96
Limestone, buff, dolomitic, with abundant gypsum crystals; ripple marks near base	9.52	159.48
Limestone, grey and buff, thin- to medium-bedded, with partings and laminae of black mudstone	17.75	177.23

	Thickness m	Depth m
Limestone, grey, rubbly, soft and porous; composed almost exclusively of shells, shell debris and bryozoa	15.75	192.98
Limestone, grey, laminated (algal lamination)	2.93	195.91

BASAL BRECCIA

| Breccia of dark grey limestone with a buff, dolomitic limestone matrix | 0.47 | 196.38 |

Unconformity

LOWER FOLLIFOOT GRIT?

Sandstone, grey, fine- to medium-grained, leached and brecciated at top; cemented with quartz below 197.90 m	2.52	198.90
Mudstone and siltstone with sandstone partings	1.08	199.98
Sandstone, grey and red-brown, medium- to thick-bedded, interbedded with medium to thick beds of mudstone and siltstone	5.14	205.12
Sandstone, grey, fine- to medium-grained, bioturbated, with load casts and flame structures	3.41	208.53
Sandstone, pale brown and red-brown, coarse-and very coarse-grained, feldspathic; cross-bedded throughout; sporadic mudstone partings	18.47	227.00
Sandstone, grey, fine- to medium-grained, thin and very thinly bedded, with graded units; abundant slump structures, load and flame casts	9.40	236.40
Siltstone, grey, micaceous, with sporadic sandstone laminae and very thin beds	2.60	239.00
Mudstone, silty, grey and dark grey, with sporadic ironstone nodules and very thin sandstone beds	43.86	282.86

COLSTERDALE MARINE BEDS?

| Mudstone, dark grey, silty, with abundant brachiopods | 3.74 | 286.60 |

RED SCAR GRIT?

Sandstone, grey, fine- to medium-grained, with shell fragments and silty mudstone at base	0.97	287.57
Sandstone, grey and pale brown, coarse- to very coarse-grained; highly fossiliferous, with abundant crinoid fragments	6.14	293.71
Sandstone, fine- to medium-grained, shelly at top; carbonaceous wisps near base	0.59	294.30
Sandstone, buff to pale grey, coarse- and very coarse-grained; feldspathic, with white feldspars; cross-bedded	4.18	298.48

Sleningford Mill Borehole: BGS Ref SE 27 NE/48; [SE 2778 7841]; surface level 45 m above OD.

This borehole was sunk in 1982 by the British Geological Survey to prove the thickness and quality of the Lower Magnesian Limestone; additional details are given by Bridge and Murray (1983). The sequence present is:

	Thickness m	Depth m
Alluvium	3.25	3.25

LOWER MAGNESIAN LIMESTONE

Dolomite, dark buff-grey; laminated and stylolised throughout, with short carbonaceous streaks and some micritisation along stylolites and close to vughs; numerous vughs generally partially or fully filled with calcite, but a few with sphalerite	3.86	7.11
Dolomite, buff-yellow to grey, with numerous stylolitic partings; abundant vughs, many filled with calcite and dolomite, some slightly mineralised with sphalerite; mineralised breccias with galena at 10.43 to 10.83 m, 13.65 to 14.00 m and 15.23 to 15.50 m; this dolomitic limestone varies from fine to coarse grained and the beds are commonly undulating over and around vughs; towards the base of the unit the beds become laminated and argillaceous	13.14	20.25
Dolomite, grey, fine-grained, compact; numerous clay-covered stylolitic partings and a few cavities with calcite; generally no vughs; prominent clay partings at 28.58 and 31.20 m	12.23	32.48
Dolomite, dark buff-grey, mainly shelly, laminated in parts; patchy pseudobrecciation and scattered ooliths	5.01	37.49

MARL SLATE

| Mudstone, dark grey and carbonaceous, with some shell fragments | 0.86 | 38.35 |

BASAL BRECCIA

| Breccia conglomerate; mudstone clasts ranging from coarse sand to gravel-sized | 0.30 | 38.65 |

Unconformity

CARBONIFEROUS STRATA

| Sandstone, pale grey, medium-grained, with cross-bedding | 2.02 | 40.67 |

Musterfield Farm Borehole: BGS Ref SE 27 NE/2; [2713 7608]; surface level c.97 m above OD.

	Thickness m	Depth m
LOWER MAGNESIAN LIMESTONE		
'Magnesian' Limestone	29.90	29.90

Unconformtiy

CARBONIFEROUS STRATA		
Shale with *Lingula* sp.	12.80	42.70
Fine-grained sandstone	1.50	44.20
Shale with *Myalina* sp.	6.10	50.30
Fine-grained sandstone	1.50	51.80
Silty shale	6.10	57.90
Medium- to coarse-grained sandstone	15.30	73.20
Shale (with *Lingula* sp. reported)	1.80	75.00
Fine-grained sandstone	1.50	76.50
Silty shale	8.80	85.30
Coarse-grained sandstone	18.90	104.20
Silty shale with *Lingula* sp. to bottom	3.40	107.60

Wood Farm Borehole: BGS Ref SE 27 NE/6; [2888 7531]; surface level c.70 m above OD.

	Thickness m	Depth m
Soil	0.30	0.30
LOWER MAGNESIAN LIMESTONE		
"Marl" (weathered limestone)	1.22	1.52
"Marl" (weathered limestone) with bands of limestone	4.49	6.01
Limestone, mainly crystalline	4.01	10.02
Limestone, buff, chalky	2.17	12.19
Limestone, grey to pinkish buff, crystalline	5.49	17.68
Limestone, white to grey and buff, chalky, with black clayey partings	12.80	30.48
Limestone, as above, with brecciated bands	6.71	37.19
Limestone, grey, brown and yellow, with much carbonaceous material in places	18.28	55.47

	Thickness m	Depth m
Limestone, broken, with clayey partings	3.05	58.52
Limestone, core missing	4.57	63.09
MARL SLATE AND BASAL BRECCIA		
Limestone, grey, with several 1.25 to 2.5 cm grey calcareous bands (marl slate) containing fish and shell fragments; bottom 0.45 m with concretionary nodules	2.14	65.23

Unconformity

CARBONIFEROUS STRATA, ?MILLSTONE GRIT		
Grit, blue-grey, feldspathic	0.61	65.84
Grit and coarse sandstone with shale fragments; cross-bedded	4.26	70.10
Shale, purple, green and grey variegated, sandy, with carbonaceous fragments and a few shell casts near base (dip horizontal)	2.44	72.54
Sandstone and shale alternating in thin beds, with poorly preserved shells at frequent intervals	26.52	99.06
CAYTON GILL SHELL BED?		
Limestone, impure, crinoidal with shell fragments	0.15	99.21
Sandstone and sandy shale, alternating; thin lens of coal at base	2.59	101.80
Shaly fireclay	0.61	102.41
Shale, with *Lingula* sp. and other shell fragments	1.83	104.24
Sandstone, grey to dull reddish brown, with some shale bands	1.52	105.76
Shale with brachiopods	0.16	105.92
Sandstone, grey to dull reddish brown	0.61	106.53
Shale with 2 to 5 cm band containing bryozoa and two 15 cm limestones near base	0.76	107.29
Shale, dark grey, with some thin limestone lenses near the top; shells mainly in the bottom 60 cm	1.52	108.81

APPENDIX 3

Open-file reports

Available from BGS Keyworth.

Geological notes and local details for 1:10 000 sheets:
SE 48 NW, NE, SW, SE (Thirsk and Kirby Knowle) by J H Powell.
SE 58 NW, SW and parts of NE, SE (Hawnby and Roulston Scar) by J H Powell.

The Permian rocks of the Thirsk district. Geological description and local details of 1:50 000 Sheet 52 and component 1:10 000 sheets SE 27 SE/NE, SE 28 SE/NE, SE 37 SW/NW and SE 38 SW by A H Cooper.

The geology of the country north and east of Ripon, North Yorkshire, with particular reference to the sand and gravel deposits; description of 1:25 000 Sheet SE 37 by A H Cooper.

The geology of the country around Pickhill, North Yorkshire, with particular reference to the sand and gravel deposits; description of 1:25 000 Sheet SE 38 by A C Benfield and A H Cooper.

The geological of the country around Dalton, North Yorkshire, with particular reference to the sand and gravel deposits; description of 1:25 000 Sheet SE 47 by A C Benfield.

The geology of the country around Thirsk, North Yorkshire, with particular reference to the sand and gravel deposits; description of 1:25 000 Sheet SE 48 by J H Powell.

APPENDIX 4

Geological Survey photographs

Copies of these photographs are deposited for reference in the British Geological Survey library, Keyworth, Nottingham NG12 5GG. Colour or black and white prints and transparencies can be supplied at a fixed tariff.

All numbers belong to series L, except where shown. The National Grid references are those of the viewpoints.

PERMIAN

A5239	Well Scar Lime Kilns	
A5240	Well Scar Lime Kilns	
A7549	River Ure (west bank), 1/3 mile east of Middle Parks Farm, Ripon Parks	
A7550	River Ure (west bank), 1/3 mile east of Middle Parks Farm, Ripon Parks	
2986	Sutton Grange Quarry, Lower Magnesian Limestone	[285 745]
2987	Sutton Grange Quarry, Lower Magnesian Limestone	[285 745]
2988	Sutton Grange Quarry, Lower Magnesian Limestone	[285 745]
2989	Potgate Quarry, Lower Magnesian Limestone	[277 757]
2990	Potgate Quarry, Lower Magnesian Limestone	[277 757]
2991	Grebdykes Quarry, Lower Magnesian Limestone	[237 823]
2992	Grebdykes Quarry, Lower Magnesian Limestone	[237 823]
2993	Watlass Lime Kilns, Lower Magnesian Limestone	[223 856]

JURASSIC

3040	Corallian Group at Cleave Dike Quarry	[5074 8632]
3041	Corallian Group at Cleave Dike Quarry	[5075 8626]
3042	Birdsall Calcareous Grit, Cleave Dike Quarry	[5075 8626]
3043	Birdsall Calcareous Grit, Cleave Dike Quarry and Boltby Scar	[5086 8644]
3047	Birdsall Calcareous Grit, Limperdale Gill	[5278 8659]
3049	Birdsall Calcareous Grit, Limperdale Gill	[5278 8659]
3050	Middle and Upper Jurassic strata, Ryedale	[5320 8826]
3051	Middle and Upper Jurassic strata, Sunny Bank	[5310 8832]
3052	Lower Calcareous Grit, Peak Scar, near Hawnby	[5310 8832]
3053	Upper Calcareous Grit Formation, Snape Hill Quarry	[5088 7871]
3054	Scarborough Formation, disused quarry near High Ground Barns	[5031 8077]
3055	Scarborough Formation, disused quarry near High Ground Barns	[5031 8077]
3056	Scarborough Formation, disused quarry near High Ground Barns	[5031 8077]
3057	Scarborough Formation, disused quarry near High Ground Barns	[5031 8077]
3058	Scarborough Formation, disused quarry near High Ground Barns	[5031 8077]
3059	Scarborough Formation, disused quarry near High Ground Barns	[5031 8077]
3060	Scarborough Formation, disused quarry in Boar's Gill near Oldstead	[5186 8067]
3061	Scarborough Formation, disused quarry near Oldstead Hall	[5313 8068]
3062	Hambleton Oolite Member, disused quarry near Old Byland Grange	[5454 8567]
3063	Hambleton Oolite Member, disused quarry near Old Byland Grange	[5454 8567]
3064	Sandy oosparite, disused quarry near Old Byland Grange	[5454 8567]
3065	Sand oosparite, disused quarry near Old Byland Grange	[5454 8567]
3066	Slump-fold in oobiosparite, Shaw's Gate Quarry	5234 8236]
3067	Slump-fold in oobiosparite, Shaw's Gate Quarry	[5234 8236]
3068	Slump-fold in oobiosparite, Shaw's Gate Quarry	[5234 8236]
3069	Slump-fold in oobiosparite, Shaw's Gate Quarry	[5234 8236]
3070	Synsedimentary deformation, Shaw's Gate Quarry	[5234 8236]
3071	Synsedimentary deformation, Shaw's Gate Quarry	[5234 8236]
3072	Siliceous limestone-filled channel cut into oobiosparite, Shaw's Gate Quarry	[5235 8237]
3073	Pale grey oobiosparite, Shaw's Gate Quarry	5235 8237]
3074	Pale grey oobiosparite, Shaw's Gate Quarry	[5235 8237]
3075	Synsedimentary deformation, Shaw's Gate Quarry	[5235 8237]
3076	Hambleton Oolite, Shaw's Gate Quarry	[5234 8236]
3077	Hambleton Oolite, Shaw's Gate Quarry	[5234 8236]
3183	Oldstead Oolite unconformably overlying the Kellaways Rock (Osgodby Formation), Ravens Gill	[5295 8186]
3184	Oldstead Oolite unconformable on the Kellaways Rock (Osgodby Formation); Ravens Gill	[5295 8186]
3185	Scalby Formation; thin coals with ganisteroid sandstones in disused adit, near Oldstead Hall	5319 8066]

QUATERNARY

3048	Steepsided postglacial valley, Limperdale Gill	[5278 8659]
3085	Glacial sand and gravel, Firtree Hill Gravel Pit, Cundall	4142 7425]
3086	Glacial sand and gravel, Firtree Hill Gravel Pit, Cundall	[4142 7425]
3087	Glacial sand and gravel, Firtree Hill Gravel Pit, Cundall	[4142 7425]

GEOLOGICAL HAZARDS

3023	Subsidence hollow formed in 1982, at Sharrow, near Ripon	[324 718]
3024	Subsidence hollow formed in 1939, at Nunwick	[318 747]
3025	Three large subsidence hollows at Nunwick	[319 747]
3026	Subsidence hollow at Hutton Conyers	[3194 7316]
3027	Subsidence hollow at Hutton Conyers	[3194 7316]
3028	Subsidence hollow at Hutton Conyers	[3194 7316]
3029	Subsidence hollow formed in 1834 at Ripon	[3186 7260]
3030	Subsidence hollow formed in 1834 at Ripon	[3186 7260]
3031	Subsidence-damaged houses in Princess Road, Ripon	[3148 7175]
3032	Subsidence-damaged houses in Princess Road, Ripon	[3148 7175]
3033	Subsidence hollow on Ripon Golf Course	[3111 7338]
3034	Subsidence hollow on Ripon Golf Course	[3111 7338]
3039	Cleave Dyke Quarry, Hambleton Hills	[4941 8653]
3044	Deep camber gull, Sneck Yate Bank	[5081 8703]
3045	Deep camber gull, Sneck Yate Bank	[5083 8728]
3046	Cambered 'lower leaf' of Hambleton Oolite, Sneck Yate Bank	[5071 8750]

FOSSIL INDEX

GENERAL INDEX

BRITISH GEOLOGICAL SURVEY

Keyworth, Nottingham NG12 5GG
(0602) 363100

Murchison House, West Mains Road, Edinburgh
EH9 3LA   031-667 1000

London Information Office, Natural History Museum
Earth Galleries, Exhibition Road, London SW7 2DE
071-589 4090

The full range of Survey publications is available
through the Sales Desks at Keyworth and at Murchison
House, Edinburgh, and in the BGS London
Information Office in the Natural History Museum
Earth Galleries. The adjacent bookshop stocks the
more popular books for sale over the counter. Most
BGS books and reports are listed in HMSO's Sectional
List 45, and can be bought from HMSO and through
HMSO agents and retailers. Maps are listed in the BGS
Map Catalogue, and can be bought from Ordnance
Survey agents as well as from BGS.

*The British Geological Survey carries out the geological survey
of Great Britain and Northern Ireland (the latter as an
agency service for the government of Northern Ireland), and
of the surrounding continental shelf, as well as its basic
research projects. It also undertakes programmes of British
technical aid in geology in developing countries as arranged
by the Overseas Development Administration.*

*The British Geological Survey is a component body of the
Natural Environment Research Council.*

HMSO publications are available from:

HMSO Publications Centre
(Mail, fax and telephone orders only)
PO Box 276, London SW8 5DT
Telephone orders 071-873 9090
General enquiries 071-873 0011
Queueing system in operation for both numbers
Fax orders 071-873 8200

HMSO Bookshops
49 High Holborn, London WC1V 6HB
(counter service only)
071-873 0011   Fax 071-873 8200
258 Broad Street, Birmingham B1 2HE
021-643 3740   Fax 021-643 6510
Southey House, 33 Wine Street, Bristol BS1 2BQ
0272-264306   Fax 0272-294515
9 Princess Street, Manchester M60 8AS
061-834 7201   Fax 061-833 0634
16 Arthur Street, Belfast BT1 4GD
0232-238451   Fax 0232-235401
71 Lothian Road, Edinburgh EH3 9AZ
031-228 4181   Fax 031-229 2734

HMSO's Accredited Agents
(see Yellow Pages)

And through good booksellers